Understanding
Minecraft

ALSO EDITED BY NATE GARRELTS

The Meaning and Culture of Grand Theft Auto*:
Critical Essays* (McFarland, 2006)

*Digital Gameplay: Essays on the Nexus of
Game and Gamer* (McFarland, 2005)

Understanding *Minecraft*

Essays on Play, Community and Possibilities

Edited by NATE GARRELTS

McFarland & Company, Inc., Publishers
Jefferson, North Carolina

LIBRARY OF CONGRESS CATALOGUING-IN-PUBLICATION DATA

Understanding Minecraft : essays on play, community and possibilities / edited by Nate Garrelts.
    p.   cm.
Includes bibliographical references and index.

ISBN 978-0-7864-7974-0 (softcover : acid free paper) ∞
ISBN 978-1-4766-1815-9 (ebook)

1. Minecraft (Game)   I. Garrelts, Nate, 1976–
GV1469.35.M535U73 2014
794.8—dc23   2014033258

BRITISH LIBRARY CATALOGUING DATA ARE AVAILABLE

Cover: Digital illustration by Mark Durr

Printed in the United States of America

McFarland & Company, Inc., Publishers
 Box 611, Jefferson, North Carolina 28640
 www.mcfarlandpub.com

For Winton, Wiley,
and Herobrine

Table of Contents

Introduction:
Why *Minecraft* Matters

NATE GARRELTS

Having sold more than 48 million[1] copies across all platforms, *Minecraft* (Mojang, 2011) is one of the bestselling videogames of all time. While it still has a long way to go in order to top *Wii Sports*[2] (Nintendo, 2006) and *Tetris*[3] (1984) in sheer numbers, it has already done something neither of these games will ever do: *Minecraft* has engaged the popular imagination so profoundly that it has transformed videogame culture. Indeed, there has not been such widespread enthusiasm for a piece of entertainment software since we collectively came down with a case of "Pac-Man Fever" when the game *Pac-Man* was released by Namco in 1980. Like most of my peers, I watched the Pac-Man cartoon on Saturday morning, ate Pac-Man cereal, and slept on a Pac-Man pillow. Strangely enough, I did not own the game and only played it rarely at a friend's house. Yet *Pac-Man* captured my imagination and the imagination of the world. It was special. While there have been both popular and controversial games since *Pac-Man*, few have had such a profound cultural impact. What is more spectacular is that *Minecraft* has achieved this without fancy graphics or gratuitous violence, and the developer Mojang generously allows users to modify the game and share derivative works—two major reasons for the game's success.

The first essays in this collection contextualize *Minecraft* by explaining its origins, describing its relationship to other videogames and toys, and helping us to think about the learning models implicit in its design. Unlike other videogames that are produced by teams of programmers working largely in isolation from their audience, *Minecraft* has been shaped collaboratively with the help of the global gaming community. In the first chapter of this collection "The Videogame Commons Remakes the Transnational Studio," Dennis Redmond discusses the audience driven development of *Minecraft* initiated by its creator Markus "Notch" Persson, *Minecraft*'s relationship to the media industry and content producers, and the game's ubiquity across multiple platforms. Redmond credits these three facets with the game's success. Working from a similar premise, Peter Christiansen's essay "Players, Modders and Hackers"

1

specifically historicizes the practice of modding *Minecraft* in light of games produced by Id Software in the early 1990s. Christiansen also discusses how playing *Minecraft* prepares users with a mindset that is not all that different from that of a modder, thus fortifying the community and breeding the next generation of modders.

Minecraft can also be situated in the larger history of both education and playthings, which Colin Fanning and Rebecca Mir discuss in their essay "Teaching Tools: Progressive Pedagogy and the History of Construction Play." Beginning with the theories of Friedrich Fröbel and Maria Montessori and continuing through educational movements and toys of the 20th century, Fanning and Mir help us to understand *Minecraft's* appeal and educational value beyond simple comparisons to LEGO bricks. Building upon these very same ideas, Jeffrey E. Brand, Penny de Byl, Scott J. Knight, and James Hooper discuss how *Minecraft* can itself become a platform for learning. Their essay "Mining Constructivism in the University: The Case of Creative Mode" describes a project at Bond University in Australia where *Minecraft* was used as a Virtual Learning Environment (VLE) for students enrolled in a class on the interactive media industry. Building on constructivist theories, they encourage us to rethink space and pedagogy in the modern university.

On the surface, *Minecraft* is deceptively simple. Within a few mouse clicks new users learn that the world can be destroyed by punching, that resources can be stored in a backpack, and that these same resources can be used to construct things. Yet the various game modes, difficulty settings, and procedurally generated worlds provide users with overwhelming opportunity. The next several essays try to characterize the relationship individuals forge with a game that straddles the line between carefully structured freedom and limitlessness. For Alexandra Jean Tremblay, Jeremy Colangelo, and Joseph Alexander Brown, *Minecraft* is best described not as a work of art but as a "vocabulary and grammar through which a player may articulate the game of *Minecraft* itself." Their essay "The Craft of Data Mining: *Minecraft* and the Constraints of Play" especially connects playing *Minecraft* with the works and theories of the Oulipo group, and discusses the algorithmic nature of the game, player modeling, and modding.

Also recognizing "the façade of unfettered freedom," Iris Rochelle Bull questions the role gender plays in *Minecraft*. In her essay "Just Steve: Conventions of Gender on the Virtual Frontier," she proposes that simply reading the world of *Minecraft* as being genderless ignores the way gender is constructed outside of the game. In drawing parallels to the American frontier myth, Bull reminds us that we are influenced by cultural ways of seeing and doing and limited by the relationships and resources presented in the game. In her essay "(Queer) Algorithmic Ecology: The Great Opening Up of Nature to All Mobs" Amanda Phillips likewise acknowledges the constraints of the "algorithmically generated and procedurally expanding environments" and our proclivity for enacting colonial and capitalists fantasies. However, Phillips contends that the "algorithmic ecology" of the game presents users with "queer embodiments and relations" that can help them rethink reproduction, time, structure, and our relationship to the algorithms of the game.

The seeming dissonance between the two previous essays exists largely because *Minecraft* does nothing to orient players on how they should interact with the software. There are no written instructions, video cut scenes, or training sessions to help the player along. When confronted with this situation, I drew on my past knowledge of construction toys and videogames, experimented within the virtual world, and searched discussion boards. In order to better understand "commonalities and problems with communicating play experiences for such an open-ended game," Michael Thomét studies two online communities where players discuss *Minecraft*. His essay "Look What Just Happened: Communicating Play in Online Communities" shows that how people talk about the game is as important as what they are talking about.

Much different than my approach to *Minecraft*, my son learned to play from watching YouTube videos by webcasters like stampylongnose and CaptainSparklez. *Minecraft* has a robust online community of fans who produce art, fan fiction, game mods, and many different types of video content. In her ethnographic essay "A Craft to Call Mine: Creative Appropriation of *Minecraft* in YouTube Animations" Jandy Gu uncovers the social relations between content creators and the ways they "negotiate legitimacy in the highly contested space of creative appropriation." She draws on her experiences with her brother, Dillon Gu, who created the *Gods Don't Bleed* YouTube video, as well as interviews with other popular animators. Esther MacCallum-Stewart's essay "'Someone off the YouTubez': The Yogscast as Fan Producers" gives readers more insight into the origins of the Yogscast, one of the most successful groups of fan-producers. MacCallum-Stewart demonstrates how *Minecraft* has stimulated a change in the way fans approach games and, in doing do, created a new domain for "gaming criticism and entertainment."

Many of the essays in this collection hint at the relationship between *Minecraft* and other types of media; Michael St. Clair makes this relationship explicit in his essay "Videogames in the White Cube." In this essay he links *Minecraft* to the larger history of "anti-pictorial trends in modern art," and shows how it "works as a radical gesture in sculpture, performance, and most specifically, installation art." Evidence of St. Clair's claims can be found in James Morgan and R. Yagiz Mungan's essay "Fine Arts, Culture and Creativity in *Minecraft*." In their essay, Morgan and Mungan discuss collaborating in *Minecraft* with international artists on both art and music projects. They have found that not only does creation and collaboration thrive in the intuitive sandbox environment, but the data itself "resonates as a source of intellectual and artistic inspiration."

Because it combines elements of many different types of software while at the same time offering users its own unique experience, *Minecraft* is not a game that can be easily classified by players or theorists. The final two essays in the collection attempt to understand the special interactivity characteristic of *Minecraft*. Adam L. Brackin's essay "Building a Case for the Authenticity vs. Validity Model of Videogame Design" discusses how concepts of authenticity and validity intersect with story and game mechanics in *Minecraft*, while Rémi Cayatte's essay "Where Game, Play and Art Collide" unites concepts that are discussed throughout the collection.

In short, *Minecraft* offers us something far more significant than pretend bowling in our living rooms, and the essays in this collection are a testament to this. *Minecraft* weaves playing, gaming, roleplaying, image manipulation, chatting, and programming all into a bundle that people write about, create videos about, and use as inspiration for other types of projects. *Minecraft* is something else—a glimpse into the future of videogames.

Notes

1. On April 9, 2014, Jens Bergensten announced on his Twitter feed that sales of *Minecraft—Pocket Edition* had reached 21 million. Only a few days before this, the Xbox Wire (2014) reported that sales of *Minecraft* for the Xbox 360 had surpassed 12 million copies. As of February 2014, PC sales of *Minecraft* were 14 million and climbing (Persson, 2014). *Minecraft* was recently released for the PlayStation 3, with sales already reaching 1.5 million (Hill, 2014). The game is slated for release on both the PlayStation 4 and Xbox One, which will no doubt further inflate these numbers.

2. With 81.99 million copies sold ("Top Selling," 2013), *Wii Sports* is often cited as one of the best selling games of all time. People are quick to point out that the game was initially bundled with Wii consoles, which skews actual consumer demand for the game. For example, while I thought the game was novel, I never would have purchased it separately from the Wii console.

3. According to the official *Tetris* website ("Tetris Overview," 2014), the game has sold 125 million copies. However, estimates on the internet fluctuate by the tens of millions. Regardless of the exact figure, it is clear that *Tetris* has been wildly popular across multiple platforms for over three decades.

References

Bergensten, J. [jeb_]. (2014, April 9). MC:PE has sold over 20 million copies (actually, over 21M), so we're going to have a live broadcast on Monday [Twitter]. Retrieved from https://twitter.com/jeb_/status/453900156388528128.

Hill, O. (2014, April 16). *Minecraft*: PlayStation 3 edition gets a Blu-ray release next month. *PlayStation Blog*. Retrieved from http://blog.eu.playstation.com/2014/04/16/minecraft-playstation-3-edition-gets-a-blu-ray-release-next-month/.

Mojang. (2011). *Minecraft* [PC game]. Stockholm, Sweden: Mojang.

Namco. (1980). *Pac-Man* [Arcade]. Japan: Namco.

Nintendo. (2006). *Wii Sports* [Nintendo Wii]. Kyoto, Japan: Nintendo.

Pajitnov, A. (1984). *Tetris* [Multiple platforms].

Persson, M. [notch]. (2014, February 1). The computer version of *Minecraft* has now sold 14 million copies. Celebrating by having no idea how to play *Lego Marvel* on PS4! [Twitter]. Retrieved from https://twitter.com/notch/statuses/429665371168444416

Tetris overview. (2014). Retrieved from http://tetris.com/about-tetris/

Top selling software sales units. (2013). Nintendo. Retrieved from http://www.nintendo. co.jp/ir/en/sales/software/wii.html

Xbox Wire. (2014, April 04). *Minecraft* creeps past 12 million sold on Xbox 360. Retrieved from http://news.xbox.com/2014/04/games-minecraft-12m

The Videogame
Commons Remakes the
Transnational Studio

DENNIS REDMOND

Over the past three decades, videogames have evolved from electronic toys into complex digital worlds, teeming with sophisticated narratives and hosting millions of player interactions. Yet one of the most fascinating innovations of videogame culture is also one of its most recent. This is the rise of the videogame commons, best understood as a subset of Yochai Benkler's (2006) digital commons.[1] Today's videogame commons is comprised of the non-commercial institutions, communities and practices of digital artists, videogame players, and videogame fan communities. Far from being a marginal phenomenon or a relic of the videogame industry's start-up era, the videogame commons has become an increasingly powerful and pervasive feature of videogame culture. In fact, today's videogame commons is radically democratizing nearly every aspect of digital media production, distribution, and consumption. There is no better case study of this transformation than Mojang's *Minecraft*.

Minecraft was created almost single-handedly in 2009 by Notch, the pen name of Markus Persson, a Swedish software coder. In subsequent years, the franchise was refined and expanded by Mojang, the software studio Notch founded in 2010. By January 2014, fans had purchased at least 13.7 million official copies of the game on various computer platforms, while the unofficial user base is in all likelihood three to five times larger (i.e., 41 million to 69 million users).[2] Yet the true importance of *Minecraft* is not merely its impressive sales results. It is the fact that it embodies a radically new type of digital media production, or what we will call audience-led production.

Certain aspects of audience-led production have been theorized by Henry Jenkins (2006) as "convergence culture" and "transmedia," namely the fact that digital networks have allowed non-commercial fan communities and fan media production to become influential players within some of the largest contemporary media franchises. Other aspects of audience-led production

7

have been explored by Mia Consalvo's work on the wide range of social behaviors (some benevolent, some predatory) exhibited by player communities inside their favorite digital worlds (Consalvo, 2007).

Yet what makes audience-led production truly new is the presence of the transnational audience. This audience consists of the approximately 2.4 billion citizens able to access the internet in mid–2013, a number which is likely to double over the next five years.[3] What makes this audience so important is not just its impressive size and growth potential. It also has two structural features that radically differentiate it from all previous mass media audiences.

The first feature is open source proliferation. This audience is connected via a wide range of digital networks that are not controlled by any single national government, regulatory body, or commercial entity. Put bluntly, there is no internet equivalent of Great Britain's control over the telegraph during the 19th century or to the overwhelming dominance of the U.S. film or broadcast television industry over all other competitors for much of the 20th century.[4]

This is because the internet is not a single technology, but a vast digital eco-system of multiple technologies, including cellphones, tablets, personal computers, and portable storage media of all kinds. No single nation-state or commercial enterprise has a monopoly over any layer of the hardware or any node of the software of this eco-system. Perhaps the closest any company came to achieving such a monopoly was Microsoft's dominance in desktop computing in the late 1990s and Nintendo's dominance in videogame consoles in the late 1980s and early 1990s. Both quasi-monopolies faded away, thanks to the proliferation of rival platforms as well as the rise of mobile digital devices. This proliferation has reached the point that the open source Android platform, a variant of the open source operating system Linux which was specifically designed for mobile devices, now has the largest market share of the cellphone and tablet markets ("Gartner says," 2013).[5]

The second feature is transnational diversity. Only thirty percent of this audience resides in the fully industrialized nations of the U.S., Japan, and the countries of the European Union. Seventy percent—approximately 1.68 billion individuals—reside in the industrializing nations. More specifically, close to half of that 1.68 billion are clustered in the four nations of the BRICs, a.k.a. Brazil, Russia, India and China, the four largest emerging markets in the world. Since the industrializing nations have lower per capita incomes than the fully industrialized nations as well as less stringent copyright enforcement regimes, their digital audiences rely overwhelmingly on file-sharing and informal digital media distribution.[6]

As it turns out, the combination of open source proliferation and transnational diversification played an indispensable role in *Minecraft*'s success. The official development of *Minecraft* began on May 17, 2009, when Notch released the earliest version of the game as a free download to the online gaming community (Persson, 2009a). The response of the audience was positive, and Notch began to devote significant amounts of time to polish and expand the code. Initially, development of the game was financed by Notch's own personal savings, and later by digital pre-orders for the full game which Notch began to accept on June 13, 2009 ("Minecraft Wiki," 2013). However, the first official release of the game did not occur until November 18, 2011, some two and a half years after its development began, and eighteen months after *Minecraft* had become a massive cultural phenomenon.

This is the sort of multiyear development cycle typical of large-scale, blockbuster videogames. For example, Sony Santa Monica's *God of War 3* (2010) took three years to develop, while Hideo Kojima's *Metal Gear Solid 4* (Kojima Productions, 2008) took four years to develop (2004–2008). Needless to say, Notch did not have the enormous financial and cultural resources available to these studios (e.g., the official credits for *Metal Gear Solid 4* list almost five hundred actors, artists and programmers) ("Metal gear," 2014). The key factor which granted *Minecraft* the time and resources it needed to become a world-class franchise was the engagement of the transnational audience.

We are fortunate to have a detailed record of this engagement in the form of Notch's English-language Tumblr blog, *The Word of Notch*. Notch created this blog on May 13, 2009 to keep fans informed about the development of the game, and the account has remained active to this day. What the blog reveals is that the secret of *Minecraft*'s success was its open and democratic development process.

From the very beginning, Notch did not simply write and debug code. He listened carefully to player feedback on message boards and listservs, participated in online social networks, and read vast amounts of fan email. In addition, Notch sought out—and deferred to—the collective wisdom and judgment of the fan community, by means of online polls, email and chats (Persson, 2010b). Finally, Notch employed the tools of social media, by uploading demonstration videos of *Minecraft* to YouTube[7] and encouraging fans to do likewise (Persson, 2009a).

At first, the role of fans was limited to providing basic feedback and assistance with debugging. As the fan base expanded, however, its structural importance increased, to the point that its members became a key source of inspiration as well as information. Indeed, if there is one single factor that differentiates *Minecraft* from other commercial videogames that integrate fan labor and user-generated content into their core experience, e.g., Sony Media Molecule's popular and well-constructed *Little Big Planet* (2008), it is *Minecraft*'s bedrock egalitarianism.

Put bluntly, most videogame fan communities are external structures wrapped around a core commercial entity. Since this entity is controlled by the commercial studio or corporation which owns the franchise, fans are structurally disempowered from the beginning.[8] By contrast, *Minecraft* is a commercial franchise wrapped around a core non-commercial fan community. While the fan community does not legally own the franchise, this lack of formal ownership is also irrelevant. The reason is that fans co-produce, co-regulate, and co-distribute the videogame in close concert with the commercial franchise. To borrow a metaphor from banking, an official purchase of the game by fans functions like purchasing an ownership share in a credit union. It is a vote of confidence in the ability of Notch and his co-workers at Mojang to be effective stewards of the underlying code base.

To be sure, this official purchase option did not exist in the earliest phase of *Minecraft*'s existence. The closest approximation of the membership share was *Minecraft*'s registered user count. On his blog, Notch noted there were already 4,200 registered users by June 9, 2009, an impressive number for a newly-created independent videogame. However, *Minecraft* never stopped growing. The numbers of registered users increased to over 15,000 just three weeks later, and passed the 100,000 mark by January 2010. Interestingly, the number of official purchases of the game occurred much later than the registered user base, but subsequently followed a similar exponential growth trajectory with 4,818 copies sold by February 14, 2010, and 37,906 by July 29, 2010 (Persson, 2009i; 2010b; 2010f; 2010m).

What this means is that the growth of the user base during the critical period between May 2009 and early 2010 was almost entirely non-commercial in nature. What convinced large numbers of fans to become *Minecraft*'s unpaid co-creators was not just the franchise's core values of openness and respect for fan labor, or the fact that Notch and the Mojang staff consistently put the needs of the player community ahead of the quest for maximum profit. Above all, it was Notch's capacity to articulate a clear and compelling vision of an audience-led development process to large numbers of fans.

This vision can be summarized in the form of three core strategies inaugurated by Notch, and then carried out by Mojang. The first strategy was extensive cooperation with a wide range of digital media artists, coders, and mod-makers throughout the digital commons. The second was the decision to expand the *Minecraft* eco-system across as many digital platforms as possible. The third was the decision to allow fans to govern the development cycle of the franchise through collective forms of decision-making (a.k.a. digital democracy), rather than by simply following market signals.

The benefits of cooperating with the digital commons are most apparent in the multimedia aspects of *Minecraft*, particularly its sound and music design. On June 7, 2009 Notch announced that German artist C418 (the pen name of Daniel Rosenfeld) would create the music and sounds for *Minecraft*. While a basic set of sounds were introduced to the game on June 28, 2009, C418's memorable and haunting score would be added a year later, on July 7, 2010 (Persson, 2009i; 2009l; 2010l). As an independent artist, Notch could and did grant C418 the development time needed to create a top-notch soundtrack. The implementation of sound also required a specialized sound engine, which was created by fellow programmer Paul Lamb and added to the code on January 5, 2010 (Persson, 2010a).

The benefits of the second strategy, an expanding eco-system, were initially more diffuse, but would generate a significant long-term payoff. For one thing, Notch made the source code available to as many personal computer platforms as possible, and did not criminalize file-sharing or modding (the structural importance of modding to *Minecraft* will be described in just a moment). For another, Notch understood the immense potential of open source mobile platforms, expressing his desire to have *Minecraft* ported to Android devices as early as May 22, 2009—a goal which was finally realized two years later on October 2011 (Persson, 2009f). Most of all, Notch designed the game's pricing strategy to maximize the accessibility of the *Minecraft* eco-system to fans, rather than maximizing profits.

On June 10, 2009, Notch announced that pre-orders of the alpha code would be available for 9.95EUR ($12.94) to help finance development. Beta copies would eventually be available for 14.95EUR ($19.44), while the full game would cost 20EUR (about $26) (Persson, 2009j). Mojang followed this strategy precisely, releasing *Minecraft*'s beta version on December 20, 2010 for 14.95 EUR, and releasing the official version of the game on November 18, 2011 for 19.95EUR (U.S. $26.99). These prices are far lower than the $70 typically charged for newly-released blockbuster console videogames, though they are in the general range of used copies of console videogames two or three years old.

Currently, copies of *Minecraft* for personal computers running Apple's Macintosh OS, Microsoft's Windows, and Linux operating systems are available for $26.99. The mobile versions of *Minecraft* for Android released in October 2011 and Apple iOS devices released in November 2011 are available for $6.99 ("Pocket edition," 2014), while copies for Microsoft's XboxLive download service released in May 2012 are available for $19.99 ("Xbox360 edition," 2014).[9] The logic behind this pricing is that the marketplace for mobile devices is the largest and most diverse in the world, with large numbers of consumers in the industrializing nations. For consumers in Russia, a middle-income nation where per capita incomes are about one quarter those of the U.S., the price tag of $6.99 is affordable, the rough equivalent of a $30 media purchase for a U.S. or EU consumer.

These prices are especially interesting given the fact that the size of *Minecraft*'s software code is quite small. The personal computer version of the game takes up only 150 megabytes of space, and the mobile versions of the game are even smaller. This is a tiny fraction of the size of contemporary console videogames, some of which require gigabytes of data. The small size of the code and Mojang's principled refusal to criminalize file-sharing means there are almost no technical barriers for users who wish to download unlicensed copies of the game for free.

If the lobbyists of the RIAA who argue that non-commercial file-sharing is criminal and destructive piracy were correct, then *Minecraft* should not exist. Yet Mojang's business model has flourished precisely because audience-led production does not need to monetize every single transaction between digital artists and the fan community.[10] Whatever sales Mojang may lose by permitting fans to share digital copies of the game is compensated for several times over by a variety of savings. These savings include not paying outlandish sums to lawyers for copyright enforcement, not paying for expensive public relations campaigns and commercial advertisements, not paying retailers for stock placement, and not paying for parasitic layers of rentiers, Wall Street operatives, and stock-obsessed executives. Instead, all of these services are provided by the *Minecraft* community.

To understand how this community self-management works in practice, we must turn to Mojang's third core strategy, namely digital democratization. One of the most typical examples of this democratization was an early update which added water and lava to the alpha code on May 20, 2009 (Persson, 2009d). The very next day, Notch described a number of additional blocks he planned to incorporate into future versions of the game, and asked for further community input (Persson, 2009e). After sifting through the community's responses, Notch added blocks of sand, gravel, trees, coal, and iron and gold ore to the game-world two days later, on May 23, 2009 (Persson, 2009g).

Since these blocks are the fundamental basis of *Minecraft*'s game-world, the fan community had effectively been given the status of co-creators of the game, a structural power almost never granted to fans of any other mass media. The fan community responded with a remarkable outpouring of productivity and participation. By June 9, 2009, less than three weeks after the public launch of the project, *Minecraft* had grown to 4,200 registered users (Persson, 2009i). On June 25, 2009, just three weeks later, *Minecraft* had grown to 15,185 registered users, while 587 consumers completed pre-order purchases (Persson, 2009k). This level of community interest was extraordinary considering that the game still had major bugs, lacked many key features, and would not have functioning sound-effects until its June 28, 2009 release.

This democratization had profound effects on the evolution of *Minecraft*'s game-play. Notch's original code presented players with a world comprised of square blocks of material, wherein each block is a one-meter cube, and where these blocks could be obtained through mining (clicking on a block with a tool) and then placed elsewhere. This potentially made the entire game-world interactive, i.e., the world was a giant set of building-blocks which could be acquired, stored, and transformed via a simple crafting system into useful tools and items.

What the audience did was to co-invent creative uses for this originally static block-world. While Notch did suggest various modes of game-play as early as May 16, 2009, most aspects of game-play were determined through a process of community-based iteration (Persson, 2009b). Late in 2009, the block-world was diversified into a tripartite system of collectible blocks, in-game tools and items, and a more refined crafting system. By January 30, 2010, the game had expanded to include 59 block types, 34 item types, and 36 crafting recipes. The vast majority of these innovations were suggested by the fan community, implemented by Notch, and then play-tested and refined by the community (Persson, 2010c). Over the next two years, this basic schemata would expand further to include in-game weather effects and climatic zones, and still later bands of hostile enemies and friendly animals. The below chart illustrates some of the main features of the evolution of *Minecraft*'s alpha version:

Table 1.

Selected events discussed on The Word of Notch during the alpha version of Minecraft

Chronology	Event
May 17, 2009	First public release of *Minecraft*.
May 21, 2009	Notch discusses block types, asks for community input.
June 7, 2009	Digital artist C418 begins work on *Minecraft*'s sound-track.
June 9, 2009	4,200 registered users.
June 10, 2009	Tiered pricing strategy announced (preorders, beta, official).
June 25, 2009	15,185 registered users and 587 purchases.
June 28, 2009	First sound-track added to game (C418's work would be added in 2010).
June 29, 2009	Registered users pass the 35,000 mark.
August 28, 2009	Survival mode (i.e., single-player mode) added to game.
January 13, 2010	Registered users pass the 100,000 mark.
January 29, 2010	Crafting added to game.
February 4, 2010	Bows and enemies ("mobs") added to game.
February 12, 2010	Day-night cycle added to game.
February 14, 2010	317 users are online on 253 servers. There are now 116,504 registered users, and 4,818 official purchasers of the game.
February 21, 2010	Notch polls the community on enlarged maps, 64.7 percent of 5,358 voters approve.[II]
June 17, 2010	630 players are online on 429 servers. There are now 233,538 registered users of *Minecraft*, and over 20,000 have purchased the game.
July 29, 2010	933 players are online on 553 servers. There are now 297,648 registered users, and 37,906 have purchased the game.

Note: The alpha version of *Minecraft* ran 19 months from May 17, 2009, to December 19, 2010.

By the beginning of 2010, the massive growth of the fan community, along with an equally impressive flood of community-created content, presented Notch with an enormous managerial challenge. It was becoming increasingly difficult for a single person to balance the needs and interests of the player community—or more precisely, the needs of the specific groups which made up an increasingly diverse player community—with the collective needs of the game-world as a whole.

One example of this growing tension was Notch's February 17, 2010 post asking fans whether they wanted experience points in *Minecraft*. Since experience points are a central game mechanic of role-playing videogames, the real issue was whether the player community wanted *Minecraft* to be more of a role-playing experience or not. Two successive polls showed that the player community was deeply split. Out of the 3,969 votes cast for the first poll, 53 percent voted yes and 47 percent voted no. Out of the 4,444 votes cast for the second poll, 54 percent voted yes and 46 percent voted no (Persson, 2010e).

The only problem with assuming that this slim majority was correct was that the user base was already larger than one hundred thousand. Just four months later, *Minecraft* would reach 233,538 registered users and 20,000 official purchasers on June 17, 2010 (Persson, 2010k). Conscious that the online vote was not representative of the fan community, Notch introduced a watered-down version of experience points, which would reward player activity but not be fundamental to the game experience.

While this deft compromise solved the short-term problem, it did not solve the long-term issue of how to engage with a fast-growing fan community numbering in the hundreds of thousands and soon the millions. In the past, the only choice for digital artists who managed to create such a popular videogame would have been to either monetize their game themselves in order to pay for the ever-increasing costs of development, or to have someone else monetize their work by selling the game to a commercial publisher.[12]

Notch rejected both alternatives. Instead, he made two key decisions. The first decision was to leave his job at another Swedish company in April 2010 in order to devote himself full time to *Minecraft* (Persson, 2010j). The second was to begin to replace the individualized, ad hoc democracy of online polls, personal updates, and social media conversations with a more permanent and collective division of digital labor. This transformation did not occur overnight, but through a process of reflection, trial and error, and community interaction lasting several months. In a post dated August 19, 2010, Notch informed the fan community about the possibility of creating a studio to help run *Minecraft*, and more importantly, what the core values of this studio would be:

> I would love to hire some people and set up a small development studio in Stockholm. This would include additional programmers, and someone in charge of the website and community features. And an artist that can make a nicer glass texture.

I am not interested in changing the openness of how minecraft [*sic*] is developed, nor do I have any intention of selling the product to anyone else; I want to be the one developing it. My development speed has gone down lately because of all this crazy cool but scary stuff happening, but I promise you it will go up again soon, regardless of what happens [Persson, 2010n].

There is strong post facto evidence to suggest that the *Minecraft* fan community played a decisive role in shaping Notch's final decision. The very first *Minecraft* fan convention, called MinecraftCon 2010, was a spontaneous and unofficial gathering of fans on August 31, 2010 in Bellevue, Washington. At the time, Notch was visiting various software companies in the region. When fans discovered Notch was in town, they quickly organized a meeting. Around fifty fans showed up, including one in costume ("MineCon," 2014).

What these fans could not have known, however, was that Notch's real reason for visiting Bellevue was that he had a job interview at Valve Software, one of the most influential and successful firms in the videogame industry. In his post on August 19, he was still deciding whether to join Valve as an employee, or else to start his own company. Thanks at least in part to the outpouring of fan support and the accelerating expansion of the fan base, Notch decided to stay independent and found Mojang as a company on September 6, 2010 (Persson, 2010o).

The crucial lesson Notch learned during the first year and a half of *Minecraft*'s development, a lesson he subsequently put into practice at Mojang, was that it was indeed possible to maintain the balance between the needs of a fast-growing player community and an ever-expanding game-world without becoming just another transnational media corporation. What was needed was the replacement of the infrastructures of corporate capitalism by those of community self-regulation. *Minecraft* would succeed not by compromising its core values or by offering consumers a slightly less exploitative form of digital hucksterism, but by replacing neoliberal capitalism with digital democracy on every level of its production, distribution, and consumption.

We will conclude with two examples of this digital democratization. The first is the field of fan-created custom game modifications or mods, a.k.a. the practice of modding. As a programmer, Notch had always been sympathetic to the practice of modding, which has a rich history within the digital commons.[13] Various versions of *Minecraft* have incorporated especially creative player mods, e.g., on April 8, 2010, Notch incorporated an improved tree generation mod, created by Paul Spooner, into *Minecraft*'s beta code (Persson, 2010i).

That said, the single most important form of modding in *Minecraft* has been the ability of players to customize a given game-world to fit their specific online or offline community. On April 11, 2011, Notch gave Mojang's official blessing to mods, and permitted mod developers to sign up without any financial fees or other costs.[14] Unofficially, Mojang had been providing moral and symbolic support to modders for some time, e.g., the Minecraft Coder Pack (MCP) project, which began in 2010.[15]

The result is an astounding profusion of mods, comprising everything from in-game mapping systems to game-play alterations. Indeed, these mods form an eco-system which is so large and complex that it deserves further study in its own right.[16] In an online conversation with Searge, the user name of the lead coder behind MCP, Notch admitted that even he was surprised at the productivity of the modders:

> Searge: What is your personal opinion about the MCP project and its ability to decompile the game and make the source code kind of available to everyone? And how much do you think the fact that modding is made easy by systems like bukkit and MCP (and the number of available mods) affects the sales of Minecraft.
>
> Notch: Personally, I used to feel threatened by it as I felt it challenged my "vision," but on the other hand I also know how wonderful mods are for games. We decided to just let it happen, and I'm very happy we did. Mods are a huge reason of what Minecraft is [Persson, 2012].

To facilitate modding, Mojang issued a clear and transparent set of rules governing mods to fans.[17] The basic idea is that fans who purchase the game are permitted to play with and modify the underlying code as they wish, on condition that such modifications remain primarily non-commercial. Commercial uses are still possible, but require official authorization from Mojang. The same conditions apply to fan-created tools, mods and plugins, i.e., these tools, mods and plugins belong to the coder who created them and may be shared freely in non-commercial form, but may not be commercialized without Mojang's permission. The bottom line is that nearly all non-commercial uses are acceptable, while nearly all commercial uses require permission from Mojang.[18] Where most transnational media corporations explicitly restrict the right of their consumers to copy and share media content, Mojang explicitly gives consumers the freedom to share what they wish, while restricting the ability of commercial enterprises to exploit the *Minecraft* fan community for profit.

The second example of digital democratization is the expansion of the multiplayer fan community. This community will continue to grow in the future, due to the fact that the total number of computer and mobile device users in the industrializing nations, where 85 percent of all human beings reside, will increase significantly over the next five years.

One of the bellwethers of this expansion is the commercial server tracking site Gametracker (www.gametracker.com), which listed 10,349 active servers running *Minecraft* as of September 2013. This made *Minecraft* the third most popular game or software utility on Gametracker's list. While the bulk of these servers were located in the industrialized nations (primarily the U.S. and EU), Russia had 314 servers, underlining the rapid growth and increasing importance of Russia's digital media culture (by contrast, Brazil had 49, not far above Argentina's 32, and less than Chile's 58). While these servers capture only a small percentage of the activity of the fan base, they do indicate the vitality of a key segment of the *Minecraft* community, namely fans of online multiplayer games.

This expansion of multiplayer content is significant because it points to a new kind of collective gaming experience, one with low barriers to entry (the *Minecraft* code can easily run on mobile devices as well as older and slower computers, and does not require powerful servers) and one that the fan community can customize and modify as it sees fit. Mojang does not operate these servers or regulate their content, but simply gives the fan community the tools it needs to create its own multiplayer game-worlds. While the operation of multiplayer servers and the creation of single-player mods currently require significant amounts of programming skill and technical expertise, these barriers to content creation are likely to diminish significantly in the near future, as the videogame commons further democratizes the tools of interactive media content creation.[19]

To conclude, what makes *Minecraft* so important is not just its extraordinary past growth trajectory or its contemporary success. Its very existence proves that non-commercial networks of artists and fans now have the digital tools, production skills, and demographic weight to co-determine the norms and policies governing corporate control over digital media production and distribution.[20] While transnational media corporations remain influential, they are no longer the only game in town. Henceforth they must contend with vast new transnational audiences, which are beginning to organize themselves via new types of digital mobilization.

This cultural watershed has an important geopolitical corollary. During the thirty year reign of neoliberalism, defined as the transnational, plutocratic form of capitalism that dominated the world economy from the mid–1970s until the 2008 crisis, the most powerful and pervasive forms of mass media were under the exclusive control of transnational media corporations. These corporations drew the bulk of their revenues from world commercial advertising expenditures, which analyst firm ZenithOptimedia has estimated at $503 billion in 2013 ("Executive summary," 2013). They also had near-exclusive control over the platforms and technologies of media production and distribution. What *Minecraft* suggests is that the videogame commons, in lockstep with the institutions of the larger digital commons, is beginning to break the chains of corporate advertising and corporate oligopoly over media production. Most remarkable of all, it is achieving this not where neoliberalism is weakest, but precisely where it is strongest: in the very heart of the $74 billion annual videogame industry.

Notes

1. Yochai Benkler's (2006) *The Wealth of Networks* remains the indispensable theory of the digital commons. See especially Chapter 3, "Peer Production and Sharing."

2. According to Mojang's company website (https://minecraft.net), there were 13.7 million official owners of *Minecraft* as of January 11, 2014.

3. This is data aggregated by http://www.internetworldstats.com/, which compiles the data from the relevant national regulatory agencies. For the sake of comparison, note that the 27 nations of the European Union had 368 million internet users, the U.S. had 245 million, and Japan had 101 million as of mid–2013.

4. This is not to imply that national authorities are powerless, or that national regulations do not matter. Nor does this excuse the deeply problematic monitoring of allegedly private email and messages by America's NSA, Britain's MI5, Russia's FSB, and countless other national spy agencies revealed by Edward Snowden and other digital dissidents. The single greatest strength of the Internet, however, was never its ability to encrypt secrets, but its ability to disseminate information to the broad public at an exponentially decreasing cost.

5. According to analyst firm Gartner (2013), tablets and cellphones comprised 83 percent of all digital device shipments in 2012, while desktops and laptops were only 15 percent.

6. For a fuller account of copyright enforcement and file-sharing in the industrializing world see Karaganis (2011).

7. One of the most famous of these is a demonstration video of *Minecraft*'s first-person, block-based world found at http://www.youtube.com/watch?v=F9t3FREAZ-k.

8. It should be noted that this commercial control was never absolute, but was significantly constrained by some key structural aspects of videogame culture. Since almost every digital device nowadays is capable of running videogames and accessing the internet, and since digital media by their very nature are both copyable and sharable, the distribution model of videogames operates very differently from the advertiser-led, oligopoly-controlled models of distribution typical of television and cinema. Videogame studios earn the overwhelming majority of their revenues from final sales to consumers and are largely independent of advertising revenues. As a result, they do not face the subtle forms of commercial censorship that police broadcast television and Hollywood cinema. Indeed, the long-term evolution of videogame culture since the mid–1970s, shows a consistent pattern of the decline of proprietary platforms and the corresponding rise of open source multiplicity.

9. On August 20, 2013 Notch confirmed via his official Twitter account that *Minecraft* will be available for the PlayStation 4, Xbox One, and PlayStation 3 platforms in the near future.

10. One of the reasons that media scholars have not paid sufficient attention to audience-led production is that we have been looking in the wrong places. It is true that the most expensive and heavily-advertised videogame franchises have some of the characteristics of corporate-dominated oligopoly media production, i.e., dependence on expensive studio talent, heavy publicity and marketing, and a brief window of highly profitable sales, followed by falling sales and price cuts. None of this applies, however, to audience-led models of media production. These latter can take full advantage of the comparative autonomy of interactive media from advertising expenditure, as well as the exponential increase in digital storage, the spread of social media networks, and the increasing distribution of open source and low-cost digital editing tools to engage with transnational audiences.

11. A total of 5,358 fans voted, and the response was overwhelming positive (45.9 percent of voters said it was a must-do, 18.8 percent said it was worth doing, 14.5 percent were neutral, and only 13.5 percent were against it). Also note the 125 comments on the poll, some of which were quite thoughtful (Persson, 2010h).

12. In an online interview with the fan community in 2012, Notch acknowledged that commercial companies had offered to buy the franchise (Perrson, 2012).

13. For the classic analysis of modding, see Postigo, H. (2007).

14. Notch's post is worth reading (Persson, 2011).

15. The *Minecraft* Coder Pack (MCP) gave potential modders who had limited programming experience a toolkit to help create their own mods. It was first released on October 17, 2010, and has subsequently flourished since then. The current Coder Pack is located here: http://mcp.ocean-labs.de/page.php?4. Note that the site indicates the current version of the MCP software has been downloaded 59,024 times as of September 29, 2013. This number counts only downloads of the most recent version of MCP, and does not include past downloads, which suggests the total number of MCP downloads may be in the hundreds of thousands.

16. While there are far too many mods to list, two of the most creative are Nuchaz' *Bibliocraft* mod and Atomic Stryker's *Pet Bat* mod.

17. See Mojang's policies governing fan labor: https://minecraft.net/terms.

18. Mojang's policy governing the more commercial uses of *Minecraft* is described in their online description of the *Minecraft* brand: https://minecraft.net/brand.

19. One sign that this is beginning to happen is the Portal Gun mod, a project where modders recreated certain game-play features of Valve's *Portal* (2007) videogame franchise inside of a version of *Minecraft*. This is significant because it points to the diffusion of state-of-the-art game-play innovations within the *Minecraft* fan community ("Mods/Portal," 2013).

20. In May of 2013, Microsoft announced significant new restrictions on the ability of consumers to share purchased media content for its Xbox One console, due to be released in the fall of 2013. Fans were outraged at the decision, and launched a media campaign against these policies. The resulting negative press most likely severely impacted pre-orders for the console, forcing Microsoft to cancel its proposed policies in June 2013. Microsoft's original proposal: "While a persistent connection is not required, Xbox One is designed to verify if system, application or game updates are needed and to see if you have acquired new games, or resold, traded in, or given your game to a friend. With Xbox One you can game offline for up to 24 hours on your primary console, or one hour if you are logged on to a separate console accessing your library. Offline gaming is not possible after these prescribed times until you re-establish a connection, but you can still watch live TV and enjoy Blu-ray and DVD movies" ("Xbox One," 2013). For an example of the sophisticated media fans produced to critique Microsoft's policies, see: Angry Joe Show, http://www.youtube.com/watch?v=ryB-hdtpQRw

References

Benkler, Y. (2006). *The wealth of networks: How social production transforms markets and freedom.* New Haven: Yale University Press.

Consalvo, M. (2007). *Cheating: Gaining advantage in videogames.* Cambridge, MA: MIT Press.

Executive summary: Advertising expenditure forecasts December 2013 (December 2013). *ZenithOptimedia.* Retrieved from http://www.zenithoptimedia.com/wp-content/uploads/2013/12/Adspend-forecasts-December-2013-executive-summary.pdf.

Gartner says worldwide PC, tablet and mobile phone shipments to grow (2013, June 14). *Gartner*. Retrieved from http://www.gartner.com/newsroom/id/2525515.

Jenkins, H. (2006). *Convergence culture: Where old and new media collide*. New York: New York University Press.

Karaganis, J. (Ed.). (2011). Media piracy in emerging economies. *Social Science Research Council*. http://piracy.americanassembly.org/wp-content/uploads/2011/06/MPEE-PDF-1.0.4.pdf.

Kojima Productions. (2008). *Metal Gear Solid 4* [PlayStation 3]. Konami.

Media Molecule. (2008). *Little Big Planet* [PlayStation 3]. Sony Computer Entertainment.

Metal Gear Solid 4: Guns of the Patriots. (2014). *Internet Movie Database*. Retrieved from http://www.imdb.com/title/tt0462423/fullcredits?ref_=tt_cl_sm#cast

MineCon. (2014, January 4). *Gamepedia*. Retrieved from http://minecraft.gamepedia.com/MineCon#cite_ref-3.

Minecraft Wiki. (2013, September 20). Retrieved from http://minecraft.gamepedia.com/Minecraft_Wiki.

Mods/Portal Gun. (2013, September 30). *Gamepedia*. Retrieved from http://minecraft.gamepedia.com/Mods/Portal_Gun.

Mojang. (2011). *Minecraft* [PC game]. Stockholm, Sweden: Mojang.

Persson, M. [notch]. (2009a, May 13). Cave game tech demo [Tumblr]. Retrieved from http://notch.tumblr.com/post/107315028/cave-game-tech-demo.

Persson, M. [notch]. (2009b, May 16). Some thoughts on games modes [Tumblr]. Retrieved from http://notch.tumblr.com/post/108596899/some-thoughts-on-game-modes.

Persson, M. [notch]. (2009c, May 17). *Minecraft* 0.0.11a for public consumption [Tumblr]. Retrieved from http://notch.tumblr.com/post/109000107/minecraft-0-0-11a-for-public-consumption.

Persson, M. [notch]. (2009d, May 20). 0–0–12a is up [Tumblr]. Retrieved from http://notch.tumblr.com/post/110175116/0-0-12a-is-up.

Persson, M. [notch]. (2009e, May 21). My list on tile types so far [Tumblr]. Retrieved from http://notch.tumblr.com/post/110762705/my-list-on-tile-types-so-far.

Persson, M. [notch]. (2009f, May 22). I set up an irc channel for *Minecraft* [Tumblr]. Retrieved from http://notch.tumblr.com/post/111362732/i-set-up-an-irc-channel-for-minecraft.

Persson, M. [notch]. (2009g, May 23). So I didn't do multiplayer code by I had fun [Tumblr]. Retrieved from http://notch.tumblr.com/post/111691116/so-i-didnt-do-multiplayer-code-but-i-had-fun.

Persson, M. [notch]. (2009h, June 7). C418 starts work on the music and sounds for *Minecraft* [Tumblr]. Retrieved from http://notch.tumblr.com/post/119457666/c418-is-making-the-music-and-sounds-for-minecraft.

Persson, M. [notch]. (2009i, June 9). Oops I meant GPU not CPU [Tumblr]. Retrieved from http://notch.tumblr.com/post/120755152/oops-i-meant-gpu-not-cpu.

Persson, M. [notch]. (2009j, June 10). In the spirit of the new economy [Tumblr]. Retrieved from http://notch.tumblr.com/post/121044061/in-the-spirit-of-the-new-economy.

Persson, M. [notch]. (2009k, June 25). Some conversion rate math [Tumblr]. Retrieved from http://notch.tumblr.com/post/129864371/some-conversion-rate-math.

Persson, M. [notch]. (2009l, June 28). Client update tomorrow with the basics for sound [Tumblr]. Retrieved from http://notch.tumblr.com/post/131385451/client-update-tomorrow-with-the-basics-for-sound.

Persson, M. [notch]. (2010a, January 5). New sound engine implemented [Tumblr]. Retrieved from http://notch.tumblr.com/post/316961243/new-sound-engine-implemented.

Persson, M. [notch]. (2010b, January 13). Member number 100000 was jostvice3d [Tumblr]. Retrieved from http://notch.tumblr.com/post/332684203/member-number-100000-was-jostvice3d.

Persson, M. [notch]. (2010c, January 30). Phew last indev update for today [Tumblr]. Retrieved from http://notch.tumblr.com/post/360469298/phew-last-indev-update-for-today.

Persson, M. [notch]. (2010d, February 6). Polls and farming [Tumblr]. Retrieved from http://notch.tumblr.com/post/374446728/polls-and-farming.

Persson, M. [notch]. (2010e, February 7). Poll time [Tumblr]. Retrieved from http://notch.tumblr.com/post/395030658/poll-time.

Persson, M. [notch]. (2010f, February 14). My god [Tumblr]. Retrieved from http://notch.tumblr.com/post/389606025/my-god.

Persson, M. [notch]. (2010g, February 17). OK here's what I was thinking for the xp levels [Tumblr]. Retrieved from http://notch.tumblr.com/post/395114400/ok-heres-what-i-was-thinking-for-the-xp-levels.

Persson, M. [notch]. (2010h, February 21) Should I spend time to rewrite the game for infinite maps? Polldaddy.com. Retrieved from http://polldaddy.com/poll/2736635/?view=results.

Persson, M. [notch]. (2010i, April 8). Still going slow but here's a new screenshot [Tumblr]. Retrieved from http://notch.tumblr.com/post/506311060/still-going-slow-but-heres-a-new-screenshot.

Persson, M. [notch]. (2010j, April 30). One month until full time [Tumblr]. Retrieved from http://notch.tumblr.com/post/560997676/one-month-until-full-time\.

Persson, M. [notch]. (2010k, June 17). 20000 wow [Tumblr]. Retrieved from http://notch.tumblr.com/post/709098848/20000-wow.

Persson, M. [notch]. (2010l, July 7). All credit for the awesome new sound goes to c418 [Tumblr]. http://notch.tumblr.com/post/782386369/all-credit-for-the-awesome-new-sound-goes-to-c418-btw.

Persson, M. [notch]. (2010m, July 29). I'm going all gaga now 1000 sales in 24 hours [Tumblr]. Retrieved from http://notch.tumblr.com/post/875499109/im-going-all-gaga-now-1000-sales-in-24-hours.

Persson, M. [notch]. (2010n, August 19). Lots of stuff going on behind the scenes [Tumblr]. Retrieved from http://notch.tumblr.com/post/977394407/lots-of-stuff-going-on-behind-the-scenes.

Persson, M. [notch]. (2010o, September 6). Hiring some people getting an office and all [Tumblr]. Retrieved from http://notch.tumblr.com/post/1075326804/hiring-some-people-getting-an-office-and-all-that.

Persson, M. [notch]. (2011, April 11). The plan for [Tumblr]. Retrieved from http://notch.tumblr.com/post/4955141617/the-plan-for-mods.

Persson, M. [notch]. (2012, July 31). I am Markus Persson aka Notch, creator of *Minecraft*—ask me anything! *Reddit*. Retrieved from http://www.reddit.com/r/Minecraft/comments/xfzdg/i_am_markus_persson_aka_notch_creator_of.

Persson, M. [notch]. (2013, August 20). *Minecraft*+Sony=true [Twitter]. Retrieved from https://twitter.com/notch.

Pocket edition version history/ Development versions. (2014, January 4). *Gamepedia*. Retrieved from http://minecraft.gamepedia.com/Pocket_Edition_version_history.

Postigo, H. (2007). Of mods and modders: Chasing down the value of fan-based digital game modifications. *Games and Culture, 2*(4), 300–313.

Sony Computer Entertainment Santa Monica Studio. (2010). *God of War 3* [PlayStation 3]. SonyComputer Entertainment.

Valve Corporation. (2007). *Portal* [PC game]. Valve Corporation.

Xbox360 edition version history. (2014, January 18). *Gamepedia*. Retrieved from http://minecraft.gamepedia.com/Xbox_360_Edition_version_history.

Xbox One: A modern connected device. (2013, June). *Microsoft*. Retrieved from http://news.xbox.com/2013/06/connected.

Players, Modders
and Hackers

PETER CHRISTIANSEN

You wake up on a small grassy island, only a few meters across. On every side, there is nothing but open sky. There are no other signs of land—not even a hint of ground below you. The only other things on the island are a small oak tree and a chest. Inside, you find a bucket of lava, a block of ice, and a few other small trinkets. With the lava, the ice, and some careful planning, you can create cobblestone, but in order to mine it, you must take wood from your precious tree to fashion tools. Wood can be generated indefinitely, but doing so depends on the player carefully collecting saplings as the tree's leaves fall. Although the odds of getting at least one new sapling from each tree are in the player's favor, there is still a considerable amount of chance involved. This task is made even more difficult by the tree's proximity to the edge of the island. There is also a single piece of melon in the chest that the player could eat, but her continued survival depends on using that melon for its seeds in order to produce a steady supply. Growing melons requires a hoe, which requires even more wood. Thus, the player must strike a careful balance between stone production, melon farming, and woodcutting in order to ensure that neither her resources nor her own stamina run out before a sustainable system can be achieved. It is a game in which every block counts. A single item carelessly washed over the edge could mean the difference between starving to death in complete isolation and eking out a meager living in a world where a block of dirt is worth more than a chest full of gold.

Although *Minecraft* (Mojang, 2011) is often noted for its sense of emptiness conveyed through its vast wilderness landscape, the Skyblock mod (Noobcrew, 2011) takes this aesthetic to the extreme, placing the player in an expanse of endless sky, with just enough materials to survive. In some ways, Skyblock is a very simple mod. Indeed, the single player version would more accurately be called a custom map, as there are no new mechanics *per se*. Every item and material functions in the same way it normally does. Apart from the very specific rules for generating the world, there is very little that has changed from the unmodded or "vanilla" version of *Minecraft*. The kind of precise

Figure 1. The Skyblock mod places the player on a tiny floating island with barely enough resources to survive (Minecraft *®/TM & © 2009–2013 Mojang / Notch).

design demonstrated in Skyblock is only possible due to certain conditions present in the complex system that makes up *Minecraft*. It relies on the confluence of a number of different mechanics whose effects upon the gameworld are normally quite subtle—the way that liquid "source" blocks differ from flowing liquid, the way fire spreads, the way that plants grow, the way that mobs spawn, and so forth. Likewise, the emergence of a game such as *Minecraft*, along with its thriving modding community, depends on a similarly favorable alignment of conditions within a different system, the large socio-technical system that makes up the modern videogame industry.

Mod Culture

In the years since the advent of the World Wide Web, modding, or the modification of existing videogames by players, has become both more prevalent and more visible. Although a number of different games are often put forward as the first example of a videogame mod, the practice goes back much further than the game industry itself. As I have previously argued, the practice of modding goes back all the way to the beginning of videogames as a medium, with games like *Spacewar!* (1962) and *Colossal Cave Adventure* (1976) (Christiansen, 2012, pp. 31–32). These examples preceded the commercialization of videogames, which meant that modders and developers maintained a very different relationship. At that point in time, most games were shared freely over early networks such as the ARPANET, and many computer users were strongly motivated by the hacker ethic, or the idea that access to computers and information should be unlimited and total (Levy, 2010, p. 28). Game designers didn't expect to make any money by making games. To them, making a game was just a brilliant hack, as was taking someone else's game and giving it a new twist (Kent, 2001, p. 17). Some of these mods were simple aesthetic additions to the game, such as Pete Sampson's "Expensive Planetarium," which added a starfield to the background to *Spacewar!* (p. 19). Other mods drastically changed the way a game was played—what might be dubbed a "total conversion" in today's terminology. This was the case with *Adventure*, one of the earliest text adventure games. The original game, *Colossal Cave Adventure*, was created by Willie Crowther as a simple cave exploration game. It wasn't until Don Woods, a computer science graduate student and avid *Colossal Cave* fan, added on to Crowther's original code that the game acquired its familiar fantasy elements (King & Borland, 2003, pp. 30–32).

With the rise of early videogame companies like Atari, Sierra, and Sega, the once close relationship between game development and modding was suddenly problematized by economic interests. Although many game developers were pleased to see players dedicated enough to modify their games, others, particularly those more closely involved with the business and legal aspects of game development, saw mods as potential threats (Kushner, 2003, pp. 115–116). These threats included seeing mods as direct competition (p. 116), as threats to their copyrights (Altizer, 2013, p. 24), or even as potential sources of copyright conflicts with other intellectual property (IP) holders (pp. 19–21). These conflicts transformed modding from a natural part of the development process into a clandestine art, traded underground across BBS systems. In many ways, the technology itself both reflected and reinforced this attitude toward modding. Whereas many early games like *Spacewar!* were spread by distributing the source code itself, commercial games were compiled into impenetrable files that resisted modification. While ingenious hackers created many programs to unpack and alter game files, this process was destructive by nature (Kushner, 2003, p. 166). In order to generate new content, the old content had to be destroyed. Modding was stigmatized both culturally and technologically as digital vandalism.

One of the biggest forces to push back against both the cultural and technological barriers to modding was Id Software, the creators of *Wolfenstein 3D* (1992) and *Doom* (1993). At a time when the mainstream videogame industry had become so defensive of its patents and IP that companies like Nintendo were said to be in the business of "video games and litigation" (Sheff, 1993, p. 259), Id went against conventional wisdom. Although some members of Id were worried about the consequences of fan modded *Wolfenstein* games, John Carmack and John Romero, the two most prominent founders of the company, were believers in the hacker ethic that had driven early game developers (Kushner, 2003, p. 116). When they created their next game, *Doom*, the ability to mod the game was built into the very architecture of the software. Data was now stored in separate files, known as WADs, allowing modders to create their own WAD files without damaging the original game. Id gave modders an unprecedented amount of freedom to do what they wanted with the game. The only stipulations the company made were that the mods require the full version of the game in order to be played and that modders make it clear that their products were not created or supported by Id (p. 169). This meant not only that modders could openly modify the game without fear of being shut down by Id, but that they could even charge money for their mods if they wanted.

When the plan for mods in *Minecraft* was first announced (Persson, 2011a), it was very similar to Id's announcement. Eager *Minecraft* players, like the *Doom* modders before them (Kushner, 2003, p. 167), had already begun to tinker with the alpha version of the game. Mojang's response came as a rather informal notice, taking the form of a post on Notch's blog. This was later codified into a more official (though still relatively informal) End-User Licence Agreement (EULA) laying out the rights of modders and players (Mojang, 2013). As with *Doom*, modders are allowed and even encouraged to tinker with the game, as long as their mods still require players to purchase *Minecraft* first and that the modders don't directly make money from their mods (although many modders support themselves through donations or advertising on their websites).

Despite a difference of nearly twenty years between the founding of the two companies, Id and Mojang share a number of similarities in addition to their stances on modding. Both companies were founded by developers who share many of the same values as the early hackers of the 1950s and 1960s. This is perhaps most clearly demonstrated in the firm opposition to software patents by both John Carmack (Kushner, 2003, p. 205) and Notch (Persson, 2012). Additionally, both companies made use of unconventional distribution channels in order to sell their games. Although Id wasn't the first company to use shareware and Mojang wasn't the first to use direct downloads, both companies were able to take advantage of these distribution channels in a way that no other company had before.

The experiments in self-publishing by Id and Mojang have been unequivocal successes, taking the companies from obscure independent studios to major institutions within the videogame industry. While the most visible result of this success are the huge profits the companies have made from their games, I would argue that this is not their most important legacy. Rather, I suggest that the freedom that these companies have maintained from game publishers and console manufacturers has allowed them to push back against many of the problematic cultural aspects of the videogame industry itself.

The videogame industry is a large socio-technical system—a complex network of people, technology, laws, and ideas (Hughes, 1987, p. 51). The workings of such systems are incredibly complex, often masking the underlying power structures that favor certain groups at the expense of others. For example, the shift in power away from small studios and independent designers toward a handful of large publishers has had a number of problematic effects on the industry. Corporate policies and the excessive use of non-disclosure agreements (NDAs) have created a culture of secrecy that often hinders development (O'Donnell, 2008, pp. 229–230). Increasing budgets have demanded larger returns, making the industry more and more risk-averse and making publishers more likely to only finance derivative works such as sequels or film adaptations (Deuze, Martin and Allen, 2007, pp. 337). Meanwhile, the risks associated with developing new IP has been delegated to independent developers, with publishers taking over only after the game is successful (O'Donnell, 2008, pp. 160). These issues (along with many others) are perpetuated in part by the one-sided relationship between developers and publishers.

By achieving success outside the standard industry system, Id was able to exercise a degree of freedom that other development studios didn't have. This meant not only the creative freedom to make games that were much too violent and gory for the conservative standards of the early 1990s game industry but also the ability to control how they wanted their proprietary code to be used. This included supporting the modding community as well as licensing out their engines to other companies—eventually even releasing them as open source software. Breaking with the standard industry practice of jealously guarding their code benefited both small independent developers as well as companies such as Valve, which based its own engine after Id's *Quake* (1996) engine, even recruiting many of its first developers from the *Quake* modding community (Christiansen, 2012, p. 36). To this day, many 3D engines can trace their lineage back to those created by Id.

As with Id, Mojang's success has allowed the company to place values such as openness above economic concerns. Sometimes this means causing small issues, such as trying to deal with other developers and companies with Mojang's "no NDA" policy (Notch, 2012). Other times, it entails major financial decisions, such as not releasing a version of *Minecraft* on Steam (Persson, 2011b) or even Mojang's high profile cancellation of a potential version of the game for the Oculus Rift after Oculus was acquired by Facebook (Persson, 2014). It is also notable that despite Mojang's refusal to work with Facebook, the company made no attempt to shut down Minecrift, a mod that enables Oculus Rift support for the vanilla version of *Minecraft*. In fact, Notch even suggested that players try it out.

It remains to be seen if Mojang will have the same lasting influence on the videogame industry as Id. Given the amount of attention that a single sen-

tence from Notch can generate, it's certainly not an unlikely scenario. Still, if *Minecraft* has no other influence on the direction that videogames take, the sheer number of aspiring game developers currently getting their start modding the game are enough to place it alongside the likes of *Doom* and *Quake*.

Building Blocks

As previously mentioned, the culture of the videogame industry makes it a secretive place, which makes it difficult for outsiders to learn the kind of skills needed to participate. The modding community, on the other hand, thrives on openness and sharing in the same way that early hacker communities did. This makes the barriers to entry into modding considerably lower than those of traditional game design. Those interested in modding can find hundreds of resources online, including forums, tutorials, videos, and even custom software. One need not be an experienced programmer to create a *Minecraft* mod. In fact, it's possible to start learning without any background in programming at all. Although programming knowledge certainly accelerates the process, anyone can create a mod with enough patience and hard work.

Minecraft is written in Java, a language popular due to its ability to run across multiple platforms. Java takes its syntax from earlier languages like C and C++, as do other languages, such as ActionScript, C#, and JavaScript. This means that anyone with expertise in one of these languages is likely to find Java code somewhat familiar. Beginning programmers may find that most *Minecraft* forums and tutorials assume a basic understanding of Java. Fortunately, online resources for learning Java are even more abundant than those for learning *Minecraft* modding. There are also countless books and courses available for those who prefer a more structured approach.

Although writing Java code doesn't require anything more than a basic text editor, modders often use an integrated development environment (IDE), a specialized piece of software designed specifically for writing code. IDEs provide additional tools for compiling code, finding bugs, and other tasks that can be difficult using a text editor alone. A number of IDEs exist for Java coding, and many of these, such as Eclipse (www.eclipse.org) are free to download.

Many mods for *Minecraft* are created to run in isolation—modifying the game in one specific way. However, with different mods changing different aspects of the game, modders have banded together to write their own interfaces to allow multiple mods to be in use at the same time without conflicting with one another. This also allows modders to create mods for a very specific

Opposite: Figure 2. Eclipse is a popular environment for Java programming.

function, rather than trying to implement changes that other modders have already made in their own mods. There are APIs for the standard game, such as Minecraft Forge (www.minecraftforge.net), as well as APIs for creating server mods, such as Bukkit (bukkit.org). Each API has its own forums and wikis to help modders get started. There are also plenty of other forums, wikis, and other sites to help with general modding skills, independent of any specific API.

While there are a number of different technical ways to approach *Minecraft* modding, there are also many ways to approach it from a creative perspective. Some mods transform the game into a completely new experience, much like Willie Crowther's additions to *Colossal Cave Adventure*. Others are more like Expensive Planetarium—subtle changes that simply add to the original game. Still others operate behind the scenes, making small but significant technical changes that are barely noticeable to players during gameplay.

Bukkit is an example of this third type of mod. One of the earliest and most widely used server mods, Bukkit itself does very little to change the game. Its real power is in its ability to add other mods through the Bukkit API, allowing server operators to install and manage a wide array of mods in order to customize their worlds the way they want. This ability made Bukkit so popular that Mojang eventually hired the modders behind Bukkit, placing Nathan 'Dinnerbone' Adams, one of the modders, in charge of their upcoming Plugin API (Adams, 2013).

It's interesting to note that while most of the plug-ins for Bukkit add new functionality to the game, some actually remove features. In fact, the Bukkit website maintains an entire list of plug-ins designed to combat griefers—players who intentionally harass others by destroying their creations, killing their characters, and other malicious acts. For example, WorldGuard, a Bukkit plug-in designed primarily for anti-griefing, can be set up to prevent players from placing lava, setting fires, or detonating TNT (sk89q, wizjany, & zml2008, 2014). It can also prevent damage to structures from normally occurring mobs, such as endermen and creepers, ensuring that days or weeks of work aren't lost by an ill-timed explosion.

While mods like Bukkit are technical tools used mainly by server operators, most mods are far more visible to the player. Specialized servers exist where players can play games like Skyblock (www.skyblock.net) without having to set it up on their own machine. Although there are often hundreds of people on a server, the game generally functions mostly like the single player version, except that the floating islands of other players can be seen in the distance.

Another popular server mod is the Minecraft Hunger Games. Like many server mods, Minecraft Hunger Games isn't a single mod, but rather a category of similar mods, with different server operators creating their own custom

Figure 3. **Minecraft Hunger games on the HiveMC.eu server. Players begin on platforms surrounding a central cache of weapons and supplies (Minecraft ®/TM & © 2009–2013 Mojang / Notch).**

variations on the theme to try and attract new players. These mods, as one might suspect, are loosely based on *The Hunger Games* books and films, placing twenty-four (or sometimes even more) players in a huge arena with some weapons and supplies in the center. The objective is generally to be the last player standing, though many servers add their own twists. Most feature huge, detailed arenas where the battles take place. Some feature blood effects, special weapons, or minigames. Others offer special perks to players who donate to the server operators. As I am writing this, there are over 1,750 different *Minecraft* servers running a version of the Hunger Games, and that number is likely to continue increasing for the foreseeable future (Minecraft Server List, 2014).

Since *Minecraft* is primarily a game about building, it should come as no surprise that one of the most common ways to mod the game is simply to add new items and blocks. Many mods do little more than add a single new block, as in the piston mod that was eventually incorporated into vanilla *Minecraft* (jeb_, 2011). Other mods may add new materials to be mined that can then be fashioned into new classes of tools. Still others take it further, allowing the player to build complicated structures like factories, robots, and even spaceships. The Tekkit mod (http://www.technicpack.net/tekkit) actually combines dozens of other mods together, resulting in a world with thousands of different blocks, allowing the player to don futuristic flying armor and wield medieval weapons as she overlooks her industrial age factory.

Although the massive scope or sheer numbers of such mods may make

Figure 4. The Tekkit mod includes dozens of other mods, allowing the player to create hundreds of custom items (Minecraft °/TM & © 2009–2013 Mojang / Notch).

the idea of joining in seem daunting, it is important to remember that not every mod has to completely remake the game. Often, the simplest mods are the best. As Mojang continues to expand and improve *Minecraft* modding, the barriers to entry will only become lower for new programmers. Mojang's recent plug-in API, for example, will create new ways to alter the game.

Built for Mods

The massive size of the *Minecraft* modding community is due in part to both the popularity of the game and the supportive attitude of the game developers. It could be argued, however, that there is more to the phenomenon than simply a favorable alignment of social conditions. In many ways, the very design of *Minecraft* is directed toward modding.

A new game of *Minecraft* begins in the same way many games do, with the player setting off to gather resources. *Minecraft*, of course, is unusual in the fact that everything around you—wood, grass, cows, dirt—can be transformed into some kind of collectable item. Still, gathering wood and stone to prepare for nightfall isn't entirely different from gathering weapons and ammo in *Half-Life* (Valve, 1998), picking up useful items in *Day of the Tentacle* (Lucas Arts, 1993), or mining minerals in *Starcraft* (Blizzard, 1998).

After gathering some basic resources, the player's next task is to use those resources to craft items. Sticks and stones are turned into swords, pickaxes, furnaces, and ladders. At this point, the comparison between *Minecraft* and most other games becomes a bit strained. While it is true that a *Starcraft* player "builds" soldiers and tanks out of minerals, the experience is far removed from *Minecraft*-style crafting. There is no need to arrange, smelt, or distill resources in *Starcraft*. Resources simply function like currency, with certain quotas to be met before a certain unit can be created. *Minecraft* resources never reach this level of abstraction. They are always items that can be held, thrown, and manipulated by the player as much as any other item in the world. Although certain quotas must still be met in order for the player to create some items, there is no virtual bank account to manage resources. If the player wants a ladder tall enough to scale a cliff, she must chop down a tree, haul the wood back to her workbench, chop it into sticks and assemble the ladder herself.

By the time the player begins using her resources to shape the landscape of her new virtual world, the experience of playing *Minecraft* is so unusual that it might seem more akin to playing with LEGO or using a clunky 3D modeling program than to playing another videogame. It is also at this point that individual play styles start to take the game in drastically different directions. Whereas there is only one way to craft an iron pickaxe, there are limitless ways that a player could construct her home. She could build a small wooden hut or a huge Gothic cathedral. Likewise, this freedom could be used to build an obstacle course, giant pixel art, or a scale model of her home town. The player can even choose to play in creative mode, rather than survival, taking out the most game-like mechanics in favor of using *Minecraft* for pure creation.

The creative aspects of the game are further enhanced with the addition of redstone, which allows the player to turn her static creations into active machines. The mechanics of redstone circuits mimic physical electronic circuits so accurately that various players have built functional CPUs out of redstone, creating virtual computer chips the size of cities (fortunately, herds of cattle and pigs roaming through your computer chip don't seem to interfere with its function). While there are occasional projects of this massive scope, more common devices include automated farms, secret passages, and mob grinders—devices that kill enemies and collect their valuable items for the player. Since redstone devices can become quite complex, it's not uncommon for people to share their designs outside of the game, in forums, videos, and tutorials. Within these communities, designs are refined, new ideas are tested, and innovative players are able to show off their creativity and technical know-how.

By the time a player has progressed to this point in the game, the jump from player to modder is surprisingly small (and in relation to some redstone creations, modding is probably quite a bit simpler). A modder looking for help creating new mobs and a player trying to build a proper redstone logic gate will likely follow similar processes—searching wikis, asking on forums, and so forth. The mechanics of the game shape the behavior of the player, configuring her not only as survivalist or an adventurer, but as a builder, a programmer, and a hacker.

This almost seamless continuum between player, modder, and developer illustrates a different way of thinking about digital practices such as work, play, and ownership. Baldrica (2007) has argued that user contributions to digital media should be considered along a similar scale. He divides user-created content into four categories: Normal game content, derivative content, games created by modifying the game, and non-games created by modifying the game (Baldrica, 2007, pp. 687–693; Altizer, 2013, p. 30). In *Minecraft*, players create work in all four categories. The castles, cities, and machines that players create in vanilla *Minecraft* fall into the first category, while screenshots and YouTube videos would fall into the category of derivative works. Mods generally fall into the third category, while other transformative works, such as machinima, would fall into the final. Baldrica makes the case for the rights of creators in all four groups, with those in the latter categories being particularly deserving of creative rights. Mojang, to its credit, has a reputation for supporting modders and YouTubers, demonstrating how such a conception of digital labor and ownership can not only be possible, but beneficial to the company in the long run.

Perhaps even more importantly, this blurring of lines between players, modders, and developers serves a pedagogical function. As players learn to play the game, they are also learning about the process of game making. The skills learned through normal play move slowly from game-specific skills, such as how to craft better armor or build a zombie-proof house, to more general or abstract skills, such as how to create a device that turns off after a certain amount of time or design a structure out of square blocks that mimics a smooth curve. This steady progression can eventually lead players to think like programmers and move from in-game tinkering to actual coding.

While this kind of technical learning is quite novel in the videogame industry of today, such was the norm in the culture of early computer games in the 1970s. Before the widespread use of either the Internet or floppy disks, games were widely distributed in print magazines, which simply listed the full code of the game. In order to play, the player had to first type the code into her computer. This process both forced the player to acquire a basic understanding of how computer programs functioned and provided an opportunity for "unguided learning" (Montfort, et al. 2012, pp. 183–184). Likewise, *Minecraft* requires the player to gain a certain amount of technical learning in order to play the game, while providing an open space for her to experiment with new ideas.

Built for Hackers

Minecraft is a game for hackers. It encourages players to investigate its world, tinker with it, and ultimately take that world apart to see how it works. Indeed, despite being a commercial game that has sold millions of copies worldwide, the development of *Minecraft* in many ways more closely resembles an open source project than a triple-A title. Notch has openly acknowledged his inspiration from other independent games like *Dwarf Fortress* (Adams, 2006) and *Infiniminer* (Barth, 2009) since the beginning (Persson, 2009). The game was released early, and continues to be updated often. Players in many ways are treated more like co-developers than customers, particularly in the case of modders. Finally, when Notch, the lead developer, was ready to move on from the project, he found a competent successor in proper hacker fashion (Raymond, 1998).

Given the current culture of the videogame industry, dominated by massive corporations, proprietary secrets, and derivative projects, a game like *Minecraft* is an anomaly. Through a convergence of heterogeneous factors, it not only survived under such conditions, but grew into a massive cultural force of its own. It now serves as a counter example to much of the conventional industry wisdom on subjects like ownership and openness.

Although the modding community has enjoyed a greater degree of security and stability since the days of *Doom* and *Quake*, its future is far from certain. Despite generally good relations between modders and developers, the current legal system often does little to protect the rights of modders (Altizer, 2013, pp. 3–5). Additionally, many studios seem to be less willing to support modding, with some games, such as *Diablo III* (Blizzard, 2012), banning mods completely (Meer, 2011). If we want mods to remain a part of videogame culture, we need to support their creators, as well as the developers who make modding a part of their games. It also couldn't hurt to have a few more games like *Minecraft* out there.

References

Adams, N. (2013). The story of the bone and the bukkit. *Dinnerblog*. Retrieved April 1, 2014 from http://dinnerbone.com/blog/2013/01/06/story-bone-and-bukkit/

Adams, T. (2006). *Dwarf Fortress* [PC game]. Bay 12 Games.

Altizer, R. A. (2013). *A grounded legal study of the breakdown of modders' relationships— with game companies or legal threats shake moral beds* (Ph.D. dissertation). University of Utah.

Baldrica, J. (2007). Mod as heck: Frameworks for examining ownership rights in user-contributed content to videogames, and a more principled evaluation of expressive appropriation in user-modified videogame projects. *Minnesota Journal of Law, Science & Technology 8*, 681.

Barth, Z. (2009). *Infiniminer* [PC game].

Blizzard Entertainment. (1998). *Starcraft* [PC game]. Irvine, CA: Blizzard.

Blizzard Entertainment. (2012). *Diablo III* [PC game]. Irvine, CA: Blizzard.

Christiansen, P. (2012). Between a mod and a hard place. In E. Champion (Ed.). *Game mods: Design, theory and criticism*. Pittsburgh, PA: ETC Press.

Deuze, M., Martin, C., & Allen, C. (2007). The professional identity of gameworkers. *Convergence, 13*(4).

Hughes, T. (1987). The evolution of large technological systems. In W. Bijker, T. Hughes & T. Pinch (Eds.), *The social construction of technological systems: New directions in the sociology and history of technology* (pp. 51–82). Cambridge, MA: MIT Press.

ID Software. (1992). *Wolfenstein 3D* [PC game]. Apogee Software.

ID Software. (1993). *Doom* [PC game]. GT Interactive.

ID Software. (1996). *Quake* [PC game]. GT Interactive.

jeb_. (2011, June 9). Attribution of the piston mod in vanilla *Minecraft*. Reddit. [Reddit]. Retrieved from http://www.reddit.com/r/Minecraft/comments/hvkmo/attribution_ of_the_ piston_mod_in_vanilla_minecraft/.

Kent, S. (2001). *The ultimate history of videogames*. London: Three Rivers Press.

King, B., & Borland, J. (2003). *Dungeons and dreamers: The rise of computer game culture from geek to chic*. Emeryville, CA: McGraw-Hill.

Kushner, D. (2003). *Masters of Doom: How two guys created an empire and transformed pop culture*. New York: Random House.

Lucas Arts. (1993). *Day of the tentacle* [PC game]. Lucas Arts.

Meer. A. (2011). *Diablo III*: No mods, online-only, cash trades. *Rock, Paper, Shotgun. Online.* Retrieved April 3, 2014, from http://www.rockpapershotgun.com/2011/08/01/ diablo-iii-no-mods-online-only-cash-trades/.

Minecraft Server List. (2014). Retrieved April 2, 2014, from http://minecraft-server-list.com/sort/HungerGames/.

Mojang. (2011). *Minecraft* [PC game]. Stockholm, Sweden: Mojang.

Mojang. (2013). *Minecraft* End User Licence Agreement. Retrieved March 29, 2014, from https://account.mojang.com/documents/minecraft_eula.

Montfort, N., Baudoin, P., Bell, J., Bogost, I., Douglass, J., Marino, M. C., ... & Vawter, N. (2012). *PRINT CHR $(205.5+ RND (1));: GOTO 10*. Cambridge, MA: MIT Press.

Noobcrew. (2011). Skyblock. [*Minecraft* Mod]. Available online at http://www.skyblock. net/ downloads/

O'Donnell, C. (2008). *The work/play of the interactive new economy: Video game development in the United States and India*. Troy, NY: Rensselaer Polytechnic Institute.

Persson, M. [notch]. (2009, October 3). The origins of *Minecraft*. [Tumblr]. Retrieved April 3, 2014, from http://notch.tumblr.com/post/227922045/the-origins-of-minecraft

Persson, M. [notch]. (2011a, April 26). The plan for mods. [Tumblr]. Retrieved March 29, 2014, from http://notch.tumblr.com/post/4955141617/the-plan-for-mods

Persson, M. [notch]. (2011b, August 29). Why no Steam, Notch? [Tumblr]. Retrieved March 30, 2014, from http://notch.tumblr.com/post/9550850116/why-no-steam-notch

Persson, M. [notch]. (2012a, July 22). On patents [Tumblr]. Retrieved March 29, 2014, from http://notch.tumblr.com/post/27751395263/on-patents

Persson, M. [notch]. (2012b, July 31). Our "no nda" policy is already starting to cause trouble, haha. Totally worth it, though [Twitter]. Retrieved from https://twitter.com/notch/status/230248774864359424

Persson, M. [notch]. (2014, March 25). Virtual Reality is going to change the world. *Notch.net*. Retrieved March 30, 2014, from http://notch.net/2014/03/virtual-reality-is-going-to- change-the-world/

Raymond, E. S. (1998). The cathedral and the bazaar. *First Monday.* Retrieved from http://firstmonday.org/ojs/index.php/fm/article/view/1472/1387

Sheff, D. (1993). *Game over: How Nintendo zapped an american industry, captured your dollars and enslaved your children.* New York: Random House.

sk89q, wizjany, & zml2008. (2014). WorldGuard. *Bukkit.* Retrieved April 2, 2014, from http://dev.bukkit.org/bukkit-plugins/worldguard/

Valve Software. (1998). *Half-Life* [PC game]. Sierra Entertainment.

Teaching Tools

Progressive Pedagogy and
the History of Construction Play

COLIN FANNING *and* REBECCA MIR

Participating in a secret chain letter circulated among German artists and architects between November 1919 and December 1920, architect Wenzel Hablik encouraged his colleagues to dream of a fantastical rebuilding of their nation after World War I (Figure 1). He addressed his correspondents:

> Children! What magnificent materials our earth still has as "material for our building games!" Just think: We have rock! Metal and diamonds! And many beautiful sands! And water! Fire and air! We can blow—suck—hit—bore—lift—press—smelt—and soon we shall also be able to fly! We can live in the air! [translated in Whyte, 1985, p. 28].

In the so-called "Crystal Chain Letters," the post-World War I German avant-garde envisioned future utopian structures and cities without limiting themselves to practicalities, drawing inspiration from the inquisitive nature of children's play (Kinchin, 2012a, p. 60). Children and adults today live out a version of Hablik's description of unfettered, creative construction in the videogame *Minecraft* (Mojang, 2011).

Given his prediction in the Crystal Chain, perhaps Hablik would not have been surprised by *Minecraft*'s success, only by the digital form this "building game" has taken. The freedom to build with nearly unlimited materials, the complexity—and occasional levity—of the crafting system itself, and the memorable retro appeal of the game's graphics have all garnered praise since its first release in 2009. *Minecraft*'s overwhelmingly positive reception relies on historically well-established ideas about play, building, and architecture, especially those promoted through the long-standing genre of construction toys. Broadly defined, construction toys and games encourage players to build, tinker, and create new objects or structures from modular units. Construction *play* occurs when people engage in this kind of building, tinkering, and creating with certain objects (often, but not necessarily, toys and games).

Historically, the act of building and the manipulation of objects have

Figure 1. Wenzel Hablik, *Große bunte utopische Bauten (Great Colorful Utopian Constructions)*, 1922. Oil on canvas (Wenzel-Hablik Foundation, Itzehoe).

formed an integral part of progressive educational theory on the role of play in human development. Reformers like Johann Heinrich Pestalozzi, Friedrich Fröbel, and Maria Montessori contributed to contemporaneous *and* contemporary views of the interrelationship between building, playing, and learning through their varying approaches to the "object lesson." This concept, which holds that active engagement with material things unlocks an individual's higher faculties and allows sensory information to be transformed into concrete knowledge, has become a foundational tenet for childhood development and education for learners of all ages (Krusi, 1875, reprint 2010; Fröbel,1904; Kinchin, 2012c). Progressive pedagogues inspired by the object lesson often taught with materials designed specifically to encourage constructive learning.

Building on these nineteenth-century educational theories, the discourse of construction play underwent significant changes during the twentieth century. In the postwar era, a particular mode of thoughtful, creative play advocated by designers and educators arose as part of a widespread preoccupation—especially in northern Europe—with "good toys" (Ogata, 2012, p. 171). The Danish LEGO bricks are perhaps the best-known construction toys to profit from careful marketing that promoted the wholesomeness of construction play, but earlier examples like Erector Sets or derivations of the long-lived German *Anker* building blocks hold equal relevance for the study of *Minecraft*'s historical underpinnings. Parallel to these postwar commercial developments, a novel vision of construction play emerged through the inventive reuse of rubble and spare building materials in the "adventure playgrounds" of wartorn European cities. Philanthropists and designers crafted these environments to foster an active, messy process of creativity and self-determination through play for urban children (Kozlovsky, 2008).

We argue that *Minecraft* unites this active, open-ended concept of the adventure playground with the tradition of educative play promised by the manufacturers of construction toys. *Minecraft*'s manifold play experiences, its ability to bridge generational gaps, and the increasingly widespread educational uses of the game (well documented in online forums like YouTube and MinecraftEdu) enable an intriguing reading of the game itself as a "good toy" that encourages creativity, rewards independent development, and evokes longstanding notions of productive play and its social benefits. In demonstrating the connections between *Minecraft* and enduring theories of education and design reform, and by surveying the critical and testimonial rhetoric about the game, we aim to complicate the pioneer discourse that surrounds it, while elucidating *Minecraft*'s important place in both the history of playthings and contemporary game studies.

Progressive Pedagogy and the Object Lesson

While children have been playing and building without the help of manufactured toys for most of human history, modern notions about the role of playthings in childhood development can be traced to a more recent period. Historians of childhood consistently credit the widely reproduced theories of Enlightenment scholars in the seventeenth and eighteenth centuries with consolidating and disseminating the paradigm of valuing children's individuality and the formative qualities of joyful play, especially in the middle classes of Europe and North America (Cunningham, 2005, pp. 59–64).

John Locke's influential *Some Thoughts Concerning Education* is perhaps best-known for promulgating the notion of the child as a *tabula rasa*, or blank slate, to be filled by a moral and intellectual education. While his prescriptive advice may seem strict by today's standards, he nevertheless advocated for the importance of toys and play in fostering a child's curiosity and skills (Locke,

1693; Cross, 1997, p. 19; Ogata, 2013, p. 36). Later, Jean-Jacques Rousseau's *Émile, or: On Education* played a prominent role in establishing the romantic notion of the child as an innocent entity living in harmony with the natural world, a concept that remains deeply ingrained in Western culture. For Rousseau, the purpose of a child's education and play was to foster individuality and exploration (Rousseau, 1762, reprint 2009, pp. 94, 249; Cunningham, 2005, p. 63).

By the early nineteenth century, pedagogues were increasingly codifying these ideas about the nature of childhood in theories and instructional methods that ran counter to prevailing trends at the time. The Swiss reformer Johann Heinrich Pestalozzi's enduring concept of *Anschauung*—later known in English as the "object lesson"—combined Rousseau's emphasis on the individuality of the child with a strong belief that the sensory (rather than verbal) faculties as the fundamental basis of human learning (Krusi, 1875, p. 163; Ogata, 2013, p. xiii).

FRIEDRICH FRÖBEL AND BLOCK PLAY

A student of Pestalozzi, Friedrich Fröbel (1782–1852) was a German educator and the inventor of the kindergarten. He ensconced the notion of the object lesson in the novel system he developed for young children's education. In contrast to educational tendencies in the early nineteenth-century European classroom, he believed that allowing children to act spontaneously on their creative impulses and curiosity would provide them with an early comprehension of what he believed to be the underlying spiritual unity of all things. Accordingly, he designed a series of objects he called Gifts and Occupations to facilitate his approach (Brosterman, 1997, pp. 32–4).

Sensory experience and manual manipulation were the key vehicles for Fröbel's pedagogy. Interacting with the material forms of the Gifts, often directed by a (usually female) educator, children progressed through a sequence of activities that increased in complexity, building upon the lessons of the earlier, simpler tasks. Fröbel designed the Gifts to introduce gradually the various properties and dimensions of geometric shapes: the third Gift, for example, comprised a set of uniform cubic wooden blocks, the fourth Gift contained rectangular prisms, and the fifth Gift provided cubes halved or quartered on their diagonals (Fröbel, 1904; see also Brosterman, 1997, pp. 50–7). In Fröbel's kindergarten, children experimented with shape, size, and volume through block play, building knowledge that connected back to the whole forms (Figure 2). The parts of each individual Gift could be recombined into a single larger cube, underscoring their connection to the Euclidean shape. As Fröbel writes:

After comprehending the *outside* of the object, the child likes also to investigate its *inside*; after a perception of the *whole*, to see it separated into its *parts*; if he obtained a glimpse of the *first*, if he has attained the *second*, he would like from the parts again to *create the whole*. (pp. 117–8, emphasis in original)

Later in the sequence, kindergartners used the shapes to build structures independently, and the Occupations provided materials children could alter themselves to create patterns and pictures from paper, string, or cloth (Fröbel, 1904, pp. 173–4).

The manual and metaphysical lessons Fröbel aimed to draw forth with his building blocks were not wholly abstract. In his instructions on the use of the fourth Gift, he narrates a scenario in which a mother or nurse plays with the child, using the blocks to build objects and portray scenes from domestic work and life: a fireplace for cooking transforms into a turf-bench for gardening, which in turn becomes a small house for shelter (Fröbel, 1904, pp. 179–81). The operative factor, for Fröbel, is the inherent flexibility and mutability of these abstract objects in representing concrete ones, and the gradual, iterative process of the block play (Fröbel, 1904, p. 180). A sense of interconnectedness also runs through Fröbel's advocacy of nature study for children, which itself became a prominent part of educational discourse in the nineteenth century. While subsequent education reformers particularly valued the scientific knowledge gained from observation of the natural world, Fröbel saw encounters with nature and its hidden systems as important spiritual lessons and a key symbolic corollary to the growth of the child (Brosterman, 1997, p. 34).

Toward the end of Fröbel's life, the kindergarten was victim of a backlash against progressive education reform; the Prussian government and other German states banned the system in 1851 (Allen, 1995, p. 87). Although Fröbel did not live to see the kindergarten movement flourish, it would eventually reach most of the Western world. In the process, the quasi-spiritual lessons Fröbel expounded in his teachings, and the careful sequence of object encounters he intended for the Gifts, were largely forgotten. His kindergarten Gifts and Occupations became viewed more as conventional toys than tools for

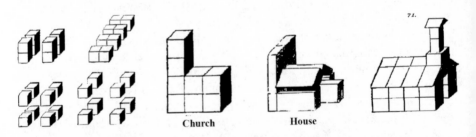

Church   House

Figure 2. Examples of different shapes made with Fröbel's third, fourth, and fifth Gifts from *The Kindergarten Guide* (Kraus-Boelté & Kraus, 1881) (From left to right: third Gift cube divisions [p. 30], third Gift church [p. 36], fourth Gift house [p. 72], and fifth Gift structure [p. 91]).

unlocking metaphysical knowledge (Brosterman, 1997, p. 13). What remained in teachers' use of these objects, however, was the unwavering belief that early and frequent encounters with tangible things—especially small, modular units that could be combined in numerous ways—constituted an essential part of children's physical and mental growth.

MONTESSORI'S "FREE WORK"

Working later in the nineteenth century and into the early twentieth, the well-known Italian physician and educator Maria Montessori similarly placed early childhood education on an explicitly material basis. Where Fröbel ultimately intended his kindergarten to impart metaphysical lessons to the child, for Montessori the classroom was an environment for training children's senses, manual dexterity, and practical skills. In opposition to what she saw as the "sentimentality" and the child's dependence on the educator in Fröbelian pedagogy, Montessori maintained that children should have freedom in both work and play, but only within a curricular structure facilitated by a trained instructor:

> *The organization of the work*, therefore, is the corner-stone of this new structure of goodness; but even that organization would be in vain without the *liberty* to make use of it, and without freedom for the expansion of all those energies which spring from the satisfaction of the child's highest activities [1914, reprint 1988, pp. 187–8].

This "freedom principle" allowed children to decide what activities they would carry out, when, for how long, and in what sort of social setting (Müller & Schneiger, 2002, p. 22). At the same time, the physical environment of Montessori's school, called the Casa Dei Bambini (Children's House), was arranged according to an explicitly "scientific" rationale, equipped with a carefully controlled "didactic apparatus" of teaching materials (Montessori, 1914, reprint 1988, p. 12).

Steeped in a moralizing discourse of hygiene and domestic efficiency, many of the materials Montessori prescribed were often child-sized versions of ordinary household goods, but more abstract tools played a part in the curriculum as well. Her designs for blocks comprised series of geometric solids in graduated sizes, named for the forms children were meant to construct: these included the Tower, the Broad Stair, and the Long Stair (Montessori, 1912, reprint 1988, pp. 192–5). Part of Montessori's larger project in developing young children's motor skills and spatial awareness, the blocks ostensibly instructed their users in the concepts of counting, basic geometry, visual comparison, and ultimately self motivation. While Montessori insisted that "the aim of the exercise ... is *not* that the rods be arranged in the right order of gradation, but that the child *should practice by himself*" (Montessori, 1914, p. 76, emphasis in original), the act of creative building was backgrounded by the developmental purpose of the blocks. Montessori's didactic apparatus, then, lay wholly outside the discourse of imaginative play, which formed the basis of some critiques that other pedagogues leveled at the method (Müller & Schneiger, 2002, p. 30). Nevertheless, the subtext of the object lesson underlined Montessori's notions of "free work" and the toy-like objects in the Casa Dei Bambini. The method, still prevalent in many places today, has had an enormous impact on early-childhood education around the globe (Kinchin, 2012e, p. 47).

Pedagogical Legacies and *Minecraft*

While both Fröbel and Montessori planned for adults to facilitate activities in the classroom, they hoped that allowing children to instigate their own play would encourage the child's curiosity and sense of motivation (Müller & Schneiger, 2002, p. 13). One of the reasons we believe *Minecraft* became so popular among educators and people of all ages is that the game allows for a similar kind of exploration, freedom, and skill development. *Minecraft* does not require an adult facilitator, but the structure of the game world itself provides a framework that places restrictions on the player. Additionally, a robust Internet culture of collaboratively edited wikis, discussion forums, and instructional fan-made videos replicates, in some ways, the role of an adult educator. *Minecraft* users must seek instruction themselves, allowing them to determine their own level of autonomy in discovering the inner workings of the game. Thus *Minecraft* could be considered the "object" that helps players unlock a higher knowledge or "lesson," in the language of Pestalozzi *et al.*, but "technical fluency" or "informational literacy" would be more appropriate using contemporary educational terminology.

Similarly, traces of the material components of these progressive pedagogies appear in the gameplay experience. Like Fröbel's Gifts, block play in *Minecraft* proceeds from the basic geometric manipulation of whole cubes to a freer type of building with more diverse shapes and sizes. As subsequent Gifts were introduced in the kindergarten, the potential outcomes increased in complexity; *Minecraft*'s crafting system represents an intriguing parallel to this progression of form. Wood, one of the first resources players must acquire and manipulate for survival in the game, is an evocative example not only for its material connection to the Fröbel Gifts, but also for the way in which its crafting generates an expansive set of variations on the initial cubic form. Players craft the raw blocks they gather by punching trees into wood planks, and from there into sticks, doors, buttons, and other rudimentary tools (not to mention the all-important crafting table).

The constructions children created with Fröbel's Gifts, as illustrations of a larger cosmic unity, were meant to both signify their full-sized counterparts and, through the material properties of the blocks, exercise a "generality of form" that is "easily put together and joined" (Fröbel, 1904, pp. 121–2). The same "generality of form" is at work in the cubic world of *Minecraft*, and its vast landscapes and flexible physics foster what Fröbel might call an "excellent means of awakening the inner world" (1904, p. 122) of the player's creativity. While Mojang almost certainly did not consciously model *Minecraft*'s central play mechanic on the theories of nineteenth-century pedagogues, Western educational models have been so thoroughly steeped in the work of Pestalozzi, Fröbel, and Montessori that the parallels are neither likely to be entirely coincidental.

Postwar Construction Play

Manufactured toys had historically been the playthings of wealthy children, but the spread of Fröbel's and Montessori's systems, coupled with industrial advances in manufacturing and printing, contributed to a proliferation of building blocks (alongside board and quiz games, puzzles, and other amusements) in late nineteenth-century Europe and North America (Brosterman, 1997, p. 50). Manufacturers' claims that these games would provide moral instruction and keep children happy and at home with their families dovetailed with similar claims by advocates of educational playthings (Hofer, 2003, p. 53; Cross, 1997, pp. 21–2). One of the earliest construction toys to be both mass-produced and mass-marketed, the German *Anker-Steinbaukasten* (Anchor Stone Blocks), provides an explicit example: Richter's, the firm that manufactured the *Anker* blocks, sold them with promotional language linking them to Fröbel's pedagogy (Williams, 1999, pp. 21–2, 31). In contrast to Fröbelian pedagogy, however, these stone-composite blocks were highly representational and adorned with classicizing motifs; the packaging indicated they were meant primarily as an architectural toy, far removed from the intentionally ambiguous formal language of Fröbel's Gifts.

As these toys and amusements entered the homes of a wider economic spectrum of consumers in the early decades of the twentieth century, the positive connotations and creative value of construction play were perpetuated by manufacturers, parents, and educators alike—a narrative that, indeed, continues today (Lauwaert, 2009, pp. 46–7). Building toys specifically, in both Europe and the United States, promoted open-ended play to their largely middle-class audiences, but the design of the toys themselves often attempted to prescribe what children could build. Alice T. Friedman argues that many building toys in this period constituted "miniature play houses which mimic[ked] the appearance of the freestanding, 'comfortable' homes associated with the families of successful businessmen and prosperous citizens" (1995, pp. 8–10). At the same time, a class of toys like the innovative and popular Meccano, designed in the United Kingdom near the turn of the twentieth century, or the American Erector Sets (1913) were intended as "instructive and amusing" exercises in mechanical engineering (Pasierbska, 2004, p. 3; Lauwaert, 2009, p. 47). Playthings that represented specific kinds of architecture, civic design, or engineering were steeped in solidly middle-class cultural values of domesticity or rational construction, and often, as with the *Anker* blocks, featured historicizing ornament and realistic detail (Brosterman, 1997, p. 50; Williams, 1999, p. 21). These interrelated genres of playthings carried implicit (or sometimes explicit) lessons of "what parents once thought their children should know about the built world" (Centre Canadien d'Architecture, 1991, p. 8).

A Mind for Design: Postwar "Good Toys"

After World War II, the tenor of discussions on childhood play shifted away from specifically didactic toys toward a growing emphasis on creativity and individual expression. In both Europe and North America, larger efforts toward postwar regeneration informed a widespread discourse on "good toys." Designers and psychologists alike increasingly held abstraction and simplicity in children's things as the keys to unlocking the child's imaginative powers, qualities that recalled Fröbel's Gifts and Montessori's didactic apparatus. These postwar playthings often constituted a rejection of what parents and designers saw as the counterproductive realism or overemphatic novelty of many other mass-market toys; as a guide to architectural toys in the American periodical *Progressive Architecture* argued, "Process becomes as important as product in a construction toy" and "the last thing a child needs in a toy is utter realism" (E.P., 1966). The concept of the good toy took hold particularly strongly in Scandinavia, tied in part to craft traditions and notions of quality production that countries like Sweden and Denmark cultivated in goods for international markets (Ogata, 2012, pp. 171–3). Inspired by the sociological study of children's play, this discourse positioned creativity itself as both an agent and goal of children's development (Nicolopoulou, 1993; Ogata, 2013).

It was in this cultural milieu of postwar regeneration and self-consciously creative—rather than strictly educative—play that the now-iconic LEGO bricks had their beginning. The history of the Danish toy is worth dwelling on in some detail, not only for the comparisons between it and *Minecraft* that regularly appear in the discourse surrounding the game, but also because LEGO itself provides a case study in many of the larger cultural narratives attached to the design and marketing of construction toys in the postwar era.

Initially introduced as "Automatic Binding Bricks" in 1949, the toys were an early experiment in plastic manufacture for Ole Kirk Christiansen's small company in Billund, Denmark. LEGO had previously been known for well-made wooden toys that fit neatly into Scandinavian tradition, but after purchasing a plastic molding machine, Christiansen copied a manufacturer's sample of plastic bricks that the British designer and child psychologist Hilary Page had been selling since at least 1946 (Hughes, 2010). Notably, Page later authored a text on the role of play in child development; his ideas and toy designs for his company Kiddicraft echoed both the longstanding belief in designed objects to instill specific skills and knowledge in children, as well as the growing emphasis in twentieth-century psychology on creativity and open-ended play (Page, 1953).

LEGO refined the brick's design further in 1958, and both historians and fans have credited the new brick and its interlocking mechanism with ensuring LEGO's immense popularity, by expanding its construction potential beyond that of its competitors and precedents (Lauwaert, 2009, pp. 47, 53–6; Hughes, 2010). But that success came only gradually, and it was not until

Figure 3. Bifold cover for the 1955 LEGO *System i Leg* Catalog (Reproduced in Hughes [2010]; photograph by David Shifflett. LEGO is a trademark of the LEGO Group of Companies. © 2014 The LEGO Group. Photograph used by permission).

the toys had been on the market for nearly a decade that they began to achieve wide recognition outside Denmark (Weincek, 1987, pp. 46–52). The growing sophistication of LEGO's marketing played an important part in the toy's international reception as well. In 1955, the company refashioned the plastic bricks into the *System i Leg* (System of Play), which positioned the existing products in a larger "Town Plan" conceit (Figure 3) (Lipkowitz, 2009, pp. 18–9). This new play narrative evoked contemporary trends in modern architecture, and the refocused marketing contained exhortations to parents about the benefits of thoughtful, quiet play and creative construction. A 1960s LEGO advertisement in a Danish magazine, for example, reads in translation:

> It's a pleasure to see children playing with LEGO—LEGO play is quiet and stimulating. Children learn to grapple with major tasks and solve them together. When LEGO's urban system comes into play, children built not only houses but entire cities with streets and traffic. One day, a LEGO city, the next a doll, ships, trains or planes. ALL ARE BUILT OF LEGO [reproduced in Hughes, 2010; trans. by author Fanning].

As LEGO continued to diversify its product line in the second half of the twentieth century, the construction potential of the toy relied increasingly on the idea of a *system* of abstract, modular components. While LEGO has consistently been packaged and sold with specific building suggestions derived from existing tropes of construction toys, the dominant marketing narrative has often focused on the potential for children to build anything at all. This was consistent with a variety of mid-century toys in both Europe and the United States that stressed the importance of a creative childhood (Ogata, 2013, pp. 50–1). At the same time, the modular logic of the individual components also allowed LEGO to package the toy in both large and small sets, a savvy strategy that allowed the toy to reach a wider spectrum of consumers and provided more opportunities for children (and adults) to enlarge their collections (Kline, 1993, p. 158). In 1962, LEGO codified its aspirations into a series of ten "Principles of Play" that crystallized the dual educative and economic ambitions of the company:

Unlimited play potential
For girls, for boys
Fun for every age
Year-round play
Healthful, quiet play
Long hours of play
Development, imagination, creativity
The more LEGO, the greater its value
Extra sets available
Quality in every detail [quoted in Weincek, 1987, p. 48]

As these principles worked their way into LEGO's marketing, advertisements for the toy dealt in an explicit rhetoric of nonviolence and creativity that came to characterize the postwar construction toy, often casting the bricks as innately superior to other kinds of playthings (Seiter, 1993, p. 71).

Historians of childhood and children's toys have argued that the toy industry in the latter half of the twentieth century gradually moved away from the class of "creative" playthings that appealed to parental notions of tradition and educational value, instead designing and selling toys that traded on novelty and appealed directly to children's tastes and desires. Cross argues that as a result, children's play became the locus of parents' anxieties about media consumption and differing generational values (Cross, 1997, pp. 6–9). The persistence of the positive connotations of wholesome, creative construction play is perhaps all the more understandable. Twentieth-century construction toys like LEGO, while they are indebted to the long history of the material object lesson, have helped propagate the perceived positive values of construction play to a global audience, assisted by mass production, corporate marketing, and deeply ingrained assumptions about creativity. LEGO's success has, in part, helped distribute the building block and construction toy conceit thoroughly in popular visual culture, setting an important precedent for *Minecraft's* blending of new media and "old" toy concepts. Indeed, many of the company's Principles of Play apply equally well to Mojang's game: players commonly mention its cross-generational appeal and opportunities for exploration and creation (Robertson, 2010; Kurs, 2011; Gambell, 2013; Machell, 2013).

ADVENTURE PLAYGROUNDS
AND SPACES OF PLAY

Adventure playgrounds, formally defined in 1955 at a convention organized by play leaders as the simple combination of "children, a site, and a play leader," are special places where children are encouraged to experiment, make, and destroy. The play leader helps facilitate the children's experience, but children can do what interests them most (Kozlovsky, 2008, pp. 172, 186). The Danish landscape architect Carl Theodor Sørensen first described this concept as a "junk playground" in 1939. Philanthropist Lady Allen of Hurtwood recognized its potential and suggested similar playgrounds be built on bombed-out sites in England so children could, as "post-war builders," develop a sense of responsibility and ownership toward their surroundings, learn to resolve conflicts peacefully through play, and constructively process the trauma of growing up in war zones (Kozlovsky, 2008, pp. 173–5, 179–80, 187; Solomon, 2005, pp. 12–4). Hurtwood's adventure playground ("junk" proving too unpopular a word) was seen as the playground of the future, both a critique of conventional playground design and Fascist ideology (Kozlovsky, 2008, pp.

171, 175). British architects Alison and Peter Smithson argued at the Ninth Congres Internationaux d'Architecture Moderne (CIAM) in 1953 that children's play in these kinds of open-ended spaces could also serve as an alternative source of inspiration to the "prevailing modernist orthodoxy of demarcated functions [in urban zoning]," which "threatened to create sterile cities devoid of community spirit" (Kinchin, 2012d, p. 161–2).

In 1960s America, urban planners also suggested that a new type of "creative playground" inspired by organic forms would alleviate perceived societal ailments such as juvenile delinquency and declining physical fitness. More prescriptively designed than the Danish junk or English adventure playground, these spaces still sought to give children a sense of connection to and influence over their play environments (Ogata, 2013, pp. 63–4). This is in direct contrast to most playgrounds in the United States today, as Susan G. Solomon argues in *American Playgrounds*, since fear of litigation has motivated governments to minimize risk of children's accidents; children's ability to master a succession of skills and challenge themselves and one another is consequently constrained by the limited choices these play environments provide (pp. 88–91). Open-ended construction play spaces filled with hammers, nails, and paint are perceived to be too hazardous for schools and cities in the United States, even though ostensibly safer playgrounds can result in children taking more dangerous risks (Tierney, 2011).

While *Minecraft* does not allow children to play with the materials that adventure playground advocates laud as "real stuff," it does allow them to build using varied materials (or digital representations of materials), direct their own playing and learning, and explore a space that they can identify with and own. *Minecraft* provides this without the risk of a concussion or broken bones. However, the semi-destructive character of the adventure playground resonates with *Minecraft*'s Survival Mode, in which players must first destroy parts of their surroundings to gather materials for building. *Minecraft*, due to its play mechanics, dual modes, and expansive world, can be understood as an inheritor of the adventure playground tradition.

The Rhetoric and Reception of Minecraft

Though *Minecraft*'s meteoric rise to popularity certainly sets it apart in the history of videogames, it is not the first to tap into the ideologies of open-ended play, nor the first to harness the act of building as a central gameplay conceit. *Minecraft*'s roots in historical forms of play and playthings, however, are especially evident in the way the game's users and critics have made explicit comparisons between the videogame and physical construction toys. It is perhaps unsurprising that *Minecraft*'s creator Markus "Notch" Persson loved playing with LEGO bricks in his youth (Goldberg & Larsson, 2011, trans. 2013, p. 210). But beyond this anecdotal connection, the contemporary rhetoric surrounding the game—whether critical, journalistic, or testimonial—highlights the degree to which *Minecraft* audiences themselves hold a complex understanding of the game's connections to its analog precedents. For example, in the 2012 documentary *Minecraft: The Story of Mojang*, game developer Peter Molyneux compares the videogame to the Danish toy:

> It is, in a way, a social LEGO, *when LEGO used to be a creative toy*, which I don't think it is so much anymore, it's much more prescriptive ... LEGO at the moment is like traditional games design, it's: buy the box, open the box, turn to the instruction sheet, make the model, stick it on the shelf, buy the next box... Where LEGO used to be just a big box of bricks, and you used to take the bricks, pour them on the carpet and then make stuff. And that's exactly what *Minecraft* is [2 Player Productions, 2012, 33:15–35:02, emphasis ours].

Molyneux's critique of LEGO is founded in a common perception that the Danish toy has lost touch with its original appeal, partially owing to its licensing deals with major entertainment properties like Star Wars and Harry Potter (Hjarvard, 2004, pp. 51–2). Ironically, this could include Mojang's own licensing agreement with LEGO in the same year, which resulted in *Minecraft*-themed LEGO sets (Goldberg & Larsson, 2011, trans. 2013, p. 210). Daniel Goldberg and Linus Larsson seem to agree with Molyneux when they write that *Minecraft* can be thought of as "LEGO pieces on steroids; LEGO pieces that you can build larger and more advanced buildings with ... true creativity isn't unleashed until they're lying all over the place" (Goldberg & Larsson, 2011, trans. 2013, p. 24). Similarly, a YouTube video from PBS Digital Studios' *Idea Channel*, asking whether *Minecraft* is "the ultimate educational tool," describes the game as "first-person Legos [sic], with a dash of husbandry, a heaping helping of architecture, and a pinch of slay-the-dragon" (PBS Digital Studios, 2013, 0:15–0:21).

This explicit rhetoric of creativity and wholesome play has pervaded the wider reception of *Minecraft*. A writer for the *Canberra Times*, in a holiday guide for parents, approvingly mentions the game's stylization and open-endedness, the same traits parents and educators most valued about the good toy genre: "Although *Minecraft* is the opposite of the uber-realistic, theatrical and often violent games like *Grand Theft Auto* and *Call of Duty*, its quirkiness and lack of realism or constraints are largely the reason for its popularity" (Gamble 2013). Even earlier reviews, from the game's long open-development period, take note of its reliance on modularity and how it enables diverse forms of building: "The game's powerful, flexible physics has allowed players to do everything from constructing replicas of the Starship Enterprise to building functioning logic circuits out of the game's basic elements" (Murphy,

2010, quoting British author Tom Chatfield). The growing critical literature on *Minecraft* reveals the degree to which the positive connotations of open-ended construction play have become something of an unquestioned truth for many consumers—and producers—of playthings. This acceptance of videogames in particular as useful educational playthings has important precedent in the popular reception of other sandbox games, like game designer Will Wright's *SimCity* (Maxis, 1989) and *Spore* (Maxis, 2008) (Crescente, 2009; Ito, 2009). Mojang itself has cast *Minecraft* in terms that echo the long-running discourse of creative toys and thoughtful play, as well as the narrative of control over one's environment that guided the adventure playground movement. In an early *Minecraft* trailer Mojang uploaded to YouTube, a narrator urges: "Let's go to a place where everything is made of blocks. Where the only limit is your imagination.... With no rules to follow, this adventure—it's up to you" (Mojang, 2011). This appeal—one of the few traditional pieces of marketing the company has produced—rests on the solid foundation built by pedagogical theories and physical toys and spaces in the preceding two centuries.

Focusing specifically on the potential applications of *Minecraft* for education, *Idea Channel's* Mike Rugnetta argues that "the possibilities of what you can get into and out of a game, which you thought was just for punching trees, are *endless*" (PBS, 2013, 2:15–2:20, emphasis in original). The educational collaborative MinecraftEdu similarly emphasizes the game's applicability for teaching science, engineering, math, languages, and the humanities; it offers both extensive lesson plans and a special educational license of the game to interested teachers. These assumptions of limitless play and universal didactic value highlight the unspoken privileging of specific kinds of creativity in adult discourse. While creativity itself is a historically and culturally contingent concept, the act of building something new out of a messy array of materials has been considered, throughout much of the twentieth and into the twenty-first centuries, "more" creative than following step-by-step instructions to complete a manufacturer's predetermined design (Ogata, 2013). This theme also finds common expression in adults' nostalgic desires for the toys of their youth (Kinchin, 2012b, p. 20; Baichtal & Meno, 2011); note Molyneux's emphatic comment on what "LEGO used to be." This view of the past, however, is somewhat selective: many older construction toys were in fact sold with highly specific building suggestions, and even the prepackaged sets and detailed instructions of many of today's toys do not ensure that a child (or adult) will follow those directives. Despite the contradictions embedded in this constructed idea of creativity, the rhetoric surrounding *Minecraft* is rooted in many of these key notions.

Conclusions

A common thread that runs through many of these recent assessments of *Minecraft* is the idea that the game contains enormous social and creative value somehow greater than its constituent parts. The alchemy of the game's unrestrictive mechanics, the labor and originality of its players, and the participatory spirit Mojang encourages all foster a vast array of inventive constructions and bring together a diverse community of crafters in a horizonless digital landscape. This discourse places particular emphasis on the novelty of the game's unusual development process and viral popularity—and rightly so—but, as we hope to have shown, there exists considerable room for examining the complex web of historical associations a digital artifact like *Minecraft* possesses.

It is thanks to these associations that *Minecraft* seems to counter contemporary anxieties censuring videogames as inherently antisocial or violent (e.g., Frost, 2010). James Gee taps into similar positive connotations in his assertion that a player's engagement with the environment of "good" videogames requires active learning and critical thinking (Gee, 2007, p. 88). Significantly, Gee stresses the importance of design in facilitating the learning process, echoing the importance earlier pedagogues placed on the material things that accompanied their curricula:

> Neither players of games, nor children in school, can learn by "playing" (i.e., immersion in rich activities) if they are forced to operate in poorly designed spaces.... Leaving children to the mercies of the real world by just letting them loose to think and explore is not education [p. 141].

This positivistic outlook on the possibilities of play to redeem digital media evokes earlier debates about the redemptive potential of play—especially play centered on the act of building—for both children and adults in real-world contexts. Block by Block, a recent partnership between Mojang and the United Nations Human Settlements Programme (UN-Habitat), for example, envisions *Minecraft* as an open-source tool for designing sustainable public spaces in poor, blighted parts of cities around the world (Mojang and UN-Habitat, 2013). Professional Block by Block facilitators solicit designs from young people who live in the project areas; in this way, the initiative recalls British architects Alison and Peter Smithsons' studies of children's play as a model for new forms of urbanism after the second World War (Kinchin, 2012d, p. 161–2).

While play, as anthropologist Brian Sutton-Smith notes, "schematizes life, it alludes to life, it does not imitate it in any very strict sense" (Sutton-Smith, 1986, p. 138), it is nevertheless noteworthy that many progressive reform efforts have sought solutions to societal problems in the conceit of playful building, from Fröbel's Gifts to popular toy designs of the twentieth century. *Minecraft* represents a new and fascinating chapter in this longer history of pedagogy and playthings, highlighting both the material roots of digital play and the continued relevance of the object lesson.

Acknowledgments

The authors wish to acknowledge Amy F. Ogata, Alexander Roederer, and J.M. Wasko for their support of this project.

References

Allen, A. (1995). American and German women in the kindergarten movement, 1850–1914. In H. Geitz, J. Heideking & Herbst, J. (Eds.), *German influences on education in the United States to 1917*. New York: Cambridge University Press.

Baichtal, J., & Meno, J. (2011). *The cult of LEGO*. San Francisco: No Starch Press.

Brosterman, N. (1997). *Inventing kindergarten*. New York: Abrams.

Centre Canadien d'Architecture. (1991). *Architecture potentielle: Jeux de construction de la collection du CCA/Potential architecture: Construction toys from the CCA collection*. Montreal: Centre Canadien d'Architecture.

Crescente, B. (2009, March 3). Maria Montessori: The 138-year-old inspiration behind *Spore. Kotaku*. Retrieved from http://kotaku.com/5164248/maria-montessori-the-138+year+old-inspiration-behind-spore

Cross, G. (1997). *Kids' stuff: Toys and the changing world of American childhood*. Cambridge, MA: Harvard University Press

Cross, G. (2004). *The cute and the cool: Wondrous innocence and modern American children's culture*. New York: Oxford University Press.

Cunningham, H. (2005). *Children and childhood in Western society since 1500* (2nd ed.). Harlow, UK: Pearson Longman.

Fanning, C. (2012). *The plastic system: Architecture, childhood, and LEGO, 1949–2012*. (MA qualifying paper). New York: Bard Graduate Center.

Friedman, A. (1995). *Maisons de rêve, maisons jouets/Dream houses, toy homes*. Montreal: Centre Canadien d'Architecture.

Fröbel, F. (1904). Pedagogics of the kindergarten. (J. Jarvis, Trans.). In W. T. Harris (Ed.), *International education series* (Vol. 30). New York: D. Appleton and Company.

Frost, J. L. (2010). *A history of children's play and play environments: Toward a contemporary child-saving movement*. New York: Routledge.

Gamble, C. (2013, November 23). Not all games involve mayhem. *Canberra Times*. Retrieved from http://www.canberratimes.com.au/comment/not-all-games-involve-mayhem-20131122-2y1ew.html

Gee, J. P. (2007). *What video games have to teach us about learning and literacy*. New York: Palgrave Macmillan.

Goldberg, D., & Larsson, L. (2011). Minecraft: *The unlikely tale of Markus "Notch" Persson and the game that changed everything*. (J. Hawkins, Trans. 2013). New York: Seven Stories Press.

Hjarvard, S. (2004). From bricks to bytes: The mediatization of a global toy industry. In I. Bondebjerg and P. Golding (Eds.), *European culture and the media*. Bristol & Portland, OR: Intellect.

Hofer, M. K. (2003). *The games we played: The golden age of board & table games*. New York: Princeton Architectural Press & New-York Historical Society.

Hughes, J. (2010). *Brick fetish*. Retrieved from http://www.brickfetish.com/index.html

Ito, M. (2009). *Engineering play: A cultural history of children's software.* Cambridge, MA and London: MIT Press.

Kinchin, J. (2012a). The crystal chain and architectural play. In J. Kinchin & A. O'Connor (Eds.), *Century of the child: Growing by design, 1900–2000* (pp. 60–1). New York: Museum of Modern Art.

Kinchin, J. (2012b). In search of the modern child. In J. Kinchin & A. O'Connor (Eds.), *Century of the child: Growing by design, 1900–2000* (pp. 11–27). New York: Museum of Modern Art.

Kinchin, J. (2012c). The kindergarten movement: Building blocks of modern design. In J. Kinchin & A. O'Connor (Eds.), *Century of the child: Growing by design, 1900–2000* (pp. 30–3). New York: Museum of Modern Art.

Kinchin, J. (2012d). Reclaiming the city: Children and the new urbanism. In J. Kinchin & A. O'Connor (Eds.), *Century of the child: Growing by design, 1900–2000* (pp. 161–3). New York: Museum of Modern Art.

Kinchin, J. (2012e). Rome: Modern arts, crafts, and education. In J. Kinchin & A. O'Connor (Eds.), *Century of the child: Growing by design, 1900–2000* (pp. 47–9). New York: Museum of Modern Art.

Kline, S. (1993). *Out of the garden: Toys and children's culture in the age of TV marketing.* New York: Verso.

Kozlovsky, R. (2008). Adventure playgrounds and postwar reconstruction. In M. Gutman & N. de Coninck-Smith (Eds.), *Designing modern childhoods* (pp. 171–90). New Brunswick, NJ and London: Rutgers University Press.

Kraus-Boelté, M., & Kraus J. (1881). *The kindergarten guide.* New York: E. Steiger & Company.

Krusi, H. (1875). *Pestalozzi: His life, work, and influence* (reprint, 2010). Carlisle, MA: Applewood Books.

Kurs, S. (2011, January 16). Mighty minnows make a mint outplaying the big boys. *The Sunday Times.*

Lauwaert, M. (2009). *The place of play: Toys and digital cultures.* Amsterdam: Amsterdam University Press.

Lipkowitz, D. (2009). *The LEGO book.* London: DK Publishing.

Locke, J. (1693). *Some thoughts concerning education.* London: A. and J. Churchill.

Machell, B. (2013, December 7). How *Minecraft* creator Markus Persson built the world. *The Australian.* Retrieved from http://www.theaustralian.com.au/news/features/how-Minecraft-creator-markus-persson-built-the-world/story-e6frg8h6–1226776074148

Maxis. (1989). *SimCity* [PC game]. Maxis.

Maxis. (2008). *Spore* [PC game]. Electronic Arts.

MinecraftEdu (n.d.). Retrieved from MinecraftEdu.com

Mojang. (2011). *Minecraft* [PC game]. Stockholm, Sweden: Mojang.

Mojang (2011, December 6). Official *Minecraft* trailer [Video file]. Retrieved from http://www.youtube.com/watch?v=MmB9b5njVbA

Mojang & UN-Habitat (2013). *Block by Block.* Retrieved from: http://blockbyblock.org/

Montessori, M. (1912). *The Montessori method* (reprint 1988). New York: Schocken Books.

Montessori, M. (1914). *Dr. Montessori's own handbook* (reprint 1988). New York: Schocken Books.

Müller, T., & Schneiger, R., Eds. (2002). *Montessori: Teaching materials, 1913–1935 furniture and architecture.* Munich: Prestel.

Murphy, S. (2010, December 14). The most ground-breaking video games of 2010. *New Scientist.* Retrieved from http://www.newscientist.com/gallery/the-best-video-games-of-2010/3

Nicolopoulou, A. (1993). Play, cognitive development, and the social world: Piaget, Vygotsky, and beyond. *Human development*, 36, 1–23.

Ogata, A. F. (2012). Good toys. In J. Kinchin & A. O'Connor (Eds.), *Century of the child: Growing by design, 1900–2000* (pp. 171–3). New York: Museum of Modern Art.

Ogata, A. F. (2013). *Designing the creative child: Playthings and spaces in midcentury America*. Minneapolis: University of Minnesota Press.

P., E. (1966, April). The child at play in the world of form. *Progressive Architecture* 47,191–8.

Page, H. F. (1953). *Playtime in the first five years* (2nd ed.). London: Allen & Unwin.

Pasierbska, H. (2004). *Must-have toys: Favourites of the 20th century*. London: V&A Museum of Childhood.

PBS Digital Studios. (2013, March 6). Is *Minecraft* the ultimate educational tool? [Video file]. In *Idea Channel*. Retrieved from http://www.youtube.com/watch?v=RI0BN5AWOe8

Robertson, M. (2010, October 21). Five minutes of ... *Minecraft*. *Gamasutra*. Retrieved from http://www.gamasutra.com/view/feature/134550/five_minutes_of_*Minecraft*.php

Rousseau, J. (1762). *Émile, or: On education* (reprint 2009). Auckland, NZ: The Floating Press.

Seiter, E. (1993). *Sold separately: Parents and children in consumer culture*. New Brunswick, NJ: Rutgers University Press.

Solomon, S. (2005). *American playgrounds: Revitalizing community space*. Lebanon, NH: University Press of New England.

Sutton-Smith, B. (1986). *Toys as culture*. New York: Gardner Press.

Tierney, J. (2011, July 18). Can a playground be too safe? *New York Times*. Retrieved from http://www.nytimes.com/2011/07/19/science/19tierney.html?_r=0

2 Player Productions. (2013, November 8). *Minecraft: The story of Mojang (official version!)* [Video file]. Retrieved from: http://www.youtube.com/watch?v=ySRgVo1X_18.

Whyte, I., ed. (1985) *The crystal chain letters: Architectural fantasies by Bruno Taut and his circle*. Cambridge, MA; MIT Press.

Wiencek, H. (1987). *The world of LEGO toys*. New York: Harry N. Abrams.

Williams, A. (1999). *Towards a geometry of childhood: The visual culture of toy bricks in Britain c. 1900–1940* (MA thesis). Bath, England: Bath Spa University College.

Mining Constructivism
in the University
The Case of Creative Mode

JEFFREY E. BRAND, PENNY DE BYL,
SCOTT J. KNIGHT *and* JAMES HOOPER

The reconstruction of the modern university is under way, and it extends beyond Massively Open Online Courses (MOOCs). Just as the United Nations Human Settlements Program (UN-Habitat) has re-imagined urban spaces in *Minecraft* (Mojang, 2011) through the Block by Block initiative (blockbyblock.org), so too have educators re-imagined the space and meaning of the University Campus. This chapter presents the potential of *Minecraft* to help students and professors re-think university spaces and university education by presenting a detailed case study of the integration of the standard, unmodified release of *Minecraft* operating in creative mode into an experimental university class.

This chapter focuses on a Virtual Learning Environment (VLE) created in *Minecraft* by students enrolled in a class on the interactive media industry at Bond University, a small university on the east coast of Queensland, Australia. Within this context, *Minecraft* became a subject for discussion, a tool for social cohesion, and a space to hold classes and store student authored "books." The thing we came to call "*Minecraft* University" integrated play and constructivist pedagogy to motivate students and foster learning in a collectively crafted world (Brand & Kinash, 2013).

Minecraft *as a Virtual Learning Environment (VLE)*

A virtual learning environment (VLE) is an educational platform that simulates conventional real world teaching and learning spaces through the delivery of classroom based content, chat rooms, online assessment, multimedia, discussion forums, electronic assessment and other pedagogical tools. The term VLE is often synonymous with learning management system (LMS) that refers to managed online learning systems such as Blackboard and Moodle However unlike LMSs, many VLEs deliver electronic educational content by non-traditional face-to-face methods.

Before the advent of the web, content delivery was asynchronous. In 1958, the University of Houston was the first of many to broadcast classes on television and radio (Fisher, 2012). As computing technology advanced, a suite of computer mediated learning (CML) applications surfaced. These programs delivered educational content and monitored student progress in an asynchronous application. Students could be evaluated through quizzes, tests, or other electronic document submissions. The progression began in earnest with the Optical Mark Recognition (OMR) test sheets (bubble sheets) still used today but included purpose-programmed computer text scanners and then on-screen tests and surveys based on Computer Assisted Telephone Interview (CATI) technology that later gave way to HTML forms. Similarly, multimedia learning programs such as those used for language learning, and CD-ROM multimedia tools bundled with textbooks increasingly offered rich media content and virtual learning objects, particularly in the physical sciences. Of the greatest interest to educators for teaching and learning purposes were synchronous multiuser environments that provided much of the desired collaboration and communication functionality. With the increase of exceedingly social, interactive and spatially immersive technologies, the term VLE began to cover a vast range of electronic learning environments beyond those focused on what would otherwise be termed classroom management. As such, online games began to be used as VLEs.

In the beginning, text-based MUDs (multi-user dungeons), MUVEs (multi-user virtual environments), and MOOs (object-orientated MUDs) were employed. In the late 1970s, the University of Essex developed the first MUD for use in role-playing games (Bartle, 1999). Among the first educational MOO servers were Massachusetts Institute of Technology's MediaMOO and the University of Texas' Daedalus MOO. Established before the World Wide Web, these environments, for the first time, provided students with real-time synchronous contact with lecturers and fellow students online. Although lacking visual richness, these text-based multi-user environments were found to support flourishing and effective online communities (Rheingold, 1993). From a pedagogical perspective MUDs were found to support the establishment of peer role models, allow role-play, provide student peer emotional support, enable interactive learning, and support collaboration across space and time (Riner, 1996; Bruckman, 1998).

Improved technology facilitated the rise of three-dimensional virtual learning environments (3DVLEs) with educators exploring the affordances of online multiuser 3D environments. The addition of richer visual stimuli expanded the educational benefits of VLEs to conceptual understanding through interaction with digital artifacts (Bricken & Byrne, 1994), experimentation without real-world repercussions (Bricken, 1990) and learning-by-doing (Dede, 1995). Furthermore, 3D virtual environments brought together experiential learning and information by providing transparent knowledge representation to learners as first-person non-symbolic experiences (Winn, 1993).

From the mid 1990s, the education community became engaged with a new collection of open access 3DVLEs, most notably *Active Worlds* (1995) and *Second Life* (Linden Lab, 2003). These 3D multiuser environments are not by any definition games but rather sandbox environments in which users can create their own avatars and add a limited range of content. For a paid subscription, 3D content can be added and dedicated classroom spaces established. One of the noteworthy teaching environments created in *Active Worlds* is Quest Atlantis (Barab, Thomas, Dodge, Carteaux & Tuzun, 2005). Quest Atlantis is a 3DVLE aimed at educating 9–12 year olds through transformative play that motivates students to social action through inspiring and interactive storytelling (Barab, Gresalfi & Ingram-Goble, 2010). Children are enabled to act as scientists, doctors, reporters, and mathematicians in a 3D virtual world in which they must build discipline-specific knowledge in order to act and achieve their goals.

Minecraft provides the same functionality available in other 3DVLEs such as *Active Worlds* and *Second Life* with some additional affordances that can make all the difference to teaching faculty. First, although *Active Worlds* and *Second Life* are free to use, the free usage is restricted to the creation of an avatar. Content creation and dedicated virtual spaces incur a license fee upwards of U.S. $ 200/month. The relatively universal affordability of *Minecraft* suits the normally lean finances of educational environments. *Minecraft*'s business model is more like that of videogame entertainment and less like that of enterprise virtual environments. The initial cost is minimal and servers are freely accessible or can be maintained in house by entry-level IT staff. Second, *Active Worlds* and *Second Life* maintain an authoritative server. This means the server has full control over the world and all interactions and processing within it. Clients connected to the server act merely as dumb terminals and thus response times become poor on slow Internet connections. The user-generated server functionality of *Minecraft* offers a relatively accessible and democratic basis for generating endless virtual worlds. Third, content creation in both *Active Worlds* and *Second Life* requires knowledge of 3D modeling and animation thereby creating barriers to entry of both knowledge and time, if not cost. The pre-fabricated block-building nature of *Minecraft* provides for nearly universal accessibility for those with consumer-level computer literacy. Building is literally as straight forward as placing one block on top of another. In summary, costs, technical issues and development skills of other 3DVLEs are beyond most teachers and therefore prevent their adoption in education (de Byl & Taylor, 2007).

Minecraft by its very nature is ideal as a building environment. This obvious functionality has seen it used for learning and teaching in design and architecture. However to be suitable as a 3DVLE it must be pedagogically sound and adhere to all facets of a suitable learning environment, leading to the questions at the center of this research: What are *Minecraft*'s affordances at delivery of education beyond physical construction? What are its knowledge building capabilities?

Minecraft *as a Constructivist Learning Environment*

What has attracted educators to 3DVLEs are their ability to facilitate a constructivist pedagogy, a teaching and learning philosophy based on active-learning knowledge building (Bruner, 1980). Constructivist theory argues that members of multi-participant environments negotiate symbolic representations of communication (Huitt & Hummel, 2003) where common meaning emerges for actors in the environment (Winn, 1993) rather than being determined by an authority source. Students construct knowledge through non-symbolic, non-reflective, psychological activity that occurs when they interact directly with worlds, whether real or virtual (Vygotsky, 1962; Piaget, 1926; Kolb 1984; Dewey, 2007).

Minecraft is well situated to support constructivist learning which dictates the focus of education be shifted from pre-designed interactions with a learning environment to an environment allowing students a wider range of interaction, albeit within the technical limitations of the environment. The software empowers constructivist learning by removing the traditional computer interface that sits between a student and educational material. Participants have the opportunity to inhabit the same world at the same time where they enjoy the flexibility to negotiate the meaning of that environment (de Byl & Taylor, 2007). This enables students to construct knowledge directly from their presence rather than from abstractions and descriptions. *Minecraft* can be characterized with respect to its suitability as a 3DVLE according to six fundamental characteristics that define constructivist-learning settings in that it:

• supports knowledge-building through acts of construction on conceptual or real learning objects;
• provides multiple depictions or perspectives of reality by allowing a variety of levels of detail and scale for building worlds in addition to full three-dimensional freedom of exploration;

• encourages authentic and meaningful context-based tasks through exploration of a concept within a complex environment and observations of resulting interrelationships that occur;
• provides case-based real-world inspired learning through the recreation and simulation of real-world environments and multiuser roleplaying experiences;
• encourages thoughtful reflection on experience integrating the learner's preconceived ideas and understandings into the building of worlds while allowing the learner to create a narrative from their learning journey; and
• supports collaborative construction of knowledge through social negotiation through the multiuser capabilities for synchronous building activities and chat.

Blocks in *Minecraft* are not containers of knowledge in and of themselves and have no inherent curricular power. However, they can be used as objects with which to think. Any inexpensive, available items that can be controlled, adjusted, used for experimentation and to build with are suitable for knowledge building (Papert, 1980). How the *Minecraft* blocks convey and transmit knowledge depends on what they represent in any given exercise. Blocks may represent their actual in-game objects (e.g., a stone block represents a stone and a dirt block represents dirt) or they may be purely conceptual. For example, *Minecraft* has been used in architecture classes for rapid development of designs with the blocks representing actual building materials. Conceptually, students at Miami University used wooden signs and levers to develop a game-based learning experience to explain logic operators (Duncan, 2011). *Minecraft* has also been used to teach English in which the environment was used to produce machinima (a portmanteau of machine and cinema by which a game is played and content captured on video) in which students had to demonstrate their understanding of the concepts of narrative *point-of-view* and *characterization* through role-play (Schifter & Cipollone, 2013). By using *Minecraft* as a machinima tool, students were able to experiment with telling stories from first- and third-person points of view and explore the process of creating story characters.

Since its release, many commentators have made the instant association between Lego and *Minecraft*, not only in terms of aesthetics but in overall form (Duncan, 2011). Indeed, the nature of the game in creative mode is one of imaginative, constructivist play. According to Juul (2002), *Minecraft* would be considered a game of "emergence" as it exhibits an open play schema and player self-expression is at the forefront of design (Juul, 2007). In creative mode, the joy of *Minecraft* depends on the design of a 3-D space, the "architectural simulator" dimension as Duncan (2011, p. 6) puts it, as well as a consideration of potential play functions of the space.

Educational content is not always a solid construct or series of facts, but can pertain to dynamic narrative experiences. For example, comparative religious rituals could be performed through reconstruction of events or by designing of historical artifacts. *Minecraft* has been used at the University of Applied Sciences, HTW-Berlin, as an individual interpretation tool in which students design an environment through which they can explain the concept of a hero's journey (Busch, Conrad & Steinicke, 2013).

Minecraft's multiuser capabilities, which allow students to talk and build synchronously, facilitate collaborative construction of knowledge. Such multiuser capabilities allow teachers to build educational experiences that incorporate critical thinking, group problem-solving, creativity and conflict resolution skills. At Manhattan's Columbia Grammar and Preparatory School, teacher Joel Levin uses *Minecraft* for this very purpose by placing teams of students into a world with limited resources and asking them to work together to achieve a specific goal (Webster, 2011). Beyond the confines of the virtual world, social learning activity has evolved in response to the game itself— within the communities that have formed around it, the plethora of instructional websites and the sharing of build resources (Banks & Potts, 2010).

It seems clear that educators and their institutions could make more of this moment when computer games and learning environments share something in common. Salen and Zimmerman (2004) cite Huizinga's concept of the play space of the *magic circle* (1955) and it is this idea and its subsequently contested boundaries (Crawford, 2012) that may provide an insight into learning and interaction. For Salen and Zimmerman, the magic circle is a conceptual frame in which "games take place within set boundaries established by the act of play." (p. 94). When inside the magic circle, players abide by both explicit and implicit rules agreed upon either prior to, or during gameplay.

Alternatively, applying Calleja's (2011) player involvement model, with its various dimensions of involvement culminating in his concept of incorporation, provides a more complex framework. Relevant dimensions in the context of operating a 3DVLE include:

- Kinesthetic involvement covering control and movement;
- Spatial involvement covering exploration of the game's spaces;
- Shared involvement covering co-presence, collaboration, and competition;
- Narrative involvement covering formation of an ongoing story (or curriculum?);
- Affective involvement which includes players' emotional engagement; and
- Ludic involvement which includes engagement with choices and consequences.

Calleja (2011) argues that more intensive and internal involvement has the potential to end in what he terms *incorporation*. Calleja's incorporation avoids the baggage of existing terms such as *presence* and *immersion* and attempts to include two levels—firstly that the "virtual environment is incorporated into the player's mind as part of her immediate surroundings" and second, that the "the player is incorporated (in the sense of embodiment) in a single, systematically upheld location in the virtual environment at any single point in time" (p.169).

The Minecraft *University Project*

To explore *Minecraft* as a VLE suitable for constructivism and involvement at the level of incorporation, the *Minecraft* University project was initiated in early 2013 and operated over a 12-week trimester as part of a class entitled Computer Game Industry and Policy offered to students enrolled in communication and creative media degrees at Bond University, Gold Coast Australia. The purpose of the project was to explore the proposition that *Minecraft* afforded educators with a constructivist learning environment that not only motivated students to engage with subject content, but also reimagined constructivist learning and the university as a ludic space.

Because the course focuses on the interactive media industry, is taken by a wide range of students self-identified as both gamers and non-gamers, and tends to be small with between 15 and 30 students each trimester, exploring *Minecraft* as a 3DVLE in this environment was ideal. The class description reads:

> The composition and size of the computer game industry is undergoing rapid change. This subject examines the relationships among developers, distributors, publishers retailers and regulators in global and Australian contexts. Issues such as technological change, trade practices, intellectual property, genres and platforms, production and publishing, monetization, value chains and economics are examined. Case studies of major computer game-related companies, organizations and regulatory bodies including current market data provide students with a contemporary and systematic overview of the industry. On completion of this class, successful students will have a high level of industry and policy knowledge necessary to work strategically in the interactive entertainment industry.

Teaching methods include a weekly two-hour traditional lecture and one-hour small-group tutorial; assessment included tutorial leadership, two short researched analyses of 1,500 words each, and a two-hour final exam.

The project progressed along three phases that were set out by the rules articulated on two signs at the spawn point instructing students to play in a magic circle and be bound by three rules:

"Welcome to *Minecraft* University:
1. Build the University,
2. Write Books,
3. Play Nice."

These simple rules provided elegant guidance for the phases such that:

- **Phase one** of the *Minecraft* University project involved world-making and the relationship between the actual built environment of the university campus and its reimaged, abstracted, analogous space within *Minecraft*.
- **Phase two** explored the re-imagination of authorship and authorial control in relation to virtual books embedded in the *Minecraft* universe with up to 256 characters per page and up to 50 pages per book.
- **Phase three** explored the articulation of multiple intelligences, meaning-making, and involvement that were negotiated as the *Minecraft* University narrative unfolded and student behavior developed to encourage and extend learning during and beyond the trimester.

DESIGN-BASED RESEARCH

We framed the project using design-based research (DBR) methodology first to ensure that the 12 students were involved in the project as learners and second to explore a curriculum innovation (Kelly, Lesh & Baek, 2008; Wang & Hannafin, 2005). This meant that students spent no more time on this proj-

Figure 1. **View of the university from above in Google Earth.**

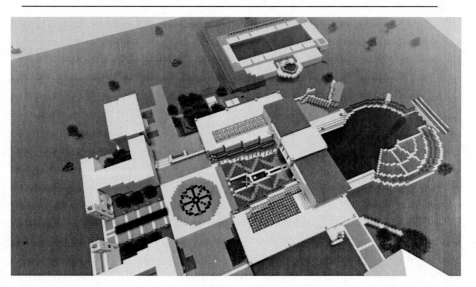

Figure 2. **View of the university from above in** *Minecraft* **(Minecraft °/TM & © 2009–2013 Mojang / Notch).**

ect than time normally spent engaged in class activities, and the trial of the 3DVLE was contextually relevant to the phenomena studied in the class—in this case, computer games. We chose not to collect data at the time of the study except to observe routine class performance outcomes such as 1) engagement observed through class attendance and class discussion and participation, and 2) performance observed with deadline submission compliance rates and grade outcomes applying standard rubrics used in earlier trimesters. Following the study, we collected qualitative student feedback about the experience of using *Minecraft* in the context of a university class.

PROCESS

Figures 1 and 2 present top-down views of the central spine of the campus from *Google Earth* and *Minecraft* respectively. The main arch building and basic structure of the lake were prepared before class began. In the first lecture students were informed about the project. Excitement and disbelief was expressed by two-thirds of the class while reservation and concern about lack of experience was communicated by a third. One student had over a year of experience working as his own server operator and administrator. Students were given the server address, which was set to run 24/7 in creative mode with peaceful difficulty, and a summary of the reasons for building the campus in *Minecraft*. These reasons included: 1) an opportunity to understand *Minecraft* as a disruptive innovation in the games industry, 2) an opportunity to develop a social and cultural connection for the class, 3) the ability to better understand the potential for games to be used for serious purposes, and 4) to explore the potential for 3DVLEs as points of intersection between books and games.

Many scholars privilege the significance of space in videogame form (Newman, 2013; Aarseth, 1997). In the case of *Minecraft* University, the digital creation of the space of a university campus was the starting point for the project. On the first afternoon following class, six students had already taken control of building and had outlined the foundations of other campus buildings and grounds. By recreating the campus students were given the ability to consider the nature of the familiar classrooms, study areas, and outdoor environments in a way that promoted a kind of hyper-spatial engagement. Indeed, within three hours the teaching lab in which the class was held and all the rooms on that floor in the building had been mapped and re-created. Students went to great effort to furnish the lab with objects, including wall art and lighting that mimicked the real-world space.

Others explored the joy of re-thinking the university space and player agency by adding fantastically new spaces including a Nether portal in a dungeon below the lab. Within days, one student had also succeeded in crashing the server with a high volume of TNT which he had quietly amassed. The operating memory on the server was expanded and the student awarded respect from all—including his professor. As word spread, two students enrolled in the class and by the end of the week, all (save one student) were working in creative mode.

Minecraft demonstrates the dominant game space aesthetic of an "open-landscape, found mostly in the 'simulation-orientated' games" (Aarseth, 2000, p. 159), making it ideal for modeling both real-world and fantastic world spaces. The major features of the campus were modeled in scale. Familiar spaces like the university library became repositories for students' class notes. In the case of *Minecraft* University, due to the familiarity of students with the spaces they were modeling. It would be fair to consider the term place as this was a representation of perceptions of a known environment. Nitsche (2009) quotes architectural theorist Norberg-Schultz (1980): "The existential purpose of building (architecture) is therefore to make a site become a place, that is, to uncover the meanings potentially present in the given environment" (Nitsche, 2009, p. 161). Because *Minecraft* natively allows for multiplayer interactions, it easily becomes a communal site for gathering and presenting knowledge. It offers a playful space for digital classes that take place in a parallel location resulting in more playful virtual collaboration (Taylor, 2006; Wang & Braman, 2009).

In the third week of the trimester, record rainfall forced closure of the physical university. The professor contacted students through the LMS and suggested holding class in *Minecraft*. On the morning of the class, nine of the

12 students were online in *Minecraft* University. In-game text chat was used to communicate lecture content, students followed along with the slides, which were hosted in Prezi (prezi.com), and answered questions. The group had the run of the virtual campus and could well have held the class in the administration building; instead, the virtual world lab representing the regular class location was chosen (Figure 3). Avatars were present and in traditional classroom configuration, and despite a few loose pigs and bubbles, the class ran for 1:38 with no break—roughly the same duration as a normal class accounting for the mid-class break. Students were slow to participate until the professor discovered the power of awarding XP with the command "XP {amount}" as students answered questions. In the remaining weeks of the trimester, attendance was nearly universal. One student who had been quiet in a different class held in a previous semester had become quite vocal and engaged throughout the remainder of the term. It seemed to the staff that with very few resources and minimal scaffolding, *Minecraft* University was meeting the criteria of an "incorporating" VLE with constructivism at its core.

Building slowed significantly by mid-term as students turned their attention to writing well-researched and written analyses of the games industry. Students opted to fit out the library with bookshelves and chests in which

Figure 3. Class was held in the virtual equivalent of the regular teaching lab (Minecraft ®/TM & © 2009–2013 Mojang / Notch).

class notes and the reports they wrote were placed as books (Figure 4). Moving their work from word-processing documents to the *Minecraft* book format required a tedious and time-consuming process of copy-paste actions (Figure 5). Books in *Minecraft* can contain up to 50 pages and each page can hold up to 256 characters, tables are near impossible and figures are not possible. Stu-

Figure 4. Library and chests for storing 1500-word essays as 50-page "books." (Minecraft °/TM & © 2009–2013 Mojang / Notch).

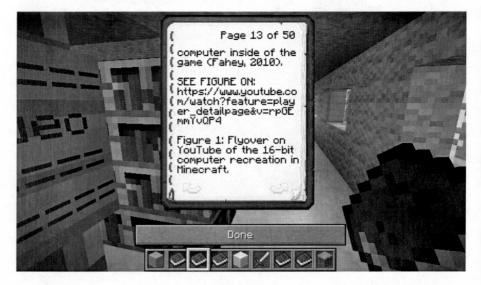

Figure 5. A *Minecraft* "book" produced by a student for the class (Minecraft °/TM & © 2009–2013 Mojang / Notch).

dents learned to make backup copies of their hard work in their own inventory and to place multiple copies of their work for others to read in different chests on library shelves. It is worth noting that not one paper was submitted late for this assignment.

A number of concepts and issues covered in the curriculum and presented in the class and assigned readings were also incorporated into the architecture of the *Minecraft* campus by students. Without instruction from the professor, students began placing signs in different locations that presented labels and concepts from course readings and lecture slides. Although a simple action, the playfulness of linking conceptual labels with the paradigm of 3D abstraction in *Minecraft* illustrates interplay between abstraction and mimesis in the aesthetics of *Minecraft* University. Notions of mimicry and mimesis flowed through the spatial design of *Minecraft* University and the signs nodded to the posters and communications common in universities the world over.

The virtual place, however, ultimately became an extraneous layer in much the same way a new game ultimately is played out and shelved for the next experience. As the space of *Minecraft* University grew over the course of the trimester, interest in building the VLE waned. Similarly placement of the second round of research papers into books at the end of the trimester was completed by only two students; the heavy load for exams and assignments at the end of a trimester, students were not pressed to follow through. Nevertheless, students offered positive qualitative reports in the end-of semester teaching and class evaluations. During the flood event, international news coverage of the class held in *Minecraft* quoted students saying they hadn't before been so motivated to learn a subject, attend classes, and look for other opportunities to use games in new ways. The conclusion of the trimester left us in no doubt about the value of *Minecraft* as a 3DVLE and why it worked well early on as a place of incorporation: Play.

Minecraft *as Play Learning*

Play is a crucial element in constructivist theory. It argues that individuals are compelled to explore their world and the various components within it through play and experimentation. The creative mode of *Minecraft*, and the structure of *Minecraft* University enables rule-governed cognitive and developmental play considered as essential elements in learning through which a blend of cooperative, parallel and solitary play occurs (Parten, 1962; Piaget, 1962),. For play environments to be truly educational they should allow:

- a variety of play forms narratives and information exchange occur (Paley, 1992);

- social and cultural behaviors and attitudes to form (Gaskins & Miller, 2009);
- knowledge to take on additional meaning and value (Leslie, 1987); and,
- the development of cognitive, emotional and motor skills (Piaget, 1962; Vygotsky, 1986).

Play, therefore, becomes a logical tool for extending learning beyond a didactic classroom and positions *Minecraft* as an obvious tool for providing students with opportunities to interact with one another while contributing and transforming knowledge through constructive play.

Inherent in play is the often unnoticed and unexpected learning outcomes associated with the playful activity. It is commonly accepted that many great discoveries have been made through playful experimentation and exploration, and it is through this type of play that humans begin to understand the function and the rules of the real world, and many of the same opportunities for learning and engagement can be found through systems like *Minecraft* (McGonigal, 2006). Had the floods not occurred, the story of the project might have been less dramatic. However, it highlights the value of experimentation and exploration in otherwise conventional practices, such as university courses.

The simplistic aesthetic of the *Minecraft* world, paired with the task of reconstructing the university campus, appeals to Huizinga's (1955) notions that play offers uniqueness and separation from the common world. By asking students to construct the university, educators afford students latitude to form a sense of

Figure 6. Students play with course concepts such as regulation addressing moral panics (Minecraft ®/TM & © 2009–2013 Mojang / Notch).

authorship and pride over the interpretive reconstruction of their learning. The open world of *Minecraft* affords a deceptively endless space in which the virtual campus can be constructed on any scale. Students are at liberty to construct fictional places and elements through which they may experience further incorporation and exploration of the academic subject. Specific applications of the *Minecraft* world to otherwise non-game based realms becomes more readily accessible due to diverse range of modifications produced by users, with many of these being readily and easily integrated into a constructivist pedagogy as needed.

The play-learning workability of *Minecraft* operates precisely because *Minecraft* exhibits a type of "caricaturism" by virtue of the game's exaggerated blocky abstraction (Jarvinen, 2002). In several ways *Minecraft* has a playful graphical relationship to games like *Animal Crossing* (Nintendo, 2001) which Sondergaard (2006) considers "simplified realism," the essence of which is increased contrast, fewer and distortedly large details, and color ranges, patterns and shapes simplified to cliché. In short, *Minecraft* mimics a triangular relationship between abstraction, reality, and language reminiscent of McCloud's (1994) well-known picture plane (Sondergaard, 2006). The nearly absurd evidence of this caricaturism and abstraction produced by *Minecraft* University was the representation of the virtual campus on a giant outdoor screen at a university open day in the subsequent trimester (Figure 7).

Figure 7. An outdoor screen promotion of the *Minecraft* campus (Minecraft ®/TM & © 2009–2013 Mojang / Notch).

Conclusion

Minecraft University presents students with an environment for traditional classroom activities, as well as the self-directed teaching and learning processes observed by Piaget, Erikson and Vygotsky in which fantasy play allowed real world situations, theories and concepts to be represented, analysed and understood (Sutton-Smith, 1980; Vygotsky, 1987; Piaget, 1968; Erikson in Hoare, 2001). The hands-on, collaborative, design-based research nature of constructivist pedagogies logically flows from Huizinga's conceptualization of play. These include the "formation of social groupings" allowing for types of play in which information and knowledge can be shared (Huizinga 1955, p. 13). Although we observed many text chat exchanges among the students in *Minecraft* University, it was clear in real-world classes that online discussions flowed over into classroom conversation that might well not have taken place without a playful incorporating place. In this way, we argue the nature of creative mode in *Minecraft* provides affordances for constructivist learning beyond that of any traditional classroom pedagogy (Smilansky, 1968).

Minecraft is a uniquely open, accessible, world-building tool that provides multiple opportunities for play-learning including ludus—structured activities with rules (Huizinga, 1955, 13), *paidia*—spontaneous and free activities (Caillois, 1961), and free movement within structures (Salen & Zimmerman, 2003). The combination of these affordances suggests an environment that is functionally limitless (Hooper, 2014) where the creative and novel applications of the game begin to extend it for other applications.

We conclude that *Minecraft* promotes education as a ludic activity for which we suggest a provisional portmanteau: ludopedagogy. Evoking scholars who have investigated the nature of learning and play (c.f., Gee, 2003; Prensky, 2001; Piaget, 1962; Dietze & Kashin, 2011; Vygotsky, 1962), ludopedagogy is a system of education whereby gameplay is at the core of the learner's development. It encompasses a framework supported by learner-centered teaching (Weimer, 2013), research-based activity (Dewey, 2007), game-based learning (Prensky, 2001), and constructivist pedagogy in an accessible 3DVLE, unabashedly a caricature of real-world educational space.

Acknowledgments

The authors wish to celebrate and promote the intellect and energy of the students who contributed to this project by building the virtual campus, writing great papers, and transferring them 256 characters at a time to books, and even crashing the server once or twice with a healthy dose of TNT. And, yes, we found the massive glass library in the Nether— nice! We'll never forget the look on their faces when we said the class would run in *Minecraft*. The cast and crew were (in alphabetical order) Rajpal, "Crash" Dallas, Alex, Samir, Andrew, Christopher, Steven, Mario (yes, Mario), Mehta, Ashley, Jeremy and Hannah. Thanks to David Bodnar for maintaining the server and setting up a virtual machine with auto reboot to keep the world up and running in the face of TNT. Thanks also to three pre-college kids who helped their dad set out the campus from Google Maps and for re-educating him on the meaning of constructivism: Erik, Alec, and Ian Brand.

References

Aarseth, E. J. (1997). *Cybertext: Perspectives on ergodic literature.* Baltimore: Johns Hopkins University Press.

Aarseth, E. J. (2000). Allegories of space: The question of spatiality in computer games. In M. Eskelinen & R. Koskimaa (Eds.), *Cybertext yearbook 2000* (pp. 152–170). Jyvaskyla: University of Jyvaskyla.

Active Worlds. (1995). *Active Worlds* [PC game].

Banks, J., & Potts, J. (2010). Co-creating games: A co-evolutionary analysis. *New Media & Society, 12*(2), 253–270.

Barab, S., Thomas, M., Dodge, T., Carteaux, R., & Tuzun, H. (2005). Making learning fun: *Quest Atlantis*, a game without guns. *Educational Technology Research and Development, 53*(1), 86–107.

Barab, S. A., Gresalfi, M. S., & Ingram-Goble, A. (2010). Transformational play: Using games to position person, content, and context. *Educational Researcher, 39*(7), 525–536.

Bartle, R. (1999). *Early MUD History.* Retrieved from http://www.mud.co.uk/richard/mudhist.htm.

Brand, J., & Kinash, S. (2013) Crafting minds in Minecraft. *Education Technology Solutions, 55*, 66–68.

Bricken, M., & Byrne, C. M. (1994). Summer students in virtual reality: A pilot study on educational applications of virtual reality technology. In A. Wexelblat (Ed.), *Virtual reality: Applications and explorations* (pp. 199–218). Boston: Academic Press.

Bricken, W. (1990). *Learning in virtual reality (Memorandum M-90-5).* Seattle: Human Interface Technology Laboratory.

Bruckman, A. (1998). Community support for constructionist learning. *Computer Supported Cooperative Work, 7,* 47–86.

Bruner, J. (1980). *Actual minds, possible worlds.* Cambridge, MA: Harvard University Press.

Caillois, R. (1961). *Man, play and games.* (M. Barash, Trans.). Glencoe, NY: Free Press.

Calleja, G. (2011). *In-Game: From immersion to incorporation.* Cambridge, MA: MIT Press.

Crawford, G. (2012). *Video gamers.* London: Routledge.

Csikszentmihalyi, M. (1990). *Flow: The psychology of optimal experience.* New York: Harper & Row.

de Byl, P., & Taylor, J. A. (2007). A Web 2.0/Web3D Hybrid Platform for Engaging Students in e-Learning Environments. *The Turkish Online Journal of Distance Education, 8*(3), 108–127.

Dede, C. (1995). The evolution of constructivist learning environments: Immersion in distributed virtual worlds. *Educational Technology, 35*(5), 46–52.

Dewey, J. (2007). *Experience and education.* New York: Simon and Schuster.

Dietze, B., & Kashin, D. (2011). *Playing and learning in early childhood education.* Stamford, CT: Wadsworth.

Duncan, S. C. (2011). *Minecraft,* beyond construction and survival. *Well Played: A Journal on Video Games, Value and Meaning, 1*(1), 1–22.

Erickson, F. H. (1958). Play interviews for four-year-old hospitalized children. *Monographs of the Society for Research in Child Development, 23*(3), 1–77.

Fisher, J. E. (2012). KUHT-TV: The University of Houston's second great vision. *Houston History Magazine*, 30–34.

Gaskins, S., & Miller, P. J. (2009). The cultural r of emotions in pretend play. In Cindy Clark (Ed.), *Transactions at play*. Lanham, MD: Rowman & Littlefield Publishers.

Gee, J. P. (2003). *What video games have to teach us about learning and literacy*. New York: Palgrave-McMillan.

Hoare, C. H. (2001). *Erikson on development in adulthood: New insights from the unpublished papers*. Oxford: Oxford University Press.

Hooper, J. (2014). *[Limitless Play]*. Unpublished Manuscript. Gold Coast, AU: Bond University.

Huitt, W., & Hummel, J. (2003). Piaget's theory of cognitive development. *Educational Psychology Interactive, 3*(2). Valdosta, GA: Valdosta State University. Retrieved from http://chiron.valdosta.edu/whuitt/col/cogsys/piaget.html

Huizinga, J. (1955). *Homo ludens: A study of the play-element in culture*. Boston: Beacon Press.

Jarvinen, A. (2002). *Gran stylissimo: The audiovisual elements and style in computer and video games*. Paper presented at the Computer Games and Digital Cultures Conference, Tampere, Finland.

Juul, J. (2002). *The open and the closed: Games of emergence and games of progression*. Paper presented at the Computer Games and Digital Cultures, Tampere, Finland.

Juul, J. (2007). Without a goal: On open and expressive games. In B. Atkins & T. Krzywinska (Eds.), *Videogames/player/text*. Manchester: University of Manchester Press.

Kelly, A. E., Lesh, R. A., & Baek, J. Y. (Eds.). (2008). *Handbook of design research methods in education: Innovations in science, technology, engineering, and mathematics learning and teaching*. New York: Routledge.

Kolb, D. A. (1984). *Experiential learning: Experience as the source of learning and development (Vol. 1)*. Englewood Cliffs, NJ: Prentice-Hall.

Leslie, A.M. (1987). Pretense and representation: The origins of theory of mind. *Psychological Review, 94*(4), 412–426.

Lien, T. (2013). Bond University conducts class through Minecraft after flood damage closes campus. *Polygon*. Retrieved from http://www.polygon.com/2013/1/30/3935576/bond-university-conducts-class-through-minecraft-after-flood-damage

Linden Lab. (2003). *Second Life* [PC game]. San Francisco, CA: Linden Lab Entertainment.

Lombard, M., & Ditton, T. (2006). At the heart of it all: The concept of presence. *Journal of Computer-Mediated Communication, 3*(2), Retrieved from http://onlinelibrary.wiley.com/doi/10.1111/j.1083–6101.1997.tb00072.x/full

Mateus, M., & Sengers, P. (2003). *Narrative intelligence*. Amsterdam: John Benjamin Publishers.

McCloud, S. (1994). *Understanding comics: The invisible art*. New York: Harper Collins.

McGonigal, J. (2011). Power up their imaginations. *The Times Educational Supplement*, (4966), 4. Retrieved from http://search.proquest.com/docview/917905142?accountid=26503

Mojang. (2011). *Minecraft* [PC game]. Stockholm, Sweden: Mojang.

Newman, J. (2013). *Videogames* (2nd ed.). London: Routledge.

Nintendo. (2001). *Animal Crossing* [Nintendo 64]. Nintendo.

Nitsche, M. (2009). *Video game spaces: Image, play and structures in 3D worlds*. Cambridge, MA: MIT Press.

Paley, V.G. (1992). *You can't say you can't play*. Cambridge, MA: Harvard University Press.

Papert, S. (1980). *Mindstorms: Children, computers and powerful ideas*. New York: Basic books.

Parten, M. (1932). Social participation among preschool children. *The Journal of Abnormal and Social Psychology, 28*(3), 243–269.

Piaget, J. (1926). *The language and thought of the child.* London: Routledge & Kegan.

Piaget, J. (1962). *Play, dreams and imitation in childhood.* New York: W.W. Norton Company, Inc.

Piaget, J. (1999). *Construction of reality in the child.* New York: Routledge.

Prensky, M. (2001). *Digital Game-Based Learning.* New York: McGraw-Hill.

Rheingold, H. (1993). *The virtual community: Homesteading on the electronic frontier.* Reading, MA: Addison-Wesley.

Riner, R. D. (1996). Virtual ethics, Virtual reality. *Futures Research Quarterly, 12*(1), 57–70.

Rose, M. (2011). *Indie games you must play.* Boca Raton: CRC Press.

Salen, K., & Zimmerman, E. (2004). *Rules of play: Game design fundamentals.* Cambridge, MA: MIT Press.

Smilansky, S. (1968). *The Effects of sociodramatic play on disadvantaged preschool children.* New York: Wiley.

Sondergaard, M. (2006). Redefining "cartoony" game art. *Gamasutra.* Retrieved from http://www.gamasutra.com/view/feature/2665/redefining_cartoony_game_art.php

Sutton-Smith, B. (2001). *The ambiguity of play.* Cambridge, MA: Harvard University Press.

Trammell, K. D., Tarkowski, A., & Hofmokl, J. (2004) *Republic of blog.* Paper presented at the 5th Annual Meeting of the Association of Internet Researchers, Brighton, 19–22 September.

Vygotsky, L. (1962). *Thought and language.* Cambridge, MA: MIT Press.

Vygotsky, L. S. (1967). Play and its role in the mental development of the child. *Journal of Russian and East European Psychology, 5*(3), 6–18.

Vygotsky, L.S. (1986). *Thought and language (2nd ed.).* Cambridge, MA: MIT Press.

Wang, F., & Hannafin, M.J. (2005). Design-based research and technology-enhanced learning environments. *Educational Technology Research and Development, 53*(4), 5–23

Webster, J. (2011) Educational building blocks: How *Minecraft* is used in classrooms. *Ars Technica.* Retrieved from http://arstechnica.com/gaming/2011/04/educational-building-blocks-how-minecraft-is-being-used-in-the-classroom/

Weimer, M. (2013). *Learner-centered teaching: Five key changes to practice.* New York: John Wiley & Sons.

Winn, W. (1993). *A Conceptual basis for educational applications of virtual reality. Report No. TR-93-9.* Human Interface Technology Laboratory. Seattle: University of Washington. Retrieved from http://ftp.hitl.washington.edu/publications/r-93-9.

The Craft of Data Mining
Minecraft *and the Constraints of Play*

Alexandra Jean Tremblay,
Jeremy Colangelo *and*
Joseph Alexander Brown

In his book *The meaning of video games: Gaming and textual strategies*, Steven E. Jones (2008) observes that "it's hard for literary scholars to understand how [games] can be truly *meaningful*, any more than a soccer game is meaningful" (p. 2). He goes on in his book to discuss some of the issues that arise when readings are derived from the rules of the game itself (p. 4). Jones is one of several people to propose reading games not merely as a list of rules and protocols, but as a set of potentialities that can come to fruition through the act of play. The anthropologist Bonnie A. Nardi (2010), for example, argues in her recent study of *World of Warcraft* (Blizzard, 2004) that "... videogames such as *WoW* are a *new visual-performative medium* enabled ... by the capacities of digital technology" (p. 7)—a position which lead her to write a full ethnographic study of *World of Warcraft*, written after several years of playing and learning the game. Meanwhile, Axel Bruns (2008), talking about *Second Life* (Linden Lab, 2003), speaks to what he called the "decentralized creativity" active within the structure of the game world (p. 1), a term that could easily be applied to *Minecraft* (Mojang, 2011) as well.

However, it is one thing say that the game becomes itself through the act of play, and another to translate that observation into a process of reading and interpretation. This problem has led to a situation where, as Jones describes, "some ludologists ... seem[m] prepared to recapitulate the history of twentieth century *literary* formalism, with 'the game itself' replacing the New Critics' 'the text itself' as the hermetically sealed object of attention" (p. 5). Likewise too is the notion of a player not as easily defined in this context as one might assume. Often times it seems like studies of videogames make the fallacy of positing an abstract, idealized player through whom the argument can be articulated, in a reversal of the much-maligned intentional fallacy—a problem present, for instance, in the otherwise very good *Storyplaying*, by Sebastian Domsch

(2013). If indeed the growing field of ludology is following the developmental arc of literary criticism, then it may be time to simply cut the Gordian knot and abandon the notion that videogames are all that different from regular texts. What we have been perceiving all this time as an essential, unbridgeable difference between the two mediums is actually the product of a question of textual authority not at all dissimilar from the problems faced by literary scholars during the rise of what we now call theory.

In "What is an Author," Michel Foucault (2010 [1984]) argues that the idea of an "author" serves as a limiting factor on the potentially infinite variety of significations that a text may open up, and in doing so is what makes reading possible, saying that "the author is the principle of thrift in the proliferation of meaning" (p. 118). Part of the problem with reading a game like *Minecraft* is determining who the "author" is. One could employ a version of *auteur-theory* and lay responsibility on its lead designer, Markus "Notch" Persson, in a manner similar to how the "authorship" of a film would be ascribed to its director, but doing so would remove from consideration the roles of the procedurally-generated game world and the creativity of the players—that is, precisely those things which make *Minecraft* interesting. If someone should start a new game in *Minecraft*, and appear in a random spot in the game world, virtually nothing which they encounter will have been placed there by Notch or any member of his development team—rather, everything encountered will either have been assembled automatically by the protocols laid out in the game's code, or by the player herself, with the gameplay being in part the result of an act of interpretation on the part of the player. We can therefore make the following assertion:

Notch is not the creator of an art object which can be analyzed like a work of literature, but is instead *the creator of the vocabulary and grammar* through which a player may articulate the game of *Minecraft* itself (if there even is a "game itself" that can be taken as a unity). This relationship is present in virtually any videogame simply by virtue of the existence of player choice, but what separates *Minecraft* from a game like *Mass Effect* (BioWare, 2007) or *World of Warcraft* is that the language created in *Minecraft*'s development is open and unrestricted enough to allow for the kind "decentralized creativity" which has made it notable. So while in *World of Warcraft* one can, within the restrictions of the game, create works of machinima, using the game as a way to produce a new work of art, but are still limited to treating the game as a kind of elaborate puppet for the will of the players, in *Minecraft* one can create just about anything—from a full-scale model of the starship *Enterprise* to a functional 16-bit processor. All of these things are ultimately derived from *Minecraft*'s code, but in largely the same way that every work of literature—this essay included—is derived from the rules of a language. Thus, the specific gameplay produced, just like a work of literature, is, as Joyce (1986 [1922]) phrased it, "an actuality of the possible as possible" (p. 21)—the act of playing, like the act of writing, takes what existed only as potential and brings it into actuality. It is thus the player who is the "author" of the game.

If we wish to take this understanding and transform it into a process of interpretation, we should take advantage of the groundwork already laid in the study of the French literary group *Oulipo*. The group, found by a collection of writers and mathematicians, comprised some of the most notable practitioners of what is called "constrained writing," or, the practice of creating literature under certain self-imposed constraints, and took their name from an acronym of the phrase "*ouvroir de littérature potentielle*," or, "workshop of potential literature." One of the most successful recent examples of this kind of writing would have to be Christian Bök's *Eunoia* (2009)—a book in which every chapter is written using only one vowel (so the first line of "Chapter E" reads: "enfettered, these sentences repress free speech" [p. 31]), leading to a kind of writing that one scholar has referred to as "constraint-based heuristics" (Betts, 2013, p. 259).

Though Bök was not a member of *Oulipo*, he is one of its more notable scholars. As he writes: "*Oulipo* regards literature as a cyberorganic phenomenon that results from deliberate collisions between poetic devices: the machinic parology of accidents.... *Oulipo* sees its work in terms of an as yet unrealized reality that exists paradoxically before its time and ahead of its time" ('*Pataphysics*, 2002, p. 64–5). Thus, for *Oulipo*, "to compose poetry is to undertake a mathematical analysis of language itself" (p. 69). Furthermore, just as a certain act of gameplay is an actualization of something which existed potentially in the rules of the game, so too is the work of art considered along these lines. We can look for instance to the "Preamble" to *Life: A User's Manual* (1987)—a novel by Georges Perec, one of *Oulipo*'s most notable members. Perec, using the example of a jigsaw puzzle, writes that "knowledge of the pattern and of its laws, of the set and its structure, could not possibly be derived from discrete knowledge of the elements that compose it.... [Y]ou can look at a piece of a puzzle for three whole days ... and be no further than when you started." This is essentially the problem faced by any scholar who wishes to derive a reading of a videogame merely from the rules and code that make it up.

By looking at the process of creating literature through the logic of machines and of constraints, the authors of *Oulipo* and their antecedents have, we think, created an aesthetic model through which videogames like *Minecraft* can be read. In particular, the way *Oulipo*'s constrained writing essentially bifurcates the creative process—*Eunoia* is as much a product of the rules it follows as of Bök's own creative decisions, to the extent that many specificities text can be said to have arisen by chance. In much the same way can an act of gameplay be said to have two parents—the decisions of the player in the act of play *and* the restraints imposed by the game world they occupy. Also important is the idea of limitation—just as one cannot write every text that is possible in a language, so too can no player ever do all of the things that are possible within the constraints of *Minecraft*'s code. What me must therefore do when reading the game is remain closely attenuated not only to the rules of the game, but also to that which results from the player's relationship to them: everything from how certain players react to particular situations they encounter, to the way players modify the game's code, to the social environment that has evolved around it—not choosing one or the other, but examining all at once and at the same time. Put more simply, we can take Jacques Derrida's famous dictum that "there is nothing outside of the text" (1997 [1967] p. 158) and say as well that *there is no metagame.*

Given the understanding of how one should approach a game like *Minecraft* outlined above, it is clearly imperative to better understand the ways in which players navigate the constraints that the game puts on them and how these constraints lead to the flowering of creativity that we have observed in the *Minecraft* community. Just as one would not undertake an analysis of a poem without knowing the grammar rules according to which it was composed, so too would it be foolish to analyze a videogame without knowing the language of its creation. Furthermore, just as critics do not limit their readings to a mere cataloguing of parts of speech, so too should videogame theorists avoid subordinating their analyses to merely describing the nuts-and-bolts of the game's composition. Knowledge of the grammar of *Minecraft* is absolutely vital to a reading of it, but this knowledge can only be used effectively if it becomes the ground on which the reading is built, and not the structure itself.

The Procedural Condition

Normally parts of games are designed by a team of artists, writers, programmers, and developers. The levels, weapons, graphics and textures, enemies, etc. are designed in order to meet with the overall world design and story. Content creation is a time consuming and expensive process, especially for the indie game developers who do not have the resources of a large design firm. Game developers, both large and small, are looking into the creation of game elements automatically. Procedural Content Generation (PCG) is the generation of elements in a game via an algorithmic process (Togelius et al., 2011). It can be stochastic and random or deterministic and non-random. It can be done prior to the game, or more commonly during the program's run. Much like player modeling there is not a pure definition where the line of PCG is made compared to content generation.

Levels (Ashlock, Lee, and McGuinness, 2011; Valtchanov and Brown, 2012), level generation based on a storyline (Dormans and Bakkes, 2011; Hartsook et al., 2011), weapons (Pace and Thompson, Brown, 2013), graphics and textures (Rhoades et al., 1992), enemies (Ashlock and Nguyen, 2011), etc. have all been designed using PCG techniques. Other creative pursuits such as poetry (Hartman, 1996), art (Neufeld, 2008), and music (Plans and Morelli, 2012) have all had PCG algorithms used for their construction to varying levels of effectiveness. In *Minecraft* the PCG is primarily concerned in the generation of the game world, i.e., which blocks are placed and where. This generation is deterministic based on a seed value of the world. This means that two players using the same seed word will create the same world. Thus, in the *Minecraft* game world, we can say: in the beginning was the seed, and the universe was memory. The question becomes how this seed moves from a string into being all the blocks in a *Minecraft* world. Two methods can do this creation, an intelligent design or an evolutionary structure. The intelligent design is the current method of level generation for *Minecraft*. The placement of blocks results from a deterministic algorithm which places them. This placement is made based upon the idea of biomes, and blocks will appear with regular frequencies based upon the biome.

The other method, not currently employed by vanilla *Minecraft*, uses certain factors to optimize the level design to the player's style and level of ability (a method present, for example, in Valve Software's *Left 4 Dead* series)(Valve Corporation, 2008). Such elements have been shown to work in modding community, and courses in AI have been using *Minecraft* as their choice of expandable platform to demonstrate such techniques (Bayliss, 2012). The specification of the world via biomes has further been expanded upon by the mod Mystcraft (XCompWiz, 2013). This mod allow for the player to generate worlds via writing a descriptive book where each page defines a feature in the desired world. The player is generating a new map or level via this process with specifications that can control the biomes, sky color, weather, etc. Any features not specified by the player are randomly generated by the system. Such a mod demonstrates how PCG can meet with the users' demands and preferences, while still having a random world.

Modeling Constrained Players

A "model" is any object or conceptual construct which can be used to approximate, understand, or simulate the appearance, actions, or properties of another object or concept. A good model allows for this approximation, understanding, or simulation to happen where the real object is too dangerous, time consuming, or impractical for the real object to be used. Models are useful for both explanation and prediction—as, for example, when an architect would make a scale model of a bridge to test a design before making a real one.

We use conceptual models in our day to day lives. Take the activity of asking someone who you have known for a few months out on a date. Before you ask the question you may consider what you will say and what their response will be, which is to say that you will model the conversation in order to prepare for it. Any thought that involves considering why an action was made, or considering an action to be done, is using a conceptual model of the world. Hence, almost all of higher level thought involves modeling.

Player modeling is a loosely defined collection of techniques for the modeling of player actions or experiences in videogames. Smith et al. (2001) bemoan the lack of a comprehensive definition and attempt to build a taxonomy of player modeling studies. They say that "[Player modeling] can equally apply to everything from a predictive model of player actions resulting from machine learning to a designer's description of a player's expected reactions in response to some piece of game content. This lack of a precise terminology prevents practitioners from quickly finding introductions to applicable modeling methods or determining viable alternatives to their own techniques" (2001, p. 301). For our purposes, we are interested in the discovery of actions of players by examining the player, not what a designer is saying about the player.

Canossa (2012) proposed that the links between player actions and a personality profile using Reiss' motivation theory would provide a model for *Minecraft* player behavior. This theory proposes a set of sixteen intrinsic motives or needs: acceptance, curiosity, eating, family, honor, idealism, order, physical activity, power, romance, saving, social contact, status, tranquility, and vengeance. There are no extrinsic motives in the model, as it is only interested in the mind in a mind-body duality. This perhaps better models the actions of a player within the *Minecraft* universe. A player does not have a physical presence inside of the game, but rather the illusion of a physical presence is attained through a mental projection, or a kind of mental modeling on the part of the player. For example, in survival mode it is possible for the player *character* to become hungry. This is not a hunger experienced by the player, but can be understood by them through a kind of modeling and the associated desire to keep the character alive.

Canossa et al. (2013) expanded this initial proposal to a set of one hundred participants self-reported for the study after a call for participation was made in a number of *Minecraft* forums. It can be assumed the respondents were all well acquainted with *Minecraft* as all gameplays of less than thirty hours of time were rejected. Each respondent was given a general questionnaire (age, sex, education, etc.), a Reiss' motivation evaluation (Reiss, 2008), and was required to submit a game log. Those with missing entries were rejected, leaving the researchers with eighty-four surveys in English and four in Spanish. These datasets were then evaluated via a Pearson product-moment correlation coefficient.

It was found that the players responding scored much higher than the average population on *Curiosity* and much lower in their desire for *Status*. The authors speculate these scores derive from the design of *Minecraft*. The game, as it is procedurally generated, gives a random world for the player to explore, providing many opportunities to explore and satisfy one's curiosity. *Status* is a difficult concept to measure in *Minecraft*; while there is an achievements tree and an ending, the structure of the game is very open, and it is impossible to "complete" *Minecraft* as one would another game. This conclusion does not take into account the wider *Minecraft* community, which might provide several opportunities to attain status—such as by producing a frequently-viewed gameplay video. However, in that case the metric for success would be largely extrinsic to the way the game is designed and coded, unlike the metrics for *Curiosity* that derive in part from the structure of the game world.

There are number of interesting correlations between player personalities and their behavior in the game. A high *Independence* is negatively associated with entering The End (that is, the conclusion of the game's simple story) or obtaining the associated achievement. Seeing as how this action is the end level of the game, more independent players are less likely to be interested in "finishing." *Curiosity* is correlated with the creation of exploration tools and use of common building tools, being positively correlated with such metrics as the number of stone axes crafted, torches used and reused, stone shovels crafted and broken, and of cobblestone used. *Tranquility* is associated with the creation of fences, as if the player is attempting to have a quiet life. *Saving* is linked with the use of cheaper materials in buildings and is negatively correlated with the use of diamond tools, which are rare and hard to replace. Those with high *Vengeance* are more likely to quit out of the game. Two very odd correlations without an obvious tie between the desire and the action exist: *Family* is negatively linked to using a gold sword and *Status* is negatively linked to mining cactus. It is noted that *Status* seekers are more likely to use potatoes, a luxury food item in *Minecraft*. Overall, the study shows that player profiling using such a model provides an ability to link a player's motivations to actions in the game.

Similar play style changes have been found to link with factors like age. In one of the largest studies of this type (Tekofsky, 2013), with 9366 responses used in the final analysis, *Battlefield 3* (EA Digital Illusions, 2011) players submitted their gameplays along with a general survey and IPIP personality test (Goldberg et al., 2006) in order to remove biases. General findings were that older players were less likely to kill or die, and generally seemed to present lower ability, but were more likely to capture objectives and focus on winning matches instead of simply accumulating a higher number of kills. Canossa et al. (2013) also showed that age was linked to more deaths in *Minecraft*. Older players in *Battlefield 3* are more commonly found in support or engineer roles, which suggest a more objective and team based play. Further, older players are found to use more defensive vehicles, like tanks, as opposed to faster offensive vehicles like jet fighters. The question remains as to whether these changes in play style are because of declining hand-eye coordination and reflexes or changing player motivations accompanying age. Iida et al. (2003) propose that older players, because of their familiarity with the game, will play in a meaningful strategy, whereas younger players are more likely to explore the various techniques allowed in the game.

Eliminating All Constraints

Minecraft's structure has allowed for a wide variety of user driven design, not only through player modification of the game code but also through the development of games within the game—for example, downloadable game worlds where players have developed mazes and puzzles for other players to solve. This kind of player-driven development is a huge part of the *Minecraft* community and is one of its primary draws.

Making modifications to *Minecraft* ("modding") is an incredibly diverse and popular off shoot to the game, so much so that it is often necessary to refer to an unmodified version of the game as "vanilla *Minecraft*" in order to distinguish it from the plethora of modded versions. The *Minecraft* code is not open source, but since it is written in java the code can be reverse engineered. Individuals who develop systems like the *Minecraft* Coders' Pack devote their time to figuring out the code so that modders can more easily create their additions (MCP Team, 2013). Modding *Minecraft* not only increases engagement in the game but also

Mojang has embraced these mods, which have opened up many opportunities for players to enjoy their game, and as of January 2014 they are currently developing the *Minecraft* Plug-in API. This is a set of tools to help modders interact with the game more easily and is currently being designed by the modders responsible for the popular mod Bukkit, who were hired by Mojang in 2012 (EvilSeph, 2012). The Mojang End User Licence Agreement (as of 2013) spells out the official stance on modding *Minecraft*:

> The one major rule is that you must not distribute anything we've made. By "distribute anything we've made" what we mean is "give copies of the game away, make commercial use of, try to make money from, or let other people get access to our game and its parts in a way that is unfair or unreasonable..."..Otherwise we are quite relaxed about what you do—in fact we really encourage you to do cool stuff—but just don't do those things that we say you can't.
>
> Any tools you write for the Game from scratch belong to you.... Modifications to the Game ("Mods") (including pre-run Mods and in-memory Mods) and plu-

gins for the Game also belong to you and you can do whatever you want with them, as long as you don't sell them for money / try to make money from them. We have the final say on what constitutes a tool/mod/plugin and what doesn't [Mojang, 2013].

Mojang's EULA makes their stance on modding clear. It also legally allows Mojang to adapt features from mods into the official game, which they have already done in the past. In fact, items like Ender Chests, Horses, Pistons and Hoppers all came from mods first before they were integrated into the vanilla game.

Mods have given *Minecraft* users the ability to make the game their own beyond the already extensible environment of the vanilla game. *Minecraft* actively encourages their users to let their imaginations run wild in any way they want, whether that be through building anything they can think of, modding the game, or participating in the active and engaging community. Combined with the active incorporation of user feedback, the success of the game is unsurprising.

Conclusion

When discussing a game like *Minecraft*, it is important to avoid a simplistic division between the gameplay and community and the coding and architecture of the game itself. Just as a work of literature must be understood in terms of its relation to the language in which it is written, so to must *Minecraft* be understood in both the way it is played and talked about *and* the way in which its structure characterizes that play. It is imperative that scholars of *Minecraft*—and, indeed, videogames in general—adopt a new, more flexible understanding of what constitutes a "game," or what falls within the bounds of discussion. If "the game" of *Minecraft* is not located in its code, but in the actualization of that code—if Notch and his team are not the makers of a game, but of a grammar—then the question of how one reads a videogame acquires many divergent possible answers. Thus, an understanding of the coding and structure of *Minecraft* must be acquired with the attendant understanding that this code does not constitute the whole game, but rather that which makes it possible for the game to exist.

We think that constrained writing, and *Oulipo* in particular, provides a useful heuristic for overcoming these problems, as its attitude towards the relationship between a work of literature and the language in which it was written is very close to the relationship between the structure of a game and how it is played. In this light, it becomes clear that there can be no easy division between the 'game itself' and an exterior world which can be ignored for the purposes of interpretation. The "game" *Minecraft* is not the code but rather an actualization of the potential within the code, and how a given player performs this actualization is conditioned by circumstances that may be far removed from the program called '*Minecraft*' on their computer. The discourse usually considered to be the metagame—the *Minecraft* Wiki, YouTube guides, modding, and the like—represent not only a community and a repository of knowledge but also alternative "readings" of the code and new heuristics of play. In this light, then, the question 'how do I read *Minecraft*?' can best be responded to with 'what exactly do you mean by *Minecraft*?' for the domain of *Minecraft*, just like the domain of a work of literature, is far more expansive than is conventionally understood.

References

Ashlock, D., Lee, C., & McGuinness, C. (2011). Search-based procedural generation of maze-like levels. *IEEE Transactions on Computational Intelligence and AI in Games, 3*(3), 260–273.

Ashlock, D., & Nguyen, S. (2011). Financial control of the evolution of autonomous non-player characters. *IEEE Congress on Evolutionary Computation* (pp. 828–835).

Bakkes, S., Tan, C.T., & Pisan, Y. (2012). Personalised gaming: A motivation and overview of literature. In *Proceedings of the 8th Australasian Conference on Interactive Entertainment: Playing the System (IE '12*). ACM, New York, Article 4, 10 pages.

Bayliss, J. D. (2012). Teaching game AI through *Minecraft* mods. In *Proceedings of the 2012 IEEE International Games Innovation Conference*, (pp. 1–4).

Betts, G. (2013). *Avant-garde Canadian literature: The early manifestations.* Toronto: University of Toronto Press.

BioWare. (2007). *Mass Effect* [PC game]. Microsoft Game Studios.

Blizzard Entertainment. (2004). *World of Warcraft* [PC game]. Irvine, California: Blizzard.

Bök, C. (2002). '*Pataphysics: The poetics of an imaginary science.* Evanston: Northwestern University Press.

Bök, C. (2010). *Eunoia.* Toronto: Coach House Books.

Brown, J. A. (2013). Evolved weapons for RPG drop systems, *IEEE Conference on Computational Intelligence in Games 2013* (pp. 259–260).

Bruns, A. (2008). *Blogs, Wikipedia, Second Life, and beyond: From production to produsage.* New York: Peter Lang.

Canossa, A. (2012). Give me a reason to dig: Qualitative associations between player behavior in *Minecraft* and life motives. In *Proceedings of the International Conference on the Foundations of Digital Games* (FDG '12). ACM (pp. 282–283). New York, NY.

Canossa, A., Martinez, J. B., & Togelius, J. (2013). Give me a reason to dig: *Minecraft* and psychology of motivation. *IEEE Conference on Computational Intelligence in Games* (pp. 97–104).

Chucklefish LTD. (2013). *Starbound* [computer software].

Derrida, J. (1997). *Of grammatology* (G. C. Spivak, trans.) Baltimore: Johns Hopkins University Press.

Domsch, S. (2013). *Storyplaying: Agency and narrative in video games.* Boston: De Gruyter.

Dormans, J., & Bakkes, S. (2011). Generating mission and spaces for adaptable play experiences. *IEEE Transactions on Computational Intelligence and AI in Games, 3*(3), 216–228.

EA Digital Illusions. (2011). *Battlefield 3* [PC game]. Electronic Arts.

EvilSeph. (2012, February 28). Bukkit Forums. Retrieved December 3, 2013, from http://forums.bukkit.org/threads/bukkit-the-next-chapter.62489/

Foucault, M. (2010). What is an author? (Josué V. Harari, trans.). In Paul Rabinow (ed.), *The Foucault reader* (101–120). New York: Vintage.

Goldberg, L. R., Johnson, J. A., Eber, H. W., Hogan, R., Ashton, M. C., Cloninger, C. R., & Gough, H. C. (2006). The international personality item Pool and the future of public-domain personality measures. *Journal of Research in Personality*, 40, 84–96.

Hartman, C.O. (1996). *Virtual muse: Experiments in computer poetry*. University Press of New England.

Hartsook, K., Zook, A., Das, S., & Riedl, M. O. (2011). Toward supporting stories with procedurally generated game worlds. In *Proceedings of the 2011 IEEE Conference on Computational Intelligence and Games (CIG)* (pp. 297–304).

Iida, H., Takeshita, N., & Yoshimura, J. (2003). A metric for entertainment of boardgames: Its implication for evolution of chess variants. In *IWEC2002 Proceedings* (pp. 65–72).

Jones, S. E. (2008). *The meaning of video games: Gaming and textual strategies*. New York: Routledge.

Joyce, J. (1986). *Ulysses*. Hans Walter Gabler et al (eds.). New York: Vintage.

Linden Lab. (2003). *Second Life* [PC game]. San Francisco, CA: Linden Lab Entertainment.

MCP Team. (2013, November 6). Mod Coders Pack. Retrieved from http://mcp.oceanlabs.de/

Mojang. (2011). *Minecraft* [PC game]. Stockholm, Sweden.

Mojang. (2013, December 11). *Minecraft* end user licence agreement. Retrieved from https://account.mojang.com/documents/minecraft_eula

Nardi, B. A. (2010). *My life as a night elf priest: An anthropological account of* World of Warcraft. Ann Arbor: University of Michigan Press.

Neufeld, C., Ross, B.J., & Ralph W. (2008). The evolution of artistic filters. In *The Art of Artificial Evolution*, J. Romero and P. Machado (eds.), (pp. 335–356). Berlin: Springer.

Pace, A., & Thompson, T. (2013). Procedural content generation and evolution within the evotanks domain. In *Foundations of Digital Games*, 439–440.

Perec, G. (1987). *Life: A user's manual*. (D. Bellos, trans.). Boston: David R. Godine.

Plans, D., & Morelli, D. (2012). Experience-driven procedural music generation for games. *IEEE Transactions on Computational Intelligence and AI in Games*. 4(3), 192–198.

"Redigit" Spinks, A. (2011). *Terraria* [videogame].

Reiss, S. (2008). *The normal personality, a new way of thinking about people*. Cambridge: Cambridge University Press.

Rhoades, J., Turk, G., Bell, A., State, A., Neumann, U., & Varshney, A. (1992). Real-time procedural textures. In *Proceedings of the 1992 symposium on Interactive 3D graphics (I3D '92)* (pp. 95–100). ACM, New York.

Smith, A. M., Lewis, C., Hullet, K., & Sullivan, A. (2011). An inclusive view of player modeling. In *Proceedings of the 6th International Conference on Foundations of Digital Games* (pp. 301–303). ACM.

Tekofsky, S., Spronck, P., Plaat, A., van Den Herik, J., & Broersen, J. (2013). Play style: Showing your age. *IEEE Conference on Computational Intelligence in Games 2013* (pp. 177–184).

Togelius, J., Kastbjerg, E., Schedl, D., & Yannakakis, G. N. (2011). What is procedural content generation? Mario on the borderline. *PCGames '11 Proceedings of the 2nd International Workshop on Procedural Content Generation in Games*, Article No. 3.

Valtchanov, V., & Brown, J.A. (2012). Evolving dungeon crawler levels with relative placement, *C* Conference on Computer Science and Engineering 2012 (C3S2E12)* (pp. 27–
35).
Valve Corporation. (2008). *Left 4 dead.* [videogame].
XCompWiz. (2013). *Mystcraft* v 0.10.5. [videogame].

Just Steve

Conventions of Gender on the Virtual Frontier

Iris Rochelle Bull

In the videogame *Minecraft* (Mojang, 2011) every player begins their adventure in the middle of a vast and unending wilderness.[1] The world exists as a crude, blocky caricature of Earth; everything from seas to deserts, plains to jungles, and more, are traversable, exploitable, harvestable, and habitable. In single-player mode, the worlds in *Minecraft* are empty frontiers on which players colonize and explore in solitude for sport. There are creatures and monsters to kill, landscapes to shape, and materials to craft—all in the name of survival, if survival is the game you want to play. *Minecraft* is also an incredibly powerful platform for players to craft art, mini-games, models, experiments, societies, and other creative endeavors. Many players young and old share videos of their time spent playing the game, and others participate in online communities focused around the consumption of fan-made productions and game screenshots. In a departure from the aesthetic design of many other videogames, parent company Mojang maintains *Minecraft* as both a sandbox[2] and a sculpting instrument that grants players an impressive amount of freedom to do as they like with the program. There are, for example, no elaborate quests to complete or explicit instructions on how to play. Not unlike a box of LEGO bricks and toys, *Minecraft* presents players with the appearance of limitless, user-generated entertainment.

The façade of unfettered freedom extends to visual representations of the player character, the evolution of which is an aspect of *Minecraft* that was unique in some ways. In the early stages of development Markus Alexej "Notch" Persson designed the game by himself, and he drew the default player avatar as a male with a goatee and jokingly referred to him as "Steve."[3] While the game was still in Alpha, Notch hired an independent artist, Hayden "Dock" Scott-Baron, to help him develop character models for the game. Older players might remember leaked art and fan videos depicting four possible character additions to the game: "Rana," "Black Steve," "Steve," and "Beast Boy." The initial design of these characters suggested that they would serve as "ragdoll" non-playable mob entities (i.e., friends, allies, or enemies), while simultaneously acknowledging the existence of femininity and blackness (e.g., Rana and Black Steve, respectively) in the *Minecraft* universe. Although the art assets were dropped after Dock's three-month stay with the project, their brief inclusion in the *Minecraft* source code inspired questions early on about the role of gender and character modeling in the *Minecraft* universe.[4] Namely, what role does "gender" serve on the frontier, if any?

Sexing Without Sexuality

Opting for a genderless design, the official "vanilla" release of the *Minecraft* PC game in 2011 did not include feminized or feminine stock models for either playable or non-playable characters.[5] While the design of playable and non-playable characters in videogames has historically privileged white, heterosexual, masculine bodies, *Minecraft* provided players with the freedom to aesthetically design their own player characters within the confines of a pixelated schema (cf. Jansz and Martis, 2007; Miller and Summers, 2007; Williams, Martins, Consalvo, and Ivory, 2009). Consequently, sexuality and gender were rendered as inert characteristics in the design of a human figure. Notch received many requests to modify the aesthetic to include feminized player character models to the game but ultimately refused. Instead, he offered these sentiments about gender on his development blog for the game:

> The human model is intended to represent a Human Being. Not a male Human Being or a female Human Being, but simply a Human Being. The blocky shape gives it a bit of a traditional masculine look, but adding a separate female mesh would just make it worse by having one specific model for female Human Beings and male ones. That would force players to make a decisions [sic] about gender in a game where gender doesn't even exist [Persson, 2012a].

In accordance with his vision, Notch designed character models and game mechanics in *Minecraft* that convolute heteronormative notions of sexuality and gender.

Referring to it as merely a "gameplay element" on his blog, Notch frames gender as both aesthetically optional, and separate from other game elements that influence player behavior, and the code underneath the game reflects this philosophy (Persson, 2012a). In *Minecraft*, there are three classes of artificially intelligent entities (also known as mobs) that simulate the mechanics of biological reproduction (via spawning and having babies): animals, villagers, and monsters. Players don't need to discriminate between distinct reproductive organs because mobs that the player can breed are unisexual. Players can coerce adult villagers, pigs, chickens/ducks, wolves, sheep, cats, horses, cows and mooshrooms into reproducing by feeding and pairing them together.[6] Penning mobs is one way players can farm them either for resources or as art installations. After being fed, a red heart animation appears above a mob's head to signal wanting affection. Lonesome mobs gravitate towards other love-struck mobs, and a miniaturized, "baby" mob spawns between them. Put simply, this system decouples the process of reproduction from biological limitations of a material body, and elides the process altogether by choosing not to animate sex acts.

The unisexual default makes it more difficult for players to negotiate heteronormativity as the dominant, cultural orientation between players. It also suggests that power relations predicated on gender and sexuality are not constituted as playable in the game space (for more on "doing" heteronormativity, cf. Schilt and Westbrook, 2009). Whatever players may think of gender and sexuality, they are encouraged to assume that those aesthetics play no role in determining what they can do on the virtual frontier.

Constructing and Locating Gender

Liberating the player character in *Minecraft* from the false biological dichotomy of two sexes is laudable, but locating gender within the player character obfuscates the ways in which social and material structures construct gender in virtual game spaces (cf. Fausto-Sterling, 1993). From a cultural studies perspective, gender is a social construction, "conceived of differently in different cultures, historical periods, and contexts" (Cassell & Jenkins, 1998, p. 4). This definition best informs the player behavior of "gender-swapping," a well-documented phenomenon wherein players adopt gendered characters that do not correspond to their cis-gender (Turkle, 1995; Cherney & Wise, 1996; Kolo & Baur, 2004; DiGiuseppe & Nardi, 2007). The cultural studies approach also allows for articulations of gender that are divorced from the material body, and it allows for broader understandings of how people might experience and practice gender in game spaces where these cultural concepts are not defined. This basic framework is supported by research conducted on gender in other virtual world environments.

In an ethnographic study of *wang ba*—Internet cafés—in China, Lindtner et. al. demonstrate how social contexts in real life (IRL) shape experiences of computer-mediated sociality and collaboration (2008). These findings complement an understanding of identity as both performative and structurally contingent. Building on the theoretical work of Hollander (2012) and West and Fenstermaker (2002) who develop a sociological understanding of performing—"doing"—gender, Stabile's research on *World of Warcraft* (Blizzard,

2004) players also articulates how gender is shaped by cooperative interaction with other players (2013, 5–6). Stabile's work shows how dominant ideologies of gender become transparent and reproduced through socialized accountability and self-referential identification (2013, 5–6). While it is possible that some players are not familiar with feeling accountable for their gendered performance, such an experience is not unique for others (Stabile, 2013, p. 7). In *Minecraft*, players may routinely ask each other about personal aspects of their lives IRL, or make assumptions about gender and sexuality based on a username, the appearance of the player character skin, or the sound of a person's voice.[7] Evidence of this phenomenon on *Minecraft* servers is scattered online across community forums, personal blogs and Tumblrs. One such example can be found on PlanetMinecraft.com, where users DerpyKat and Daisy Rose co-authored a community blog post to share their experiences as perceived "guys" and "girls." As though talking to each other, they note the different ways others police their gender within a masculine/feminine binary. Here is choice excerpt:

> I'm pretty good with a bow, so when I when I joined a RP server, I joined a town that needed a bowman. I joined as Ethan (I didn't have my account yet.) I started out a newbie of the Bow squad, and pretty soon I bumped the General out of his place and became General of Bows. I [sic] when I got my own account, I was so excited because I could finally play as a girl. I joined the town, and said I'm pretty good with a bow like I did last time. Then, he put me as town princess. I wanted to say that I was Ethan, but I didn't because they have a no multi-accounting rule … so I couldn't say "I'm Ethan." or I was banned [Derpycat and Daisy Rose, 2013].

Moments when players discriminate along the lines of assumed identities are highly contingent on how players communicate with each other and what they can sense in their interactions—not all presenting women, girls, or otherwise feminized bodies experience gendered discrimination, but some do and in different ways depending on the social makeup and historical background of the space in question (cf. Mohanty, 1988). In any cultural context, the role of the genderless human being, then, is one of a blank canvas. The avatar is presented as a white doll with no inherent cultural or historical baggage that would invite the distaste of the player.[8] As if to contrast the default, a customized avatar invites interpretation of marked denotations—customizations intend to communicate difference. What others interpret depends on the literacy of the reader and their conditioned, judgmental response; how players communicate a response depends on the tools of communication afforded to them. In *Minecraft*, outside of miming with one's avatar, players can communicate through a text channel; although unsupported by Mojang, players also use voice chat services to create private sound environments outside the game.[9] Mojang does not provide players with any means for policing player behavior, so players and server administrators are burdened with facilitating their own codes of conduct.[10] As Daisy Rose's account above illustrates, these codes can extend beyond protecting players from harassment and more formally establish expectations between players of different cultural backgrounds. Whether codes are implicit or explicit, there are consequences to playing or acting in ways that disorient or disrupt the expectations of other players (cf. Sundén and Sveningsson, 2012). Expectations are shaped in many cultural, historical, practiced, and rhetorical ways of being; they refract the practice of everyday configurations that constitute social behavior and stabilize multiplicitous categories of femininity and masculinity (Butler, 1988; Haraway, 1991; Connell, 1996; Ahmed, 2006). If players are want to reproduce those ways of being in *Minecraft*, it may be because they don't know how to feel and behave like a genderless human being. Their expectations are also in dialogue with the design of any given virtual world, so the social gendering of a player's avatar or play style can ideologically compliment the way a game rewards the completion of a particular task.

Videogames cannot be reduced to a set of rules and abstracted algorithms, but the structure of a videogame does legitimate contingent ways of being and doing that is architected with particular values and assumptions in mind (Malaby 2009, p. 13). It would be equally reductive to suggest that gender and various activities are separable from the histories that shape a person's experience with doing in and around the game space. In reflecting on their research that observes children learning how to use computers, McDermott and Varenne ask:

> When is gender anyway? On what grounds can any piece of behavior be called gendered, with those who help, by way of what interpretive categories, and in what contexts applied? The cultural question is not what do boys and girls do, but *when are the categories of male and female made relevant, in what circumstances, by virtue of what work?* [2006, p. 20; original emphasis maintained].

In virtual worlds, where contextual circumstances (i.e., narrative, setting, etc.) are frequently borrowed from mainstream cultures and sites, the virtue of work is an intensely value-laden, contingent category. Valued activities that are framed as leisure and relaxation contrast other activities or experiences as distinctly "not fun" or not "part of the game." As Squire points out: "games focus our attention and mold our experience of what is important in a world and what is to be ignored" (2006, p. 21–22). The patterned distinctions of "fun" as congruent with acting and "not fun" as congruent with being acted upon, "hardcore" games as masculine and "casual" games as feminine, highlight the ways in which "play" can engender gendered ideals of masculinity and femininity in particular cultural contexts (Anable, 2013; Vanderhoef, 2013).

In exploring the minefield women and girls navigate in the arena of e-sports, T. L. Taylor notes that the role of femininity is a markedly subjugated one because of the overt domination of men and male bodies in the competitive scene (2012).[11] Taylor relates the patterned treatment of feminine bodies to the longer history of women's bodies in athletic arenas, and observes that acculturating to the performance of being an e-sport athlete is complex; "It is never just an issue of individual skill but the ways an entire system of practices, institutions, values, and forms of identity work on, and through, that player" (2012, p. 132). As the *Minecraft* community continues to champion celebrity players on YouTube and constitute public spheres on websites like Reddit (where content is unceremoniously voted on), these idiosyncratic cultural systems and ideological values are becoming more transparent. While *Minecraft* is not yet widely conceived of as a competitive e-sport, players do engage in other forms of in-game competition. Build and mining challenges, Let's Plays, and Player-vs-Player mini-games (i.e., "Spleef," "Race for the Wools," "Ultra-Hardcore") are some of the most popular forms of player-generated entertainment enjoyed by tens-of-thousands of subscribers. With increasing regularity players are meeting in real life (IRL) at official and unofficial conferences (i.e., Cons). In these player-dominated spaces, where gender is almost unavoidably associated with appearance and body shape of the player, people find different ways of playing that I haven't been able to find in the game space—costume contests, panels and workshops, classes on *Minecraft*-themed content. Of course, conferences and other social publics are structurally different in many ways from the virtual worlds that inspire them; however, it is important to pay attention to the ways in which gender is presented in public spaces because the individual experiences that players have in those places feedback into the virtual world (Taylor, 2006, p. 9; cf. Lamerichs, 2011). A genderless avatar, for example, does not set a precedent attitude of gender inclusivity—the people playing the game must set those expectations. The design of *Minecraft* inherently consequences and rewards some ways of playing over others (e.g., dying is undesirable, therefore all players who want to avoid death harvest and eat food)—this design may not take into account the gender of a player, but these patterned ways of *doing* may resonate with histories of gendered work and play in the real world. Compared to the range of motion people have in the real world, the limitations of the game structure reflect a relatively narrow spectrum of acceptable player behaviors.

Minecraft *as a Vehicle for the American Frontier Myth*

Procedural generation may allow for more than 18 quintillion possible *Minecraft* worlds and provide players with a diverse matrix of blocks, textures, creatures, and environmental elements; but, the basic actions that many players perform remain relatively limited.[12] Players punch, place, and destroy both blocks and mobs in the service of comfortably dominating their environment without the aid of other players or non-player characters (NPCs). By hunting, mining, pioneering, railroading, crafting, and farming, players find individualized solutions for the problems all must inevitably solve—feeding, protecting, and arming oneself. A player may kill or ignore mob enemies, for example, but players cannot communicate meaningfully with them.[13] The player character is designed to always be capable of killing mob enemies, but it must scavenge for and harvest resources from the land and underground in order to protect itself—functionally, there are no other ways to survive in *Minecraft*. Cook argues that games are "simulations that facilitate and encourage a user to explore and learn the properties of their possibility space through the use of feedback mechanisms" (2006). Simulations do not exist in cultural vacuums, and their design—on mechanical and aesthetic levels—invite different epistemological interpretations from different cultural standpoints. From a Western perspective, the design of vanilla *Minecraft* distinctly privileges ways of doing and being that complement the Western Frontier Myth.[14] This resonance is significant for its ubiquity in American culture; Americans, whether they are formally aware of the Myth are not, are conditioned by symbols that evoke it.

The Myth suggests and signifies a "formative experience" on an ever-fluid landscape that constitutes an imaginary "wilderness" (Stoeltje, 1987, p. 250; Slotkin, 1998, p. 11). It is a self-legitimizing logic that frames the wilderness as a frontier that the individual is charged with colonizing. In *Minecraft*, the player character literally spawns on the grounds of an imaginary and abstract wilderness that has been designed for colonization and exploration—there is no one else to care for and there is little else to do. The constantly evolving nature of the game design and development process privileges players who are comfortable with a nomadic play style or who have a detached relationship with their colonies and homesteads. Unconventional in respect to all other videogames, *Minecraft* has always been in some stage of development.[15] Even today, two years after the "official" release of the game, Mojang continues to publish updates that alter the mechanics and asset library in the game., which often necessitates that players abandon old world files and start completely over. The burden to modify and preserve persistent civilizations falls on server administrators, though there is little that motivates this labor outside of nostalgia. This system, this play space doesn't explicitly reward players who form an emotional attachment with the landscape or the mobs on it. Mobs in *Minecraft* are not designed to be your friends; other players are supposed to offer friendship—they are the ones who are detached from the landscape and never in danger of being accidentally deleted. This isn't to say that players do not form unique relationships with mobs—certainly, some have pets and pen monsters—but, there are not consequences for killing pets. Although players may constitute their own codes of conduct and forms of governance, these civil acts are tenuous. *Minecraft* doesn't evolve with players as they construct frameworks for civilization. Rather, it provides a limbic space where the individual can act and think in ways that would otherwise threaten the stability of a society (Slotkin, 1998, p. 12). Charged with actualizing or expanding the borders of civility and order, the individual is their own governing body: this person is a cowboy, a ranger, a lone gunman, a gold digger. As a consequence to the perpetual, physical struggle that maims the Cowboy or the Cowboy's enemies, an ìinfinite distanceî exists between colonization and civilization (Celsaire, 1972).

On the frontier, the myth empowers the individual to care for and prioritize their needs over the needs of others. In caring for oneself, the Myth suggests that—by design—killing and colonizing are mechanisms that regenerate the spirit of the individual (Slotkin, 1998, p. 12). This process of *regeneration through violence* necessitates the "othering" of subjects and the extermination of the unequal (Slotkin, 1998, p. 12). In *Minecraft*, the only one who can starve is the player character. Players can easily exploit the lives of other entities by farming them as resources (villagers, sheep, pigs, cows, chickens); killing or scaring enemies (dogs, cats); or, as a means of transportation (horses, mules, donkeys, and pigs).[16] Playing *Minecraft* as a pacifist vegetarian is technically possible, but the game design generally rewards those players who murder animals for meat (e.g., meat staves off starvation longer than vegetables and bread)—put another way, players are rewarded for treating the landscape and everything on it as a resource ripe for harvesting by way of punching, stabbing, shooting, etc. Players are not encouraged to think negatively about their behavior; the animation for death is particularly benign— the virtual body simply vanishes into the digital. Nor are players conditioned to feel particularly threatened on the frontier that they spawn, the Overworld. In order to encounter entities that might overwhelm the player character in combat, that player needs to travel to the Nether—an alternate, fiery dimension made to resemble a hellish landscape.

In the Nether the player character encounters several mobs that only serve to antagonize them; Pigmen and Baby Pigmen, for example, are incredibly powerful and aggressive enemies that are otherwise peaceful creatures unless provoked by the player character. Like every other mob, they wander around aimlessly and without particular purpose. Pigmen and Baby Pigmen drop "loot" when they die, but nothing that the player character cannot find elsewhere and by other means. Players often encounter the Nether with great trepidation, but there are great rewards for those who journey to "dance with the devil," so to speak. These rewards may be aesthetically beautiful blocks that enable the player to represent different building materials, or they might constitute ingredients the player character needs in order to brew potions that allow for greater feats of strength, speed, health regeneration, and stealth. It is impossible for the player character to survive in the Nether without journeying back to the Overworld eventually because nothing grows and players cannot transport water there. However, the Nether is commonly used as a mode of transporting across large distances in the Overworld because of an odd property that connects the two dimensions; traveling one block in the Nether is the equivalent of traveling eight blocks in the Overworld. I personally have used the Nether to do this, and I'm aware of many other players who have constructed elaborate roads and transportation hubs. Colonizing the Nether for the purposes of transportation provides players with a way of utilizing this space as a tool and controlling a landscape that might otherwise serve as a persistent, overwhelming threat.[17]

In the process of overcoming enemies and colonizing the land, the player character is elevated in their heroic status on the frontier. The land and trophy items that a player collects—diamond armor, Ghast tears, enchanted weapons, etc.—further serve to symbolize power, progress, and accomplishment. The relevance of these objects varies from server to server; on some servers players are encouraged to purchase equipment (e.g., armor, weapons, hats, capes) and special permissions (e.g., flying, community membership, property, improved text chat, etc.). On other servers, where players privilege a meritocracy, accomplishments may carry more social capital. Still, in both spaces and without regard for the value of the items in a purse, there exists in *Minecraft* player communities economies of power informed by game mechanics and assets that distinguish noobs from seasoned veterans. In Western culture, constitutions of subjectivity (i.e., who gets to be a citizen) are Eurocentric and privilege white, heterosexual, property-owning males (Escobar, 2008; Castro-Gòmez, 2002). In *Minecraft*, players can self-identify as part of the larger player collective by simply playing the game—subjectivity is predicated on doing more than anything else.[18] In this way, the design of *Minecraft* does not draw relationships between gender and power; the game is not designed to privilege or restrict the bodily freedom of players based on a gendered class they may wear or adopt. However, the limitations of what all players can do in *Minecraft*— what designers choose to code—does reflect a bias that privileges a masculine constitution of subjectivity.

For some time, feminists have drawn similarities between the symbolic characteristics of the "genderless" legal person—"rationality, autonomy, self-interest, objectivity, assertiveness, self-sufficiency, self-possession"—and masculinity (Hunter, 2013). It is no coincidence, they argue, that representations of the "reasonable" liberal citizen are men, and not wives or pregnant women (Hunter, 2013). The conflation of "reasonable" with "masculine" in the constitution of a legal person elides any consideration that social differences constitute different manifestations of rational thought and behavior. The design of the game assumes that all *Minecraft* players want to engage actively and assume a dominant role at all times on the frontier—this is not inclusive to play that requires the player to assume a passive or subjugated role, and it creates an environment where the "right" kinds of labor and work have value. In privileging *Minecraft* players who position themselves within a homogenous constitution of the player character—as a weapon-wielding, diamond-mining, meat-eating machine—game designers at Mojang marginalize players who want to find other ways of surviving, community building, and playing with mobs that don't align with the dominant paradigm. This value-laden framework of labor parallels with constitutions of the hero on the Western frontier.

Stories about the Western frontier seldom highlight the labor and lived experiences of women of color, white women, and men of color. Homogeneous constitutions of heroism timelessly measure protagonists against traditionally defined and arbitrary measures of masculinity. In *West of Everything: The Inner Life of Westerns*, Tompkins writes that most western tales define their actors on a sliding scale of masculinity:

> [Westerns] create a model for men who came of age in the twentieth century. The model was not for women but for men: Westerns insist on this point by emphasizing the importance of manhood as an ideal. It is not one ideal among many, it is the ideal, certainly the only one worth dying for. It doesn't matter whether a man is a sheriff or an outlaw, a rustler or a rancher, a cattleman or a sheepherder, a miner or a gambler. What matters is that he be a man [1992, p. 17–18].

In Westerns, masculinity serves as a literary device to constitute cultural attitudes toward socio-political ideas and ideals. Sexist attitudes are used to represent cultural discourses—assumedly for audiences that would not be offended by the overt characterizations (Folsom, 1966, p. 88–90). In most Westerns, idealized men are contrasted by materialistic women for rhetorical discourse;

> Indeed, women are not absolutely necessary to the presentation of these two differing points of view, but the attitude which they are conventionally made to represent is required. The values represented by a stable society must in some way be introduced into any fictional exploration of the significance of the frontier, if only to throw into greater relief the contrasting values which the frontier represents [Folsom, 1966, p. 88–90].

In the saloons where women work they are seldom named or heard; their livelihoods and their stories are not represented nor reflected in Western mythos (Butler, 1985; Riley, 1988; Namias, 1993; Lewis, 2011). Instead, their bodies function as a reminder of what civilization has to offer cowboys after a period of wrangling on the frontier (Folsom, 1966).

As much as men in Westerns are defined by what is in their pants, their performance of masculinity must align with socially constructed values and ideas of what a man does. Men are active, aggressive, calculating, dominant, unyielding; in contrast, the unmanly are passive, weak, submissive, careless— unsuited for, and vulnerable on, the frontier. As literary devices, the social relationship between men and women stratifies, and both identities are denied "true equality ... regardless of sex or gender" (Murray, 1995). *Minecraft* may not come packaged with an explicit narrative, but the game design sets a stage in Western context for performances of gender that essentialize masculinity with activity and femininity with passivity; it is a virtual world where the nomination of princesses only comes when a women walks on stage and men are not encouraged to volunteer (cf. Confortini, 2006). In *Minecraft*, players can empower themselves, but at the expense of degrading some other doing; some other way of playing or being that falls outside of what Notch's Steve would do.

In an analysis of Abigail Scott Dunaway's suffrage speeches between 1834– 1915, Lewis discovered that Dunaway's empowerment of women on the Western frontier invariably came at the degradation of femininity and other marginalized identities (i.e., American Indians and people of East-Asian lineage):

> As Duniway implied that only the women who could 'prove their manhood' had the right to political equality, she encouraged women desiring suffrage to become more like men and less like traditionally weak women [Lewis, 2011, p. 144].

Dressing women with masculinity as a means to escape a subordinate position may constitute the possibility of an "active" femininity, but this gendering— too—reifies the subordination of femininity to masculinity (Halberstam, 1998). Playing *Minecraft* does not empower femininity, it empowers women who reject traditional roles they might otherwise be assigned. This under- standing of gender, performance, and difference does little to diffuse the danger of "coming out" as differently-gendered people IRL (cf. Sundén and Svenings- son, 2012; Stabile, 2013). In *Minecraft*, the genderless default serves as a mask to hide a person's "real world" self, and it offers players an opportunity to first prove their proficiency in privileged ways of playing the game. Eventually, though, many players must reveal various aspects of their identity to other players—through textual communication, voice-chat, or visual representation (cf. Chow, 1995).

Players who come out as women or girls in *Minecraft* must also contend with what it means, at present, to assume the feminine gender. In terms of constructing gender, the relatively few mods that do exist reproduce hetero- normative, misogynistic, and/or essentialist notions of what gender is or can be. Some mods allow users to modify the appearance of the player character's age and body type, enter marital relationships with non-playable characters, and "tame" "girlfriends." Some YouTubers have published videos of mods in development that allow the player to spawn fair-skinned, feminized character mobs that either role-play sex acts or submit to being killed with weaponized pink dildos. It is also worth mentioning that others have published videos of themselves role-playing sex acts with improvised assets provided by vanilla *Minecraft*. These improvisations overwhelmingly represent feminine character models with long, colorful hair styles and elongated eyes (where "men" have two horizontal pixels, "women" have two vertical pixels). The patterned location of gender is distinct; modders assume that the player is either interested in feminizing their avatar, or adding "girls" as a non-playable mob in the game. Instances where players record video of role-playing sex acts present the perspective of the assumed male, who performs "thrusting" (moving forward and backward) behind a crouched, stationary female.

In a Western context, mods that only add breasts to the player character seem to reinforce the insignificant role of embodied gender on the frontier, while mods that add feminized non-playable mobs seem to rely on essentialist notions of gendered performances. Essentialism reduces the role of femininity to a persistent state of subservience to the player character, wherein the non-playable character follows the player around like a pet. In both cases the player character doesn't fundamentally change the way they move through or play the game. New values and goals aren't added in such a way that the player character changes the game of survival, and the "dressing" of femininity only serves to underscore the homogeneous nature of what constitutes as valued labor in the game. This isn't to say that there aren't any mods that change the way players survive or evaluate particular resources and ways of playing. However, no one has yet crafted a mod that assumes playing as a gendered character *should* change the goals, objectives, and modes of play. In this way, players don't develop for themselves rhetorically different ways of being that disrupt a domain that has long privileged white, heterosexual men.

I Love Playing Minecraft, *But I Wish I Could Sit Down Once and Awhile*

In my time playing *Minecraft*, which began in January 2012, I have been privileged to see the game development from its later stages of Beta to the game that it is today. I have been able to observe and experience first-hand what kinds of activities are valued in and around the game. Hunting, mining, railroading, and farming, for example, have been part of the architecture of the game since Alpha. The ability to name creatures and monsters, to write books, to wield magic—these activities came much later on in the development process. Although many players have enjoyed building houses and inventing various abstractions of home decor, the extent to which players can play house has been limited in the stock version of the game. In the unmodified version *Minecraft*, players aren't explicitly allowed to perform subservient or passive roles, if they are to role-play at all. Players cannot sit down (although players have revealed code in past iterations of the game that permit users to do so). Players cannot form or express formal, recognizable relationships with each other. Players do not raise mobs or otherwise form explicitly interpersonal relationships with in-game AI. The game interface does allow for players to communicate via text, but the stock version of the game is limited in comparison to other virtual world videogames. The ways in which players can perform and tell stories in the game is limited along these lines, lines that have traditionally distinguished the frontier from civilization.

Yet, at the same time, suggesting that there is even a single, resonate quality or theme that is communicated by a videogame ignores the ways in which our own lived, cultured minds filter our experiences in a virtual world. In terms of gender, even in a virtual world that doesn't acknowledge the concept, players cannot help but experience the virtual world through the eyes and mind of a gendered person—if that is the perspective they have as a human being in the real world. Moreover, Consalvo notes that "it is foolish if not dangerous to attempt to determine with any authority the 'essential' or 'fundamental' national qualities that may be found in individual games, and how these qualities are understood by players" (2006, p. 127). However, the limit of what players can and cannot do does frame the number and kind of possible experiences a player can shape for themselves.

Popular constructions of gender and sexuality in games certainly rely on aesthetic representations and virtual performances (i.e., looks and acts), but this contrasts with lived experiences of gender and sexuality that demand a framing of these terms outside of an object-oriented, categorical model. In thinking about the range of possible experiences Western audiences have with virtual worlds like *Minecraft*, Bordo's exploration of the dualism between gender/sexuality and the body suggests that, actually, divorcing gender from the body is a fantasy seldom realized in Western culture (1993). Bordo argues that this is because people are exposed, in the process of acculturating to Western philosophies and behaviors, to powerful lessons that teach us to appropriate both our own behaviors and the behaviors of others along the lines of gender, race, and social class (1993, p. 16). In thinking about human behavior in videogames, it's important to keep in mind that videogames are reducible as another conceptual structure where people are trained to think about what is and isn't "acceptable." The ways in which "active" and "acting," "masculine" and "men" are commonly privileged in videogame design over "passive" and "being acted upon," and "feminine" and "woman" is one way this analysis can be extended to understand the ways in which gender and labor—or "doing," more simply—favors the masculinist fantasy from a Western cultural perspective.

NOTES

1. When players assume the role of a player character in *Minecraft*, they are thrust into an implicitly whitewashed system. It is a limitation of this chapter that I do not analyze the relationships players with indigenous cultural backgrounds may have with this game.

2. Sandbox games are characterized by open-ended, non-linear designs that allow players to generate unique play styles, objectives, and narratives.

3. This artifact of early design was astutely preserved in the design of another independently developed game, *Super Meat Boy* (2010). The goatee was commonly mistaken to be a goofy, hair-colored smile, but Notch confirmed the intent of the art over Twitter (Persson, 2012b Jul 28).

4. While these characters were removed from official versions of the game (content published by Mojang), fans have developed and maintained mods that make these assets available.

5. Notch himself refers to the character design as "genderless," although—as I will show later on—I believe that labeling is debatable. Associating gender with aesthetic design distracts from other performative aspects of gender that this chapter tries to address. The term "vanilla" is a colloquialism that many players use to distinguish between unmodified and modified versions of the game—vanilla *Minecraft* is, essentially, an unmodified version of the game. I try to limit my analysis to vanilla *Minecraft* because of its relative ubiquity.

6. Mooshrooms are red cows with mushrooms that appear to grow on their backs; they can be harvested for mushrooms, leather, and beef.

7. Some public servers support voice-chat capabilities using mods. Others host their own private chat channels using services like Ventrilo, TeamSpeak, or Mumble. A voice may also be heard when players record themselves playing *Minecraft* using either a live streaming service like Twitch.TV, or a public distribution channel like YouTube.

8. I don't spend enough time talking about race in this article, but make a specific reference to the notion of a "white doll" here for a few reasons. First, though the default player character avatar has a noticeably darker or tanned complexion, the overwhelming majority of advertisements that promote the game white-wash "Steve's" complexion so that he presents as a bearded, white male—evidence that white supremacy still affects promotion and marketing of the game and related paraphernalia. Second, the reference is inspired by research conducted by Kenneth and Mamie Clark on the relationship between American children, racial attitudes, and their overwhelming preference for fair-skinned dolls—how these attitudes and preferences have evolved since the 1940s is unclear but worthy of consideration.

9. Players can also crouch their character into a bent-over position in a way that might connote sneakiness, fear, or submissiveness. *Minecraft* mods or video animations that toy with abstract performances of sex (usually heterosexual) almost always feature the feminized player character in the crouching position. Jumping in the crouched position in such a way that obscures another player character is sometimes interpreted as harassment, but it is as commonly seen as a playful performance that intends to grab a player's attention by annoying them.

10. See Tucker (2011) and Kou and Nardi (2013) for more on griefing and manipulating player behaviors. Griefing and other forms of targeted harassment do occur on *Minecraft* servers, but such a survey is outside the purview of this article (for more on griefing, see also Phillips, 2011).

11. Taylor makes mention of women without distinguishing between race, which is why I similarly choose the homogeneous term "women." Mohanty (1988) emphasizes in their work the importance of distinguishing between the experiences of white women and

women of color; it is not my intention to assume all women experience public spaces similarly, and there is a significant opportunity for more research in this area.

12. This figure borrows from the estimate number of possible seeds a user can spawn from procedural generation—it takes into account possible placements that the game will spawn "organically" (i.e., there are some blocks that will not spawn in certain areas of the game unless the code is modified to do so). Of course, there are other possible estimations. My favorite extrapolation on this thought exercise is detailed in a YouTube episode titled "How many *Minecraft* worlds are there?" published on March 2, 2013 by Matt and Jord, users who publish content for the Podcrash YouTube channel. Their explanation figures that each possible permutation is dependent on the number of possible blocks placed in all possible spaces. Their first assumption is that blocks are independent of each other, meaning that a block with a door on it is not also a possible block with an open door on it—open doors are not a separate class of blocks to count. Assumption 2: Blocks do not affect other blocks. Assumption 3: the limit of space in all possible *Minecraft* worlds is $(59,999,9992)*256$ blocks (which is then converted to $9.21*1017$). Assumption 4: the total number of possible block configurations includes different orientations of blocks, which inflates the baseline 142 possible blocks to 653. They raise the number of possible blocks to the power of the number of total possible worlds (i.e., $6539.21*10^{17}$), which totals a number greater than all particles in the observable universe.

13. Players can technically "communicate" with Villagers in the game much in the same way that people "communicate" with ATM machines when they need money from a bank. This is a particularly disappointing element of *Minecraft* because the Enderman mobs repetitively recite distorted voice recordings of phrases such as "hi-ya," "hellow," and "what's up." Representing the Other on the frontier as a resource complements the frontier myth framework, and—yes—this is an extremely common convention of most other videogames that demands further analysis and research.

14. To be absolutely clear, I realize that, as an open-ended platform, *Minecraft* can be redesigned to be many other kinds of games. I am very cognizant of the mini-games and adaptations that players have established on public servers; however, this analysis is intentionally limited to "vanilla" *Minecraft* because it is the most basic design that all adaptations ultimately spawn from. Players may modify the code in ways that convolute a simulation of the frontier myth, but these modifications do not significantly deviate or undermine philosophical and algorithmic superstructures that uphold the original design.

15. Between the public release for PC and January 2014, *Minecraft* players have been offered 23 downloadable update packages, many of which required players to re-seed new maps. Players can copy certain configurations using specialized software, and sometimes merge old maps with new updates, but the game's interface does not allow for this level of manipulation with the game space. Many of these updates have added new content and architecture to the game, in addition to fixing bugs and enhancing already existing content. I wish I could append this paper with a second that explores this aspect of game play by itself.

16. Villagers are a humanoid-like mob that players can encounter (they spawn randomly and can be difficult to find at times). Players can trade goods for other goods with them. However, in my experience of playing with other people, Villagers are similarly exploited so that players can acquire better trades. The algorithm that accounts for their number in the game is predicated on a number of doors in a given location and a number of already spawned Villagers (i.e., there can only be so many Villagers given a certain number of doors in a particular square area). In order for players to filter out "bad Villager trades," a player must set up a killing mechanism that systematically murders the Villager without taking direct damage from the player character. Commonly it means that Villagers are moved

into minecarts and transported to a station that exposes them to lava. Like any other kind of coveted objects, some players make a game of amassing a population of Villagers that make good trades with the player character, but this process takes a fair amount of time, death, and luck to achieve. Along these same lines, some players collect name mobs and refer to them as "pets." However, no pet exists without some utility; even tamed cats serve to scare away Creepers, mobs that are known for sneaking up on the player character and exploding.

17. There is, obviously, an analysis to be done on the religious symbology that skirts player activities in the Nether and Overworld, and how this symbolism may further complement or play with Christian sensibilities.

18. This isn't to say that *Minecraft* players celebrate each other for simply playing the game—what you do in the game does generate social capital, and capital is valuable. There's a whole separate chapter to follow up on this single branching idea; who is the community that influences *Minecraft* development? How is this community commodified on YouTube? How do economic realities in the real world privilege the Let's Play community—a group of people that require very expensive bundles of computer hardware and software, in addition to time with which to record, edit, and upload content?

References

Ahmed, S. (2006). *Queer phenomenology: Orientations, objects, others.* Durham: Duke University Press.

Anable, A. (2013). Causal games and the work of affect. *Ada: A Journal of Gender, New Media, and Technology,* 2. Retrieved from http://adanewmedia.org/2013/06/issue2-anable/

Blizzard Entertainment. (2004). *World of Warcraft* [PC game]. Irvine, CA: Blizzard.

Bordo, S. (1993). *Unbearable weight: Feminism, Western culture, and the body.* Berkeley: University of California Press.

Butler, A. M. (1985). *Daughters of joy, sisters of misery: Prostitutes in the American West, 1865–90.* Urbana: University of Illinois Press.

Butler, J. (1988). Performative acts and gender constitution: An essay in phenomenology and feminist theory. *Theatre Journal, 40*(4), 519–531.

Cassell, J., & Jenkins, H. (1998). Chess for girls? Feminism and computer games. In J. Cassell & H. Jenkins (Eds.), *From Barbie to Mortal Kombat: Gender and computer games* (pp. 2–45). Cambridge, MA: MIT Press.

Castro-Gomez, S., & Martin, D. A. (2002). The social sciences, epistemic violence, and the problem of the "invention of the other." *Nepantla: Views from South, 3*(2), 269–285.

Césaire, A. (1972). *Discourse on colonialism.* New York: MR.

Cherney, L., & Wise, E. R. (Eds.). (1996). *Wired women: Gender and new realities in cyberspace.* Seattle: Seal Press.

Chow, R. (1995). The politics of admittance: Female sexual agency, miscegenation, and the formation of community in Frantz Fanon. In Bowman, P. (Ed.), *The Rey Chow reader* (56–74). New York: Columbia University Press.

Confortini, C. (2006). Galtung, violence, and gender: The case for a peace studies/feminism alliance. *Peace Research Abstracts Journal, 43*(6).

Connell, R. W. (1997). Teaching the boys: New research on masculinity, and gender strategies for schools. *Teachers College Record, 98*(2), 206–35.

Consalvo, M. (2006). Console video games and global corporations. *New Media & Society, 8*(1), 117–137.

Cook, D. (2006). "What are game mechanics?" lostgarden.com. Retrieved from http://lostgarden.com/2006/10/what-are-game-mechanics.html

DerpyKat & Daisy Rose. (2013, July 12). *Minecraft* sexism, a collaborative blog with Daisy Rose [Blog]. Retrieved from http://www.planetminecraft.com/blog/minecraft-sexism-a-collaborative-blog-with-daisy-rose/

DiGiuseppe, N., & Nardi, B. (2007, May 07). Real genders choose fantasy characters: Class choice in *World of Warcraft*. *First Monday*, 12(5). Retrieved from http://firstmonday.org/issues/issue12_5/digiuseppe/index.html

Escobar, A. (2008). *Territories of difference: Place, movements, life, redes*. Durham: Duke University Press.

Fausto-Sterling, A. (1993). The five sexes. *Sciences*, 33(2), 20.

Folsom, J. K. (1966). *The American Western novel*. New Haven: College & University Press.

Halberstam, J. (1998). *Female masculinity*. Durham: Duke University Press.

Haraway, D. J. (1991). *Simians, cyborgs, and women: The reinvention of nature*. New York: Routledge.

Hollander, J. (2004). "I can take care of myself": The impact of self-defense training on women's lives. *Violence Against Women*, 10(2), 205–35.

Hunter, R. (2013). Contesting the dominant paradigm: Feminist critiques of liberal legalism. In M. Davies & V. E. Munro (Eds.) *The Ashgate research companion to feminist legal theory*. Farnham, England: Ashgate, 13–30.

Jansz, J., & Martis, R. (2007). The Lara phenomenon: Powerful female characters in video games. *Sex Roles*, 56, 3–4.

Kolo, C., & Baur, T. (2004, Nov.) Living a virtual life: Social dynamics of online gaming. *Game Studies*, 4(1). Retrieved at http://www.gamestudies.org/0401/kolo/

Kou, Y., & Nardi, B. (2013). Regulating anti-social behavior on the Internet: The example of *League of Legends*. iConference 2013 Proceedings (pp. 616–622). doi:10.9776/13289

Lamerichs, N. (2011). Stranger than fiction: Fan identity in cosplay. *Transformative Works and Cultures*, 7. doi:10.3983/twc.2011.0246.

Lewis, T. (2011). Winning woman suffrage in the masculine West: Abigail Scott Duniway's frontier myth. *Western Journal of Communication*, 75(2), 127–147.

Lindtner, S., Nardi, B., Wang, Y., Mainwaring, S., Jing, H., & Liang, W. (2008). A hybrid cultural ecology: *World of Warcraft* in China. Proceedings of the ACM Conference on Computer Supported Cooperative Work, CSCW (pp. 371–381).

Malaby, T. M. (2009). *Making virtual worlds: Linden Lab and* Second Life. Ithaca, NY: Cornell University Press.

McDermott, R., & Varenne, H. (2006). Reconstructing culture in educational research. In Spindler, G., & Hammond, L. A. (Eds.) *Innovations in educational ethnography: Theory, methods, and results* (pp. 3–31). Mahwah, NJ: L. Erlbaum Associates.

Miller, M., & Summers, A. (2007). Gender differences in video game characters' roles, appearances, and attire as portrayed in video game magazines. *Sex Roles*, 57, 9–10.

Mohanty, C. T. (1988). Under Western eyes: Feminist scholarship and colonial discourses. *Feminist Review*, 30, 61–88.

Mojang. (2011). *Minecraft* [PC game]. Stockholm, Sweden..

Murray, M. (1995). *The law of the father? Patriarchy in the transition from feudalism to capitalism*. New York: Routledge.

Namias, J. (1993). *White captives: Gender and ethnicity on the American frontier*. Chapel Hill: University of North Carolina Press.

Persson, M. (2012a Jul 28). Gender in *Minecraft* [Tumblr]. Retrieved from http://notch.tumblr.com/post/28188312756/gender-in-minecraft

Persson, M. [notch]. (2012b Jul 28). @S0phieH No, it's a goatee. The default skin (and the unofficial name) is unfortunately male. I regret this. The model is genderless [Twitter]. Retrieved from https://twitter.com/notch/statuses/229146250430267392

Phillips, W. (2011). LOLing at tragedy: Facebook trolls, memorial pages and resistance to grief online. *First Monday*, 16(12). doi:10.5210/fm.v16i12.3168

Riley, G. (1988). *The female frontier: A comparative view of women on the prairie and the plains.* Lawrence: University Press of Kansas.

Schilt, K., & Westbrook, L. (2009). Doing gender, doing heteronormativity. *Gender & Society*, 23(4), 440–464.

Slotkin, R. (1998). *Gunfighter nation: The myth of the frontier in twentieth-century America.* Norman: University of Oklahoma Press.

Stabile, C. (2013). "I will own you": Accountability in massively multiplayer online games. *Television & New Media*, 15(1), 43–57.

Stoeltje, B. J. (1987). Making the frontier myth: Folklore process in a modern nation. *Western Folklore*, 46(4), 235–253.

Sundeīn, J., & Sveningsson, M. (2011). *Gender and sexuality in online game cultures: Passionate play.* New York: Routledge.

Taylor, T. L. (2006). *Play between worlds: Exploring online game culture.* Cambridge, MA: MIT Press.

Taylor, T. L. (2012). *Raising the stakes: E-sports and the professionalization of computer gaming.* Cambridge, MA: MIT Press.

Team Meat. (2010). *Super Meat Boy* [Xbox 360]. Microsoft Game Studios.

Tompkins, J. P. (1992). *West of everything: The inner life of westerns.* New York: Oxford University Press.

Tucker, S. (2011). *Griefing: Policing masculinity in online games* (Master's Thesis). Retrieved from Scholars' Bank, University of Oregon.

Turkle, S. (1995). *Life on the screen: Identity in the age of the internet.* New York: Touchstone.

West, C., and S. Fenstermaker. (2002). Accountability in action: The accomplishments of gender, race, and class in a meeting of the University of California Board of Regents. *Discourse and Society*, 13(4), 537–63.

Williams, D., Martins, N., Consalvo, M., & Ivory, J. (2009). *The virtual census: representations of gender, race and age in video games.* New Media & Society, 11(5), 815–834.

Vanderhoef, J. (2013). Casual threats: The feminization of casual video games. *Ada: A Journal of Gender, New Media, and Technology*, 2. Retrieved from http://adanewmedia.org/2013/06/issue2-vanderhoef/

(Queer) Algorithmic Ecology
The Great Opening Up of Nature to All Mobs

AMANDA PHILLIPS

In 1997, Electronic Music Foundation President Joel Chadabe described electricity's contribution to composition as "the great opening up of music to all sound." This sentiment resonates with other mid–90's techno-utopian figurations of the digital as an escape from the constraints of the physical world— a medium of endless possibility. Though such optimism has waned in the intervening decades, computational representations of natural environments open up new orientations toward nature that easily read as fantasies of capitalist frontier expansionism enabled by the reduced material constraints of the digital. The digital worlds of *Minecraft* (Mojang, 2011) "open up" both literally and figuratively, with algorithmically generated and procedurally expanding environments that are theoretically infinite but bound by the operational constraints of the software. *Minecraft*'s unfolding nature is also reflected in the game's crafting system, in which resources open up into increasingly small parts of themselves: one block of wood, for example, will yield 4 wooden planks, which can be crafted into 8 sticks total, and so on. While it is true that *Minecraft*'s generated landscapes are optimized for the calculation of yield values and have spawned countless user-generated colonial fantasies, their stunning empty vistas also substitute spawning for reproduction, versioning for evolution, and drop probabilities for history in ways that defer neat categorization. Oriented away from heteronormative and capitalist temporalities, this algorithmic ecology opens nature up not only to human occupation for productivity, but to the trivial, nonproductive wanderings of automated digital inhabitants. *Minecraft* conceals within its thoroughly exploitable mathematical models queer possibilities of reproduction, temporality, and occupation of space that move beyond the purposes for which they have been coopted.

Queering Platform Studies

The emergence of platform studies as a discipline has encouraged scholars to tease out "the connection between technical specifics and culture" (Bogost and Monfort, 2009) and offers a good starting point for thinking about the queer modalities of *Minecraft*. However, rather than appeal to the existing canon of platform studies, this chapter adds some new critics to the conversation. Computational systems operate according to logics that are normative by definition in order to guarantee a seamless modular integration with other components of the system, and feminist thinkers like Tara McPherson (2012), Wendy Chun (2007, 2011), and Lisa Nakamura (2002, 2008) have traced how these normative logics emerge from and contribute to hegemonic systems of power, containing difference within structures that are easily manageable by automated systems. These scholars map out an approach to a kind of platform studies that attends to the cultural power embedded within technical systems, from fiber optic networks or computer architecture (Chun) to user interfaces on the Internet (Nakamura). McPherson (2012) charts how the modular logics of operating systems like UNIX, which emerged alongside the Civil Rights movements in the mid-twentieth century, are part of a larger institutional trend that organizes both knowledge and populations in such a way that obscures the relationship between surface and structure. She argues that "the fragmentary knowledges encouraged by many forms and experiences of the digital neatly parallel the lenticular logics which underwrite the covert racism endemic to our times" (p. 33). For McPherson, these "forms and experiences" begin at the level of code—in this example, at the moment in which modularity became a core principle of UNIX computing—and she calls for increased attention to the mutual imbrication of culture and platform.

Kara Keeling (2014) mods McPherson's project further into what she calls "Queer OS," an approach to feminist platform studies that additionally "understands *queer* as naming an orientation toward various and shifting aspects of existing reality and the social norms they govern, such that it makes available pressing questions about, eccentric and/or unexpected relationships in, and possibly alternatives to those social norms" (p. 153). This turn toward queerness as an analytic for digital and other computational media opens up new possibilities for interpretation, which some scholars are already shaping. Jacob Gaboury (2013), for example, writes a queer history of computing that explores how the sexuality of some of the foundational mathematicians and programmers in computing history might have shaped their "mode of being in the world," and as a result, their scholarship. At one point, Gaboury (2013b) suggests that since Alan Turing's concept of the computable number, a foundational principle in the development of computing, requires the excision of entire classes of numbers from a system, we might look to locate queer computing beyond these constraints, in the computer's excess. While it is important to think through speculative technologies and develop new methods to open up more possibilities for computational expression, it is equally valuable to locate queerness in existing applications of computational logic. Following Gaboury's associative stitching together of the history of computing, the personal lives of some of its forefathers, and the material instantiations of their research, this exploration of a different kind of queer computing opens up with the algorithm, the formalization of which was one of Turing's contributions to computing history.

Turing, Gaboury points out, found no algorithm for creativity or intuition. And yet creative algorithms of a kind do exist, even if they operate within the bounds of calculable numbers and concrete tasks. In fact, Gaboury (2013c) includes in his queer history of computing an anecdote about Christopher Strachey, a gay programmer working at Manchester University in the 1950s, who designed a program that would algorithmically generate love letters dripping in "melodramatic Victorian overtones" and then posted them anonymously on the department's bulletin board for his colleagues to find.[1] This type of creative production hearkens back to analog forms—a relevant contemporary example would be the paper computational experiments of the Oulipo—but automating the process allows creative resources to be used in different ways. Randomized level generation in video games, for example, dates back to the 1980s and has been implemented in landmark titles such as *Rogue* (Toy & Whichman, 1980) or *Diablo II* (Blizzard, 2000). As a design strategy, it decreases the need for specific game assets to be stored, making it a desirable way to reduce the size of a game without sacrificing playable content, which partially accounts for its popularity in older titles that needed to use storage space more judiciously.

Ashmore and Nitsche (2007) suggest that the contemporary resurgence of procedural generation began as a result of increasing costs of production coupled with demand for more content, as well as high-profile games like *Spore* (Maxis, 2008) that renewed interest in the quirky combinations enabled by computerized creativity. *Spore*'s procedural animation techniques were a brief Internet sensation, with users creating bizarre and obscene creatures and posting videos of the suggestive ways that the software made them move. More recently, big-budget titles like *BioShock Infinite* (Irrational Games, 2013) utilized procedural generation during development to ease the task of building highly detailed, expansive cities (McMahon, 2013), while indie darlings like *Spelunky* (Yu & Hull, 2009) and *FTL: Faster Than Light* (Subset Games, 2012) have taken advantage of the efficiency that procedural generation provides in-game to allow for a variety of experiences across multiple replays and player experiences without requiring massive development resources and time. According to critic Claire Hoskins (2013), procedural generation might provide a new frontier for developers as the improvement curve of photorealistic graphics reaches its limits.

Some video game critics, such as *Indie Statik*'s Chris Priestman (2013), credit the recent boom in procedurally generated content to *Minecraft* itself, which is perhaps the most successful contemporary game to leverage the power and wonder of procedural level generation. A game that encourages the gamer to move outward into continuously changing territory benefits immensely from the sense of discovery and serendipity that random content creation provides. However, Priestman suggests that it is multiplayer activity that sustains *Minecraft* as a platform, that procedural generation is a mere "numbers game" providing "quantity over quality." And yet, the game's procedurally generated environments underwrite both single and multiplayer experiences and in fact provide the drive for much of its sociability: for example, in this author's experience, part of the pleasure of playing with others in *Minecraft* is in dividing up labor to find, harvest, and build with resources more efficiently in a vast world. The numbers game in *Minecraft* is, in fact, the heart of the platform, and its mixing with ecological aesthetics creates a strange form of nature—an algorithmic ecology—that is simultaneously ripe for capitalist exploitation and full of alternative queer embodiments and relations. It is in the spirit of Queer OS that we proceed under the hood to tease these out.

Procedural Generation and Algorithmic Ecology

What I call "algorithmic ecology" in *Minecraft* gestures toward the fact that automated computational processes govern nature in the game and in many ways, thanks to aesthetic design and game mechanics, subsume the ecological within the mathematical. This is not necessarily an anti-ecological gesture. In fact, Timothy Morton's (2007) suggestion to remove nature from ecological thinking might find unique application in looking at algorithmic ecology; while the aesthetic veneer of nature is certainly interesting in an analysis of *Minecraft*, focusing on its underlying processes and relationships with the user might be a way around the obscuring "view" of nature beyond which Morton wishes to move (2). This strategy, conveniently, also resonates with the methodologies of platform studies. By investigating the technological structures (or, in this case, the technical design decisions) that underwrite the aesthetics of this particular software platform, a more complex understanding of both will emerge.

The processes that fuel *Minecraft*'s terrain generation establish the foundation for an ever-expanding ecology that can be shaped by the gamer. Although math is ultimately the foundation of all digital games, there is something about *Minecraft*'s open dedication to cubes and crafting recipes that help bring its abstract algorithms onto the surface. Aesthetically, the world is an homage to the simplest Cartesian formulation of space, invoking the graphs and grids of childhood mathematical training. Procedurally, the symbolic weight of the algorithm exists in the crafting function itself: the drive to use resources efficiently and to create ever more complex objects in the game world. Break trees into logs into planks into sticks to recombine them again as useful tools. Use tools to gather increasingly rare resources to recombine into new tools and objects. Community members reinforce this drive with exhaustive guides that show new users how to make the most of their time and materials with elaborate formulae. *Minecraft* parlance is littered with stacks and percentages and altitudes and probabilities, and the community has experimented with the game to the point that while they may not understand everything about the code under the hood (although many of them do), they certainly have calculated its numerical impact on in-game activity.

Each new *Minecraft* world is generated using calculations driven by a "world seed," an integer converted from letters, words, or numbers that can be set by the player upon beginning the game. If the player chooses not to seed the world, the game uses a seed based on the date and time of world creation.[2] The world seed ensures a significant degree of uniqueness amongst *Minecraft* worlds, but also allows users to share with one another if particularly compelling territories emerge as a result. *Minecraft* initially spawns the player and creates a finite "chunk" of land around them, populating the world with structures like caves, lakes, ravines, and others according to the world seed. Chunks are one of the organizing units in *Minecraft*: where a block is its most basic physical form, a chunk is a 16x16x256-block pillar of land that is generated around the player. Each chunk has its own biome assignment, which dictates animal and plant life, geological structures, and local weather conditions. *Minecraft* worlds are things of voxelated beauty, with complicated environmental features emerging as generated geographical structures collide, overwrite, and blend with one other.

As a player moves through space, the program continuously generates new terrain based on the seed and current generation algorithm, which has historically been updated to increase variety and smooth out the transitions between biomes. There is some debate about the actual rendering limits of a *Minecraft* world. The game's creator, Markus Persson, went on record in 2011 to clarify that there was no hard limit to the world's size, but due to rounding errors and other mathematical effects, movement, structures, objects, and other aspects of the game may become distorted and behave erratically the farther the gamer moves from the world's initial spawn point. Currently, there is an invisible wall 30,000,000 meters in any direction from the world's initial spawn location that prevents a gamer from exploring further. In fact, avatar location is a key variable in many of the game's calculations, used to determine not only expected things like draw distances for graphics and enemy line-of-sight but also which portions of the world are loaded into memory and actively updated. "Mobs," the mobile units (mostly animals) that exist within the game, also turn off and on based on player location, and many will disappear if the player moves too far away. This operational radius is necessary for system performance in a theoretically infinite world, but it has important implications on play.

Despite the proximate relationship between gamer and environment, the game environment also operates independently of human interference. *Minecraft* isn't a persistent world that continues to function after users exit the system, but its ecology runs off of automated algorithms that do not require user input. Alexander Galloway (2006) describes a moment of gamic action he calls "pure process," in which the machine would operate on its own in the game world without input from the operator. In some games, when the operator ceases to act, the machine reaches a state of ambience, "slowly walking in place, shifting from side to side and back again to the center. It is running, playing itself, perhaps" (10). Standing still in *Minecraft* reveals these moments: animals spawn out of view and wander around, bleating and clucking in the distance. They might hunt each other or fly into a lava fall and burn up. Any crops that were planted will grow and mature. The sun rises and falls. Weather continues to change.[3]

Galloway's work also emphasizes the fact that operator and machine play the game together, something that the operational radius mechanic of

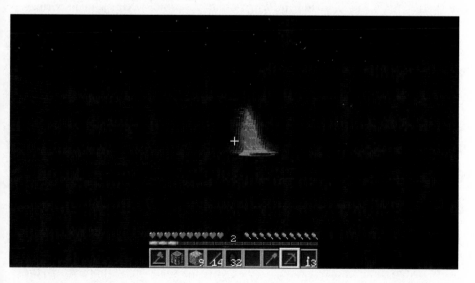

Figure 1. A waterfall and lava fall side-by-side (Minecraft®/TM & © 2009–2013 Mojang / Notch).

Minecraft deftly illustrates. In most games, this mechanism is a fairly obvious tit-for-tat of combat or other continuous stream of engagement. For *Minecraft*, operator and machine share a subtle copresence based on location, an ecological simulation that underscores both the embeddedness of the human in an environmental system as well as their irrelevance to its mundane operations. In writing about the possibility for a game that models ecological principles, Alenda Chang (2011) observes some of the fundamental mistakes that video game designers make with digital environments: the first of these is that they relegate environments to the background. As the operational radius and procedural drive to craft illustrates, there is nothing about the environment of *Minecraft* that keeps it in the background. Interaction with the world is the entire point of the game in any of its player-selected modes, whether that it comes in the form of exploration in Peaceful difficulty, daring combat in Adventure Mode, or unrestricted building in Creative Mode. [4]

Chang's second video game ecological design error is the stereotyped environment. Gaming classics like *Super Mario Bros.* (Nintendo R&D4, 1985) or *The Legend of Zelda* (Nintendo R&D4, 1986) have long-held traditions of environment types that repeat in every installment of the series: grassy over-worlds, dark caves, lava fields, oceans and lakes. While some of the biomes in *Minecraft* may draw on common environment types like forests, deserts, and jungles, it also includes less well-known varieties like taiga and tundra and makes nontrivial gestures at localizing weather, animal, and plant life, achieving a kind of environmental realism that Chang finds desirable. *Minecraft* bestiaries, for example, include information on the biomes that spawn particular species so that less common animals such as ocelots may be more easily found and tamed. Indeed, some *Minecraft* users share world seeds that generate particularly rare biomes at the spawn; the interest in these may range from aesthetics to rare resources, but it is clear that environmental variety and specificity in the game is an important feature.

By these introductory criteria, *Minecraft*'s algorithms seem to model ecology in a meaningful way. However, Chang's hope for environmental realism in video games is also connected to environmentalist politics. She asks, "Why must games replicate the same kind of costly obliviousness we see everyday in the non-digital world" when both culture and game design might benefit from seeing the consequences of environmental exploitation played out to extremes (61)? This leads to her third criterion for the failed ecological game: simplistic relations between gamer and environment, such as the "extraction and use of natural resources" (58). There is much to fail *Minecraft* on that score, and it is directly related to its algorithmic qualities. Every block is a standing reserve of materials that can be gathered and opened up, sometimes exponentially, for the purposes of production, and the continuously expanding environment gestures toward plentitude rather than consequences.

But that's not the only thing gamers can do with this particular numbers game, and that's certainly not what the game's engine, when left to its own devices, would do with itself. While it is not my intent to bracket important political critiques for the sake of a niche argument, it is important to consider that *Minecraft* as a platform makes it quite easy to turn away from the capitalist expansion narrative that so many find on its surface. In fact, the aesthetic beauty of the game's algorithmic ecology is found in its vast empty vistas that are populated by precious few sentient creatures and no industrial communities. There is plenty of space, literally and figuratively, for living life with minimal impact on the natural world, coexisting rather than conquering. This is not a sterile nature by any means, but it is not one built solely for the taking.

Queer Time, Queer Places

In *The Queer Art of Failure*, Judith Halberstam (2011) writes about the "Pixarvolt" genre of animated films, which deal on the surface with narratives of capitalist individualism but ultimately "[serve] as a gateway to intricate stories of collective action, anticapitalist critique, group bonding, and alternative imaginings of community, space, embodiment, and responsibility" (43–4). While the narrative content of these films clearly contribute to Halberstam's analysis, and while not all computer animated films have queer revolutionary potential, there are some structural aspects of computer animation that seem to distinguish the genre from traditional hand-drawn cartoons. Halberstam discusses, for example, what many others have observed about the content of Pixar's films: the narrative follows the technological breakthrough. Shiny surfaces generated *Toy Story*. Hair textures generated *Monsters, Inc.* In Halberstam's examples, the technological breakthrough was the animation of "numbers, groups, the multitude. Once you have an animation technique for the crowd, you need narratives about crowds, you need to animate the story line of the many and downplay the story line of the exception" (176). What follows are stories about ants, bees, and fish that Halberstam finds particularly compelling.

Minecraft's technological breakthrough is algorithmic ecology, the continuously generating, automated world that seems on the surface to exist purely for exploitation. What follows this innovation, however, is not a compelling anticapitalist narrative—or any narrative at all. Algorithmic ecology in *Minecraft* produces a very queer form of nature that proceeds according to its own nonreproductive rhythms.

Most discussions of queer ecologies begin with animal embodiments, from "homo or nonrepro queer penguins" (Halberstam 2011, 41) to intersex deer (Morton 2010, 276). Because the discourse of "natural" sexual orientation and gender identity drives much homo- and transphobic rhetoric, activists have pointed to the existence of queer animals to counter these claims and to generate discussions about essentialist and constructivist worldviews. *Minecraft* has its own variety of queer animal life, whose primary mode of reproduction is computer spawning. Most mobs spring into the world fully formed based on the game's algorithm for creating them: first, the player must be close enough for a chunk to be active. Next, the game checks that the mob cap hasn't been reached. Next, it attempts to spawn on a particular location, and will fail or succeed depending on the conditions of the terrain it randomly selects. Then the process repeats. The rules and caps differ based on the type of mob, and some mobs only spawn from physical spawn blocks located in the environment, but the result is fairly straightforward: baby animals do not occur "naturally" in the game.[5]

This does not mean that there is no sexual reproduction, but even breeding has some very queer features. The operator can initiate breeding in any two domesticated animals of the same species by feeding them their favorite food, a rather curious design decision that associates reproduction with nonsexual desire. Moreover, while the ability to breed gestures toward a heteronormative temporality oriented toward family units and capitalist production, it is quite queer in execution, revealing something about *Minecraft*'s world that is rare for other reproductive simulations: sexual difference does not exist. One can trace the lack of sex back to the initial *Minecraft* player character, which is androgynously blocky and has a skin that can change their outer appearance at the user's will. Unlike many games, *Minecraft* neither asks the gamer to choose a gender for their avatar nor really imposes one upon them.[6] All of the game's cows and chickens produce milk and eggs, respectively, further suggesting that there is no sexual dimorphism in this algorithmic environment. Reproduction is often a limit case in ecological simulations; virtual animal breeding games from Maxis's *SimLife* (1992) to Nintendo's *Pokémon* (Game Freak, 1996) continue to utilize an individual's sex as a major mechanic of reproduction, even when its other natural features are based on fantasy physics.

And yet, animal sex in nature is only part of what constitutes a theory and practice of queer ecology. Morton (2010) suggests complicating or even retiring the concept of the animal entirely, arguing that "queer ecology would go to the end and show how beings exist precisely because they are nothing but relationality, deep down" (277). Echoing work by theorists like Donna Haraway, Morton suggests that queer theory's expertise in questions of fluidity and relations between bodies, temporalities, and spaces, makes it an "intimate" intellectual counterpart of ecology (281). In the first multi-author collection dedicated exclusively to exploring the facets of queer ecologies, Catriona Mortimer-Sandilands and Bruce Erickson (2010) outline "a new practice of ecological knowledges, spaces, and politics that places central attention on challenging hetero-ecologies from the perspective of non-normative sexual and gender positions" (22). Their collection moves through queer animality,[7] green and pink political movements, and the queer uses of public space,[8] and it makes a compelling case for the various ways in which queer and environmentalist activisms and theories may intersect.

Algorithmic ecology provides yet another site to investigate queer environments beyond ecomimesis and queerness beyond sexual identity, as it enables plenty of nonproductive activities and is a playground to experiment with new ways of being. There is no primary life orientation in *Minecraft*; wandering, hunting, farming, building, mining, fishing, standing still, and more are all equally viable paths.[9] One may scramble to find shelter and hide to survive the first night if they desire, but the ambient electronic and piano music that accompanies the game suggests something quite different than combat for the game's primary orientation. Peaceful difficulty, which despawns hostile mobs in the game, is a simple menu switch away. This difficulty setting gestures toward something of a queer fantasy: imagine if all the hostility in the world could be turned off with the flip of a switch. The ecological utopia opened up by Peaceful difficulty offers an imaginative landscape in which one can literally pick one's own battles, in which violence does not necessarily go hand-in-hand with spatial exploration. The act of disappearing all of one's enemies can also be read as a quintessential conquering fantasy; I choose to read it in a utopian light here because the hostile mobs in *Minecraft* are themselves remnants of a fantasy of settler colonialism: the implacable Other who

Figure 2. Sheep, pigs, and chickens wandering on a rocky hillside (Minecraft */TM & © 2009–2013 Mojang / Notch).

must be destroyed as a matter of self-preservation. By despawning (rather than destroying) this myth, which motivates so much violence in society, Peaceful difficulty metaphorically restores the world to a state of peace without fear of difference.

With hostile mobs turned off, one has an abundance of time to appreciate the world's unique rhythms. Very little happens in *Minecraft* without user input or presence after the initial world spawn. This may seem to contradict earlier claims about the game's active ambient state, but the "happening" to which I refer here deals with reproductive futurity, a topic of some interest during queer theory's turn toward temporality. Halberstam (2005) notes in the introduction to *In a Queer Time and Place* that "Queer uses of time and space develop, at least in part, in opposition to the institutions of family, heterosexuality, and reproduction.... If we try to think about queerness as an outcome of strange temporalities, imaginative life schedules, and eccentric economic practices, we detach queerness from sexual identity..." (1). Both the temporal and economic aspects of this argument are relevant here, since it is possible (and common) to play the game without engaging in any (or many) of its productive algorithms and still be a functional part of its ecology. This opening up of queer identity in terms of time might apply to any number of gaming temporalities, very few of which operate according to real world rules, but this is especially so in *Minecraft* time. It is easy to recognize the drive for ecomimesis in the proliferating biomes and weather patterns added to each subsequent *Minecraft* update, but something about the world feels a bit too purposeless to be a useful ecological simulation.

If crops aren't planted, they won't grow. If animals aren't bred manually, they won't reproduce or mature. Ice might freeze and melt, and rain storms will come and go. The sun rises and falls, but time as marked by reproductive life stands still.

And yet, the game plays. The lack of a temporal movement toward the future is connected to the game's lack of a diegetic past. Queer orientations toward time and space in *Minecraft* extend to alternative relationships to history, as well. Though environmental traces, all planted by the spawn algorithms, point toward history on both geological and cultural scales, they are completely decontextualized and give little hope of ever yielding a narrative. Temples, dungeons, and strongholds appear according to how the world seed and algorithms dictate, sometimes located where no gamer will ever find them. Halberstam (2011) discusses this same type of queer haunting—"the empty promises of utopia"—in the context of the photography of queer Spanish artist collective Cabello/Carceller, who documented abandoned spaces such as swimming pools and dance clubs in California. Interested in outlining queer mobilizations of failure to thrive and engage in capitalist futures, Halberstam notes that "the empty pools stand like ruins, abandoned and littered with leaves and other signs of disuse, and in this ruined state they represent a perversion of desire, the decay of the commodity, the queerness of the disassociation of use from value" (111). While the ruins of *Minecraft* do represent an Orientalist *Indiana Jones* opportunity to retrieve rare items, their existence outside of time—literally as procedurally generated features of the landscape with the same temporality as the frozen animal and plant life—denies any sense of closure or conquering one might get from discovering their diegetic origins. For Halberstam, it is precisely the deferral of narrative that prompts the meditation on queer failure in the photographs of Cabello/Carceller.[10]

Queer Algorithmic Ecologies

We might return here to Priestman's (2013) warning about the tendency of procedural generation to get stuck in its own temporality, to fail where other games may succeed with hand-crafted content. *Minecraft*'s rise to success, in some ways, was in fact predicated on its early cyclical failures: using the paid-alpha/beta release model, it was in an extended period of public iteration that was both quintessentially capitalist and defined by the need for alternative funding models to sustain independent game development. Since its popularity was massive before an official launch version even hit the shelves, it is perhaps no surprise that the resulting play possibilities are quite wide open; here, we see a preview of what developing for the multitude might ultimately mean. If Halberstam saw queer possibilities following logically from computer rendering of crowds, then we might claim that *Minecraft*'s numbers game follows a similar path. A set of algorithms dictating the continual production of an expanding world is unleashed to an exponentially increasing group of users for whom the game is tailored and updated until official release, opening up a queer ecological system frozen in time that appeals to all ages.

So where does this leave us with an algorithmic ecology? We have explored how terrain and mob generation are governed by a complicated set of procedural rules modified by a world seed. We have seen how resources can be taken apart and added up into new formulations. We have even discussed the community's dedication to cracking open and exploiting the game's probabilities in the interest of maximizing profit. And, crucially, none of this is hidden underneath the veneer of realism or narrative like so many other simulations, instead reveling in an aesthetic that hearkens to early childhood math class and building blocks. While algorithmic ecology exists (with similar properties) in other virtual worlds like *Second Life* (Linden Lab, 2003) or *The Elder Scrolls* (Bethesda, 1994–2014) series, it is *Minecraft*'s dedication to space rather than narrative and voxels rather than photorealism that brings out both its ecological and algorithmic properties.

Figure 3. A sunset in a *Minecraft* field (Minecraft */TM & © 2009–2013 Mojang / Notch).

Minecraft's algorithmic ecology exists in a queer time that is cyclical rather than linear, one that deploys surface structures in place of temporal depth, and which produces queer forms of animal life and endless opportunity to walk hand-in-hand with the game's algorithms as they continuously open the world up and show users its awe-inspiring structures. Sitting still in a cave with bats fluttering around the avatar's head and chickens clucking somewhere up above, it is easy to see how algorithmic ecology is the source of the magic in this place. As a theoretically infinite world with inexhaustible soil and virtually waste-free resource conversion, *Minecraft* may not always provide a lesson in responsible attitudes toward nature. And yet it is more than an exploitative fantasy, full of exciting queer possibilities.

Notes

1. Gaboury traces the efforts of both Noah Wardrip-Fruin and Jeremy Douglass to analyze Strachey's program as a computational curiosity, privileging its form over content in reaching their final conclusions: the love-letter program "is a parody of the process of producing love letters" (Gaboury 2013c). However, he goes further to state that a queer approach must also recognize the critique of normative courtship procedures as well.

2. As the technical details of the game may change with updated versions of the software, some of this information may no longer be accurate. The current version as of this writing is 1.7.5.

3. Of course, *Minecraft* veterans will note that such quiet moments are only possible during daytime conditions on the surface of the world, or while playing in Peaceful difficulty, a point to which we will return later.

4. One can make the argument that the point of any game is to interact with its envi-

ronment, inasmuch as spatiality is a defining quality of digital media. However, Chang's contention specifically engages natural environments.

5. The one exception to this is the Villager, which spawns baby Villagers if there are a sufficient number of doors in its village. Like all animals in *Minecraft*, Villagers are not sexually dimorphic.

6. However, some mods of the game, such as the educational MinecraftEDU, do implement a gender choice in the game.

7. See also Chen (2012).

8. See also Gandy (2012).

9. Here I evoke Sara Ahmed's (2006) discussion of queer ways of being in terms of orientation away from prescribed life paths such as compulsory heterosexuality.

10. An additional reading that warrants further exploration is that these decontextualized ruins represent a disappearing of native peoples such that conquering space becomes a guilt-free activity. My choice to read queer temporality in these ruins rather than ultimate exploitation is not a refusal of this claim. Indeed, such contradictory strains of analysis are the lifeblood of critical discourse.

References

Ahmed, S. (2006). *Queer phenomenology: Orientations, objects, others.* Durham: Duke University Press.

Ashmore, C., & Nitsche, M. (2007). The quest in a generated world. *Situated Play, Proceedings of DiGRA 2007 Conference,* pp. 503–509.

Bethesda Game Studios. (1994–2014). *The Elder Scrolls* [PC game]. Bethesda Games.

Blizzard, North. (2000). *Diablo II* [PC game]. Irvine, CA: Blizzard Entertainment.

Bogost, I., & Monfort, N. (2009). Platform studies: Frequently questioned answers. Paper presented at *Digital Arts and Culture,* Irvine, CA, December. Retrieved from http://www.bogost.com/downloads/bogost_montfort_dac_2009.pdf

Chang, A. (2011). Games as environmental texts. *Qui Parle: Critical Humanities and Social Sciences, 19* (2), 57–84.

Chen, M. (2012). *Animacies: Biopolitics, racial mattering, and queer affect.* Durham: Duke University Press.

Chun, W. H. K. (2006). *Control and freedom: Power and paranoia in the age of fiber optics.* Cambridge, MA: MIT Press.

Chun, W. H. K. (2011). *Programmed visions: Software and memory.* Cambridge, MA: MIT Press.

Gaboury, J. (2013a, February 19). A queer history of computing. *Rhizome.* Retrieved from http://rhizome.org/editorial/2013/feb/19/queer-computing-1

Gaboury, J. (2013b, March 19). A queer history of computing: Part two. *Rhizome.* Retrieved from http://rhizome.org/editorial/2013/mar/19/queer-computing-2

Gaboury, J. (2013c, April 19). A queer history of computing: Part three. *Rhizome.* Retrieved from http://rhizome.org/editorial/2013/apr/9/queer-history-computing-part-three

Gaboury, J. (2013d, May 6). A queer history of computing: Part four. *Rhizome.* Retrieved from http://rhizome.org/editorial/2013/may/6/queer-history-computing-part-four.

Gaboury, J. (2013e, June 18). A queer history of computing, part five: Messages from the unseen world. *Rhizome.* Retrieved from http://rhizome.org/editorial/2013/jun/18/queer-history-computing-part-five.

Game Freak. (1996). *Pokémon* [PC game]. Nintendo.

Galloway, A. (2006). *Gaming: Essays on algorithmic culture.* Minneapolis: University of Minnesota Press.

Gandy, M. (2012). Queer ecology: Nature, sexuality, and heterotopic alliances. *Environment and Planning D: Society and Space*, 30, 727–747. doi: 10.1068/d10511

Halberstam, J. (2005). *In a queer time and place: Transgender bodies, subcultural lives.* New York: New York University Press.

Halberstam, J. (2011). *The queer art of failure.* Durham: Duke University Press.

Hosking, C. (2013, December 10). Stop dwelling on graphics and embrace procedural generation. *Polygon.* Retrieved from http://www.polygon.com/2013/12/10/5192058/opinion-stop-dwelling-on-graphics-and-embrace-procedural-generation

Irrational Games. (2013). *BioShock Infinite* [PC game]. 2k Games.

Keeling, K. (2014). Queer OS. *Cinema Journal, 53*(2), 152–7. doi: 10.13353/cj.2014.0004

Linden Lab. (2003). *Second Life* [PC game]. San Francisco, CA: Linden Lab Entertainment.

Maxis. (1992). *SimLife* [PC game]. Maxis Software.

Maxis. (2008). *Spore* [PC game]. Electronic Arts.

McMahon, C. (2013, April 11). *BioShock Infinite*: A city in the sky. *3D Artist Online.* Retrieved from http://www.3dartistonline.com/news/2013/04/bioshock-infinite-a-city-in-the-sky/

McPherson, T. (2012). U.S. operating systems at mid-century: The intertwining of race and UNIX. In L. Nakamura and P. A. Chow-White (Eds.), *Race after the Internet*, 21–37. New York: Routledge.

Mojang. (2011). *Minecraft* [PC game]. Stockholm, Sweden.

Mortimer-Sandilands, C., & Erickson, B. (2010). Introduction: A genealogy of queer ecologies. In C. Mortimer-Sandilands and B. Erickson (Eds.), *Queer ecologies: Sex, nature, politics, desire*, 1–47. Bloomington: Indiana University Press.

Morton, T. (2007). *Ecology without nature: Rethinking environmental aesthetics.* Cambridge, MA: Harvard University Press.

Morton, T. (2010). Queer ecology. *PMLA, 125*(2), 273–82.

Nakamura, L. (2002). *Cybertypes: Race, ethnicity, and identity on the Internet.* New York: Routledge.

Nakamura, L. (2008). *Digitizing Race: Visual cultures of the Internet.* Minneapolis: University of Minnesota Press.

Nintendo R&D4. (1985). *Super Mario Bros.* [NES]. Nintendo.

Nintendo R&D4. (1986). *The Legend of Zelda* [NES]. Nintendo.

Persson, M. [notch]. (2011, March 9). Terrain generation, Part 1 [Tumblr]. Retrieved April 2, 2014 from http://notch.tumblr.com/post/3746989361/terrain-generation-part-1

Priestman, C. (2013, December 8). Why it's best to be cautious around procedurally generated indie games. *Indie Statik.* Retrieved from http://indiestatik.com/2013/12/08/procedural-generation

Subset Games. (2012). *FTL: Faster Than Light* [PC game].

Toy, M., & Wichman, G. (1980). *Rogue* [PC game].

Yu, D., & Hull, A. (2009). *Spelunky* [PC game]. Mossmouth.

Look What Just Happened

Communicating Play in
Online Communities

MICHAEL THOMÉT

Minecraft (Mojang, 2011) can be played in a number of different official modes and difficulty settings, each of which can offer unique play experiences. The main modes of the game are creative, survival, adventure, and hardcore.[1] For the survival and adventure modes, there are four difficulties: peaceful, easy, normal, and hard.[2] To avoid confusion many acronyms are used by players to represent combinations of game settings; the most common are SMP (survival multiplayer) and SSP (survival single-player).[3] In addition to official options, there are many unofficial modes for playing the game that involve the use of game modifications (mods) to change the behavior of *Minecraft*. Mods can add new blocks, chat functions, organization methods, automation, crafting recipes, as well as restrict or remove any of the same. Further, with or without the use of mods, players can impose their own agreed upon modes on top of any game they play. Brendan Keogh's (2012) *Towards Dawn* is an example of a self-imposed nomad mode of play on an SSP game. Nomad players are forbidden from remaining in a single area of the game for more than one night.

Players often show interest in how others play the game, asking questions and sharing their play experiences over public forums. This chapter analyzes these exchanges between players in two online *Minecraft* communities and searches for commonalities and problems with communicating play experiences for such an open-ended game. In doing this, we can better understand both what *Minecraft* players value and what they find pleasurable. Ultimately, their rhetorical strategies also give us insight into player agency within and outside of the game world.

A Method for Mining Discussion Boards

Hundreds of posts from the *Minecraft* official forums (Minecraft Forum, n.d.) and the /r/Minecraft subreddit (/r/Minecraft, n.d.) were examined over the months of November and December 2013. Posts were identified for further study if they were on the topics of discussing play experiences or play styles of *Minecraft* players. This resulted in 71 total posts identified in the short time frame (46 from reddit and 25 from the *Minecraft* forums). From these, twenty of the most representative posts were captured in field notes and analyzed as observances of players communicating play to others. Nine posts were from reddit, and eleven from the *Minecraft* forums. These twenty posts are representative of how players discuss their play experiences and styles over these online communities for those two months at the end of 2013.

To situate this in *Minecraft* history, the data was collected during the time of MINECON 2013 (Bui, 2013), and immediately following the 1.7.2 version update (entitled "The Update that Changed the World"; Adams, 2013). During the collection of the data, *Minecraft* was released on the Sony PlayStation 3 (Owen, 2013), though no data was collected about this release as it happened near the end of collection period, after posts had already been identified. Most posts studied were about the PC version of the game, though in many cases it was impossible to tell which version of the game the posters were discussing.

While most of the analyzed posts were from November and December, some originated in September or October of 2013. A select few were older, referenced in newer posts, or chosen as they have a particular bearing on this study. All posts were publicly available at the time of capture.

This initial study was ethnographic in nature. It involved entering into online communities, searching for posts talking about play experiences and styles, as well as checking the most recent conversations for discussions about play experiences and styles. The study used field notes to collect and record relevant posts for analysis. The method of analysis was to apply the Player-Game Descriptive Index (PGDI; Thomét 2013b) to posts and compare what components of PGDI were talked about.

This study used the Player-Game Descriptive Index (PGDI; Thomét 2013b) as a tool to compare descriptions of play experiences and play styles made by players in both the *Minecraft* official forums (Minecraft Forum, n.d.) and the /r/Minecraft subreddit (/r/Minecraft, n.d.). As PGDI was created to describe a player's style of play and the kinds of play that a game provides, the method transfers easily to being able to describe players descriptions of how they played a game, as well as what happened to them in the game. What follows is the briefest description of the method and how it was applied.

PGDI is comprised of 26 independent components over six categories (see Table 1). Each component represents something unique about a game or a player's style of play and is measured regardless of the other components. The descriptions of all of the components can be found in Thomét (2013a).

Table 1.
Player-Game Descriptive
Index Categories and Components

Social	Participation	Mastery	Immersion	Customization	Progression
Community	Agency	Achievement	Embodiment	Building	Ability
Competition	Challenge	Collecting	Emotion	Experimentation	Character
Cooperation	Power	Discovery	Excitement	Replay	Goals
Multiplayer	Reward	Process	Instinct	Uniqueness	Plot
		Skill		Variety	

To apply PGDI for this study, the collected posts were examined and compared to the descriptions of the PGDI components to determine what kind of information was sought and what responses were given. The originating posts were first analyzed for what kind of information that player was looking for and what kind of experience or play style the player provided for others to comment on, if any. Then, each responder's post was analyzed to see if it matched what the original poster was looking for and if the response was contributing to the conversation in an expected way. Interactions between responders and the original poster were given close attention, as it was much easier to tell if a response was helpful or not if the original poster stated so.

For original posts, there were 14 identified components discussed or requested by players and 16 different types of response. Nine of the components from the index were not discussed in the posts studied. The categories of the index used most often were the following:

Community—the discussion of and fan base around a game.[4]

Challenge—the search for making a game more difficult and feeling like the game is justifiably hard without being impossible.

Process—the mastery and understanding of the internal workings of a game.

Skill—the mastery of a game's actions, and understanding how to effectively use them to a particular result.

Building—the configuration of items and the world of the game, particularly to create something out of the game's pieces.

Variety—the ability to configure the experience of the game, specifically by accessing differing modes of play.

PGDI was specifically built to be used by researchers to compare that which is usually difficult to compare (typically games to other games, or players to other players). With PGDI, it became easy to determine the aims of each post and how one post compared to others. As such, when problems in communication arose, it was more apparent as to why through the use of PGDI.

Discussing Play Experiences and Styles

This chapter examines two different kinds of posts in the studied communities: those that dealt with play experiences, and those that dealt with play styles. The original posters in these two types of posts often had very different aims, and rarely did the two mix in the same post. Both kinds of posts provide unique insight into the players of *Minecraft*. Posts about play experiences were those that discussed some kind of description or summary of actual play, and examining these posts provides insight into the experiences players of *Minecraft* find meaningful and important. Posts about play styles were those that considered *how* one plays or approaches the game in a general sense. Looking at these kinds of posts shows us what modes of play *Minecraft* players most enjoy, which modes they do not enjoy, and how players' approaches to the game change over time.

Players usually requested others to provide play experiences by first trying to situate readers in a moment of gameplay, providing a sense of embodiment. A post might provide a description of events one-after another as if it were happening as the person was writing the post. Alternatively, players also might state a very brief overview of what happened to them, followed by a question of others having had that kind of encounter, or one related to a problem or phenomenon that arose in their experience. Requests for play experiences that described a situation using one of these methods were often trying to garner responses related to the way the game works—what the PGDI would classify as a relating to *process*. Even if this was initially unstated, it usually came out in responses of conversation that the original poster's goal in requesting play experiences was related to trying to understand *Minecraft* and how it works.

Images were sometimes used to help communicate play experiences and were much more commonly found in the original posts than they were in responses, particularly on /r/Minecraft. The image disparity is likely due to the way that the two communities are set up. /r/Minecraft makes initial post images very accessible by providing a thumbnail link in the main list of posts, but the indented, threaded style of conversations in /r/Minecraft does not accommodate the large screenshot images of Minecraft. In contrast, the Minecraft official forums provide many tools to place images into posts directly, resizing the images to fit the post width. Additionally, the forums provide each response with a clearly defined space, so there is less confusion as to who is providing what image, and common etiquette in the space is to place images in a "spoiler" tag, which will hide it from view until one elects to see it.

It bears noting that Brendan Keogh's (2012) *Towards Dawn* similarly gives accounts of events, save that Keogh uses many images to create a montage of the events in his project. Keogh (2013) has a very embodied feel with his project, providing descriptions of his experiences in the game as if he were writing a travel journal and wanted his readers to join him on the experience. This is mirrored in the way that people would provide blow-by-blow accounts of an experience. Based on the language used in the posts, the players wanted to share the experience of being there. One player even called their account a tour of the world, adding to the embodied nature of the post.

One long ongoing post requested play experiences from others directly, using both a summary and an image. In addition to play experiences, the original poster also suggested that players share projects that they have completed. All of this was blanketed under a question of what players had done recently. Most responders to the question provided progress and project reports. Many reported what they had recently built in the game, using pictures to show off their creations. Others described their experiments with redstone machines or manipulations of game mechanics, either improving on old, deemed inefficient, designs, or working on something novel. The post is remarkable as it began in the middle of 2012 and was ongoing through the duration of the study, garnering many replies each day.

Another strategy used by posters to convey complex play experiences was to fictionalize an experience, adding narrative elements that couldn't exist in the game in order to explain the experience as more of a flowing story (e.g., dialogue, intricate actions, etc.). The /r/MinecraftNovels/ subreddit (/r/MinecraftNovels, n.d.) is dedicated to creating fiction around the world and concept of *Minecraft*, and often includes posts that fictionalize experiences for the sake of telling a personal story. These posters often wanted to receive feedback on the craft of their writing, and were merely using *Minecraft* as a backbone to provide content for them to fictionalize.

While /r/MinecraftNovels was not included in this study, much controversy was sparked in one of the studied posts that used this style of relating a play experience to create a historical overview of the events of a month-long multiplayer experience. The controversy arose when skeptics pointed out inconsistencies in the account and it was eventually revealed to be at least partially, if not totally, fiction. Although the post was untrue, many people initially believed the account and discussed it, generating much talk over the nature of the events and people involved, as well as the imposed rules of the style of play described. The false post inspired many players to try a different mode of play that was not their usual play style. Unlike others who wanted people to critique the quality of the writing, this poster was trying to place readers into a situation in order to start a philosophical discussion about the future of humankind in a situation like the one described. Although it was determined to be fake, the original poster did get just such a discussion. This is a rare case of a poster actually hearkening to PGDI's *community* component, by using the game as a springboard to access the community. While the poster used a falsified version of *embodiment* to generate the discussion, the goal was clearly to engage the community in a discussion about the players themselves.

As for posts in which players wanted to know *how* others played the game, being bored accounted for over half of the reasons behind inquiring about play styles. These bored posters often phrased their questions in such a way that asked responders to "fix" the boredom. They typically got many responses. One bored poster, for example, described playing only in creative mode, with survival mode boring him. This player wanted others to give reasons for playing a survival game and ways of playing where someone who plays mostly creative mode would not be bored. Some responders refused to answer bored posters helpfully, stating that they were not responsible for making the player enjoy a particular mode. Most bored posters had responses like these, in addition to helpful answers. Another notable bored poster asked instead for challenges to impose upon gameplay such as using only wooden swords for combat. In this case the player wanted to know novel ways to play the game, perhaps those that others thought were interesting but would not attempt due to the difficulty imposed. All bored posters wanted to find other, new, ways to customize their game experience—what PGDI terms *variety*.

Players responding to inquiries about play styles usually took one of several approaches. They either described how they approached a single mode of play, detailing steps to take, or they discussed how they approach the whole of the game of *Minecraft*, describing multiple modes of play in more general terms. Players responded to the question of how to stay interested in the game (i.e., bored posters) by suggesting modes of play directly, rather than providing a specific way of playing the game.

For players who wanted to discuss their approach to *Minecraft* as a whole, they typically produced ordered systems to follow. This was typically in response to questions of how people played *Minecraft*, but rarely a poster would open by describing how they approached the game. In response to a player wanting to play more survival mode games, one player reported that they approached the game by starting in creative mode, building up an interesting starting area with a village, and then switching to survival mode after, for play in the customized area. Another stated that they treated each mode of play as a completely separate game, and provided styles of play for each of the common modes. A particularly interesting response to a similar post described *Minecraft* play as cyclic. This player began in survival mode, moved on to creative mode, and then searched for a reconfigured experience with mods. After that, the responder noticed a period of boredom, followed by an interest in redstone machines. By the end of the period, the responder noted that *Minecraft* would have advanced many versions, allowing a player to begin the cycle again on survival. In the thread where this response was found, many people agreed, often chiming in as to how their own style was similar or how it differed.

Particularly in response to bored posters, some players suggested very general play styles by indicating a particular mode to try. In most situations, players offered the idea of changing from a single-player game to a multiplayer game. These players often gave support for this by describing the overall experience they had on their own multiplayer servers. Occasionally, some responders invited the original poster to their server to join them in play. This happened with one player who was having problems staying with a particular multiplayer server and was asking advice on how to remain interested in a multiplayer game. A responder directly addressed the original poster's concerns with multiplayer and suggested a particular server, to which the original poster showed great enthusiasm.

Helping Other Miners Isn't Easy

Overall, responses were most helpful to original posters when the responders paid attention to the kind of question being asked and provided a similar response. In particular, responses that fell under the same PGDI components in the original post were ones that attracted a lot of discussion and excitement. As an example, most bored poster questions were questions of the *variety* component, i.e., questions about reconfiguring the play experience. Although many responses to bored posters were to try the multiplayer mode, at the same time, many players suggested other modes of play, and others gave a number of ideas for what to do in a particular mode. Most of these responses, while similar, showed the vast number of play style options available to *Minecraft*, which harkened to the *variety* component. In short, the best responses for the variety questions were those that suggested many varied ways of playing.

Sometimes, though, it was impossible to really tell what components were governing a particular question. This was often a result of players being unclear, or providing too few details to understand the desired kind of response. The clearer a person was in asking a question, the more responses the post received. Unsurprisingly, clearer initial posts received replies that were more on target with what the original poster wanted. One player described a way for defeating one of the end-game enemies using a very unusual and inefficient method, but never explained why the description was given. This led to confused discussion as to why a person would go to the trouble to follow the method, when the point was instead an experiment of killing the enemy without the use of weapons and armor. In cases like these, players had to request and provide clarifications, which sometimes changed their reaction to the original post.

The most common problem that arose in the discussion was that of responders assuming the original poster had more knowledge about the game than he or she actually possessed. Almost every time, this was in posts related to the *process* component, that is, posts about understanding the inner workings of the game and knowing the way in which the game behaves and processes input.

In one example, a player was wondering how a particular enemy could be found in a place where it normally could not. The original poster provided no indication that they held much process knowledge, and yet the first response was a single word answer. While the response did technically answer the question, it did not provide enough context to be useful to the original poster, who had to request clarification. Eventually, another responder provided the more expanded version of the same answer. After a few more responses an even more detailed process answer appeared proving that the original one-word answer was not correct for the specific experience, but did work in general. In this case, the most helpful posts were those that attempted to provide the original poster with process knowledge that they did not possess.

Other common communication problems that arose were less spectacular, but still very prevalent. Many responders provided mostly unhelpful comments. Some challenged or denied the validity of a question, without answering it or providing a contrasting remark. In response to a question of what others do to keep from being bored, one responder simply said that he didn't do anything because *Minecraft* never got boring for him. Some others only contributed a sense of camaraderie. In response to a player seeking ways to get interested in survival mode as they mostly played creative mode, another player simply joined in to say that they too had the same problem. While this can help with a sense of not being alone with a problem, it still did not address the requests of the original poster. Although players rarely posed questions about others' play styles by asking what others liked about *Minecraft*, many responders answered posts by simply reporting what play style they enjoyed employing in the game.

Although rare, arguments sometimes broke out between responders, which took the focus away from the purpose of the initial questions or requests. One player had an experience in which they lost an ambitious building project due to a lightning strike causing fire and was asking if a particular type of placed item would be able to stop the lightning from striking. Instead of this question being answered, an argument broke out over the number of reported blocks lost and how difficult it would be to replace them. Even when the argument was quelled, other players only offered other ways to prevent the lightning from striking that ignored the players request about a specific item.

Another problem in communication that occurred was specifically tied to the relating of play experiences. Players responding to posts were typically unable to provide embodied accounts of a play experience after the fact. Instead, they often had to resort to saying what probably happened, rather than definitively saying what did happen, drawing on their past experiences and knowledge of how *Minecraft* works instead of remembered events. As a result, most original posts had more detailed descriptions of play experiences, while responders had more generalized versions.

Only a Short Trip Into the Nether

When dealing with such qualitative data as natural language text-posts, it can be difficult to find a place to start searching for commonalities and problems. By attaching PGDI components to each post, it became easier to identify patterns and search for nuances in those patterns. While the actual components had little bearing on the results of the analysis, the use of PGDI aided in conducting the analysis itself. As mentioned earlier, this is not the original purpose of PGDI, but this study has shown that it is helpful as a research tool beyond the comparison of digital games and their players.

Certainly, there is much more to learn here about how players discuss and describe play experiences and styles in *Minecraft*. Collection of data was conducted by making simple searches in each of the studied communities. This could have limited the data to researcher bias as many posts may have been lost due to the use of improper keywords. Additionally, the selection of the two communities may skew the results, depending on how other online communities differ from the studied ones. The ethnographic nature of the study notably prevented the analysis from including close readings of representative discussions, which would have been useful to perform a sociolinguistic analysis. Thus there are many ways in which the research could be conducted more rigorously and with more care for a complete picture of players discussing play experiences and styles in online, primarily text-based spaces.

Yet, this brief foray shows the unique ways players ask for and receive help, share their collective experience, and celebrate both triumphs and failures in playing a game that on the surface promises very little common experience. Even this short trip has shown us what experiences players find important enough to discuss and the modes and approaches to the game that players most adhere to. Perhaps what we have learned is that the rhetorical strategies they use give us insight into their feelings and experiences as much as the content they communicate. The more we study these exchanges, the more we will understand *Minecraft* players. Just as one step in the Nether is eight steps above ground, these few steps toward understanding players have crossed a vast distance already. While we've gone in and explored a bit, there is still an infinite landscape before us.

Notes

1. In creative mode players have an unlimited supply of every type of block, turning the game into a playground where they can build whatever they imagine. The other three modes are variations on the survival mode of play in which players must survive the experience with resources they find while balancing hunger and avoiding enemies to stay alive (although dying is only temporary). The adventure mode adds the limitation of being able to only collect resources with the proper tools, while the hardcore mode adds a restriction to the difficulty of the game and forces deletion of the save file when a player dies.

2. Peaceful difficulty is a unique difficulty where monsters are not found in the world and health replenishes slowly over time, mitigating much of the danger. The other three difficulties remove these beneficial rules, and monsters become variably stronger the higher the difficulty level. Hardcore mode is fixed to the hard difficulty level and it cannot be changed, unlike other modes. On top of all that, any combination of mode and difficulty can be played as either a single-player or a multiplayer game.

3. The acronyms usually do not indicate the difficulty of the game, suggesting that this is less important of a setting for people looking for ways to play the game. The only exception is the case of the hardcore mode of play, which prescribes the hard difficulty. The acronyms found in posts were: SSP, SMP, CMP (creative multiplayer), AMP (adventure multiplayer), and HMP (hardcore multiplayer). Creative single-player, adventure single-player, and hardcore single-player were typically shortened to their first word, i.e., creative, adventure and hardcore, respectively.

4. Obviously, players who participated in these discussions were all participating in the *Minecraft* community. However, the community component of the index was only applied to posts that took the *Minecraft* community as its subject matter.

References

Adams, N. (2013). *Minecraft* 1.7.2: The update that changed the world (updated!). Retrieved from https://mojang.com/2013/10/minecraft-1–7-the-update-that-changed-the-world/

Bui, V. (2013). Minecon live stream. Retrieved from https://mojang.com/2013/11/minecon-live-stream-2/

Karmali, L. (2013). *Minecraft* PC sales at 12 million; franchise at 33 million. Retrieved from http://www.ign.com/articles/2013/09/03/minecraft-pc-sales-at-12-million-franchise-at-33-million

Keogh, B. (2012). Towards dawn. Retrieved from http://towardsdawns.blogspot.com/

Keogh, B. (2013). When game over means game over: Using permanent death to craft living stories in *Minecraft*. *Proceedings of the 9th Australasian Conference on Interactive Entertainment: Matters of Life and Death*, Melbourne, Australia. 20:1–20:6. doi:10.1145/2513002.2513572

Minecraft Forum. (n.d.). Retrieved from http://www.minecraftforum.net/

Mojang. (2011). *Minecraft* [PC game]. Stockholm, Sweden.

Owen. (2013). *Minecraft*: PlayStation 3 edition is now available!. Retrieved January 15, 2014, from https://mojang.com/2013/12/minecraft-playstation-3-edition-is-now-available/

/r/Minecraft. (n.d.). Retrieved from http://www.reddit.com/r/Minecraft/

/r/MinecraftNovels. (n.d.). Retrieved from http://www.reddit.com/r/minecraftnovels

Thomét, M. (2013a). Player-Game Descriptive Index (PGDI). Retrieved from http://
incobalt.wordpress.com/player-game-descriptive-index-pgdi/

Thomét, M. (2013b). Using components to describe videogames and their players. In Z.
Waggoner (Ed.) *Terms of play: Essays on words that matter in videogame theory* (pp. 178–
211). Jefferson, NC: McFarland.

A Craft to Call Mine

Creative Appropriation of Minecraft
in YouTube Animations

JANDY GU

The ceiling fan was still running, each blade chasing the next in a hopeless game of tag. The air that passed between them drifted through the darkness in all directions, brushing my neck like a secret, whispering against a thin layer of condensation. The artificial breeze only served to cool the moisture on my skin, turning my sweat into something foreign. I was caught in a saran wrap trap of my own perspiration. I threw the covers off and sat up in bed. Segmented LED lights told me it was 3:45 a.m.

Carefully, I opened the door to my room and made my way past the den to the back staircase. As I passed the guest room, I noticed light seeping out from the crack beneath the door. It flickered and stretched, dancing along the wooden floorboards, the photographic negative of a shadow. My brother was still awake. Our parents didn't let us keep computers in our rooms because they believed bedrooms should be a sanctuary for sleep. Electronics remind us of everything we have to do and keep us from getting a good night's rest, they'd say. So of course, Dillon set up his desktop in the guest room. As I opened the door to poke my head in, a wave of laughter greeted me.

Dillon was squatting in his black leather executive chair, legs folded up so that his chin could rest in the valley between his knees. I recognized the position. He had adopted it from the enigmatic character 'L' in Death Note, a Japanese Anime series he convinced me to watch the summer before. Dillon was facing his desk, one arm wrapped around his shins, the other outstretched, clicking away furiously on his mouse. On the screen, I saw a pixilated world where everything was composed of cubes. He turned away for a moment to look at me.

"Hey you're still up?" He asked.

"Mm, couldn't sleep. What're you doing?"

"Playing a game."

From the speakers, I could hear a string of nonsensical phrases in a number of different voices. They were speaking English, but these were empty words—their contextual significance lost on me.

What the hell, why is this tree on fire? Oh there's lava right here. There's a spider! Get the spider, get the spider!

"Is that Danny and Brandon?" I asked, raising my voice slightly so Dillon could hear me over the effusive enthusiasm radiating from his sound system.

I want to pick some roses.

"Yeah and some other—," he starts to respond.

Guys, I'm being attacked by a skeleton.

At this, Dillon turns his full attention back to the screen.

"Oh shit! Wait, where?"

Outside somewhere.

"Get inside."

Hey guys, make some iron so I can make some weapons.

If you guys have coal, put coal in the ... thing. Dillon, do you have room for all of us?

"I'm working on it, bro!"

Man, I need to shower.

"Hey go into the farm. We've got a pool downstairs."

Everyone laughed. I gently closed the door and went downstairs to get some water.

Just by nature of being Dillon's sister, of living in the same house, breathing the same air, sharing blood and space, I have come to exist in the periphery of the *Minecraft* (Mojang, 2011) universe. There is a whole network of people who connect through playing this game and through engaging in the various creative avenues it inspires. These interactions do not simply end when both parties turn off their computers. *Minecraft* makes its way into everyday conversations with other people. There is an extension of these online relations in the way cyberspace communications and virtual life events are conveyed by those involved to the people close to them, bridging the disconnect in the virtual world/real world dichotomy. My relationship with my brother is an embodiment of this bridge and it is through such a metaphorical viaduct that I have come to understand *Minecraft* as a game, social resource, and visual aesthetic.

In the following pages, I hope to illuminate the complexities of social connections that manifest through the *Minecraft* YouTube scene and the ways in which animators like my brother negotiate legitimacy in the highly contested space of creative appropriation. This study is composed primarily of ethnographic accounts involving my interactions with Dillon as he was animating, semi-structured interviews with other *Minecraft* YouTube animators, and detailed examinations of certain videos within this genre.[1] My analysis of the sociality between animators, their viewers, and their offline personal relationships will draw on a broad range of literature including philosophy, anthropology, law, and media studies.

Making Pixels Bleed

Minecraft seems to be grounded in the everyday. It is not a game that has a linear progression, where one must defeat opponents or overcome a series of challenges in order to proceed to a higher, more difficult level until finally, the game is over. There is always more to do, more to create. In *Minecraft*, the players are expected to utilize the resources available to them, which manifest as textured cubes in a 3D generated world, in construction and combat. There are two major modes of gameplay: survival and creative. In survival mode, the primary objective is to stave off hunger and maintain health; in creative mode, one is presented with an unlimited supply of resources and neither health nor hunger is of any concern, allowing players to build as extensively as they please. A third level of gameplay, known as hardcore mode, has the same objectives and parameters as survival mode, except players are unable to respawn in the same server.[2] Dillon usually plays on a private server with several of his friends in hardcore mode, which is what I witnessed the night I first saw him play.

When Dillon told me about his ideas for a *Minecraft* inspired animation, my first question was whether anyone else had created something similar in the past. This is an essential question in an age and society where intellectual property is heavily protected and highly valued. There is something to be cherished in originality, especially in the creative arts. Yet because he would be adopting the *Minecraft* aesthetic, he would have to be innovative within that mold—a difference within a reproduction. Dillon specifically mentioned how his work would be a *Minecraft* fight animation, which meant he would be using *Minecraft* characters to tell his visual tale. But the final product aims beyond the scope of the *Minecraft* game. As an example, he showed me the music video *Fallen Kingdom* created by CaptainSparklez and animated by Bootstrapbuckaroo. The video is set to Coldplay's *Viva la Vida* and opens with the same line as the original song—"I used to rule the world"—before deviating into *Minecraft* references. It follows a King, portrayed in the *Minecraft* style, walking through his old kingdom. Periodically, the ruins trigger a flashback, the screen panning to images of the kingdom when it was prosperous until finally, the King sits down on a ledge gazing out at the kingdom. The song ends with the line "And that was when I ruled the land," a slight departure from the original closing line. Today, this video has more than 72 million views.

Shortly after *Minecraft* was made available to the public, individuals began to make animations based off the game and post them on YouTube.

These types of videos experienced a rise in popularity during the summer of 2011 (Slamacow, Interview) and varied in nature, from themed pastiches of pop songs to short episodes of a longer narrative. Many of these videos would combine elements of *Minecraft* with other references, creating intertextual connections between several digital sources. In a way, the creative nature of the game is reflected in the development of these animations, where the player draws from the available resources to build an entirely unique construct.

Dillon released his first video in July 2012. It was only twenty eight seconds long but it took him a month of eight-hour work days to create. "I'm done!" He told me, bouncing slightly as he made his announcement. He beckoned me to follow him to the guest room. Scattered across his desk, surrounding his keyboard, were pages upon pages of storyboard sketches and other scribbles. His calligraphy pen and ink set were sitting in the corner still pristine from gentle use. Plastic water bottles littered the floor, gathered around the foot of his chair. Dillon kicked a few of the empty Dasani bottles aside and scooted onto the leather cushions. Pulling up a rendered file entitled *Drunken Boxing*, he looked at me, maximized the screen, and pressed play.

Onscreen, a cubical man was depicted drinking on a movie set. He chugged what I presumed to be alcohol and stumbled into a few zombies, killing them in his inebriated state. In the meantime, an Enderman materialized and dropped a Creeper on the scene. This didn't phase the protagonist as he continued to dodge arrows, knock down more adversaries and then, after all his foes had been subdued, ride off screen on a pig, slumped against the angles of the swine's back. I wasn't sure what to make of it so Dillon explained to me how he wanted to create this character who is always drunk but in his drunken stupor, turns out to be an accidental badass. This made me laugh. "It's just practice for a larger project but I wanted to try out some stuff first. What do you think?" He asked me. "I haven't uploaded it yet, I wanted to see if you think it's okay." I thought it was great and told him so.

Dillon's next video was wildly successful. Periodically, he would burst into my room with gusto, announcing the most current update on his videos, "100,000 subscribers. 4 million views!" He would say. Today the video has over 9 million views on YouTube. As Dillon began thinking about the project that eventually became *Gods Don't Bleed*, he sat on the creased leather of his chair, swiveling it side to side as he used keyboard shortcuts to navigate the iridescent pages on the screen. He was browsing through Blendswap, a website for Blender users to share their work under a Creative Commons license, in search of materials to start with.[3] He already knew he wanted to create a video centered on Herobrine, a character recognizable to avid *Minecraft* players. Dillon found a premade Herobrine skin online, downloaded it and then double-clicked on the file to open it in Blender. Using digital tools with the ease of familiarity, he molded Herobrine onscreen to match the Herobrine in his imagination. There, the cubed figure stood, stored in the hard drive of Dillon's custom-built computer, unused. Until one day, Dillon was again browsing Blendswap and similar websites when he came across a premade three-dimensional environment resembling a cathedral with a throne at the end of a long hallway. He pulled up Herobrine's file, manipulated the character with his mouse and placed him in the throne of his newly downloaded environment. This was the scene I encountered when I was summoned, in a flurry of excitement, to Dillon's room. He pulled up the image on his desktop and then maximized the window. "How awesome does that look?" He asked rhetorically, basking in the glorious image displayed on his 32-inch screen. "Wouldn't you want to watch a video that starts off like this?"

The short storyline and fighting choreography were all developed in response to this initial screenshot, based in what was conceivable within that cathedral environment. A month later when the video was released, Dillon waited in trepidation for the Internet's reaction. He was relieved and delighted when the video's view count got incrementally higher and higher.

Not too long ago, I had mentioned casually to one of my friends that my brother makes *Minecraft* animations on YouTube. When they asked to see a video, I clicked on the red, yellow, and green vortex of Google Chrome and typed *Gods Don't Bleed* into the browser. The first link on the resulting page was Dillon's original video followed by a few re-uploads from other YouTubers. When I scrolled further down however, I noticed a link titled "Gods Don't Bleed: a Minecraft Fan Fiction." The link led me to a fan fiction website where someone had written a short story based on Dillon's video. It set the scene in "Minecrafteria" and expanded on elements of Herobrine's reputation in more explicit detail, interpretations not overtly mentioned in Dillon's animation. I called Dillon right away. "Did you know there are fan fictions based on your video?" I asked with exhilaration. When he said no, I copied the link and emailed it to him. I heard clicking sounds through the receiver on my cell phone, waiting for my brother to pull up the website.

"Whoa." We were both blown away by the impact *Gods Don't Bleed* has had on its audience.

Creative or Copied?

Sometimes I would walk past Dillon's room when his door was ajar and catch him acting out the motions in the mirror, trying to figure out the best way to imitate his actions in animation. Imitation and replication then seem an inherent part of the craft. Animation is the illusion of motion and movement—motion and movement usually based on those of humans (Broadfoot & Butler 1991; p. 264). In borrowing the *Minecraft* aesthetic, Dillon is imi-

tating a pre-existing work. He, like other *Minecraft* animators, decided to replicate the vintage cubed look of the characters because of their simple appearance
and as a platform for technical practice (Slamacow interview; Bootstrapbuckaroo interview). And the author of the *Gods Don't Bleed* fan fiction piece is
imitating Dillon's work. But how much imitation is too much in the eyes of
the law? In the eyes of society?

Digital media has fostered two similar but distinct consequences of technological advancement: reproducibility and accessibility. Walter Benjamin
addresses the first of these in his writing on how the technological reproducibility of art can cause a particular work to lose its "aura" (2008, p. 23), the
powerful impression an image can have when it necessitates individual interaction. While he speaks of this loss with some remorse, he asserts that the ease
of mass production liberates works of art from their previous "parasitic subservience to ritual" which in turn, may give rise to new artistic mediums
designed particularly with reproducibility in mind (Benjamin 2008, p. 24).
The affect of painting and sculpture are dependent upon personal access to
those works, reliant on the art form's traditional ties to religion and aesthetics
but photography and film are free of these constraining relationships because
they can address a mass audience directly. The term "reproducibility" as Benjamin uses it should not be thought of as repeated copying (even though copying is the process by which reproduction happens) so much as the simultaneous
release of multiple originals. It is important to distinguish between reproduction and piracy. Piracy is often described to include counterfeiting, copying,
smuggling, and trafficking (Johns, 2009; Dent, 2012). Reproducibility is the
result of technological advancements that allow for mass production. People
were engaging in piracy long before art became reproducible on a mass scale.

Benjamin's ideas on art and technological reproduction can certainly be
extended to include the World Wide Web. However, the Internet takes reproducibility a step further in increasing access to these works, making them
downloadable, making them malleable. Individuals now have access to copies
of these multiple originals and with digital copies it is easy to manipulate these
works. Here is where the line between piracy and reproducibility becomes a
bit blurred. Independently reproducing music, movies, videos, logos, etc. without the permission of the original creator violates the idea of intellectual property (Friel, 2007; Johns, 2009). Therefore, digital art and other creations that
borrow elements from existing works often straddle this legal/illegal divide.

The parasitic relationship Benjamin describes doesn't cease to exist
entirely; it merely becomes subject to another type of parasite. I use the term
parasite in the way Michel Serres conceptualizes the parasite, with all three of
its French connotations: the biological parasite, the social parasite, and static.[4]
In thinking about creativity, anything we create or invent comes from what
we already know, from what we see and experience around us. We are taking

in these elements from our surroundings without giving back. So when Serres orients all relations in terms of the parasite, he is not necessarily being pessimistic. He is really using the idea of the parasite to conceptualize the way humans and human products fuel each other, feed off each other, and interrupt each other. And the parasitic relation never truly stops because there is always a last relation (Serres, 1982, p. 23). Mechanical reproduction may have released art from its parasitic relationship with ritual but it is now entangled in parasitic relationships with other things, like technology or adaptable elements of other works. Here I am speaking of the parasitic relationship between various creative products, but there is a humanistic element in the parasitic relationship that will become relevant further on in this essay. The parasite parasites the parasite which parasites another parasite and so on.

This relates, in some sense, to Michel de Certeau's characterization of active reading as "poaching," a conscious interpretation of the literary text presented to the reader, taking away only the useful pleasurable elements (1984, p. 28). In this way, reading is not merely an act of passive consumption but rather active construal. Media theorist Henry Jenkins has applied this idea to fan art and fan fiction practices, orienting the authors of such works as "textual poachers" who "keep what they take and use their plundered goods as the foundations for the construction of an alternative cultural community" (1992, p. 47). Jenkins explores this relationship between text and reader, film and audience, in the process of creating stories within pre-established fictional worlds. He delves beyond the "crazy fan" stereotype of fan communities and examines the creative integrity of the work produced in participatory fandom. More recently, legal scholar Lawrence Lessig uses the term "remix" to refer to digital works created by taking snippets from various works and combining them to create a new work, with no underlying reverence for any of the sources used. In other words, remix involves appropriation without implying fandom. He traces this "cut and paste" technique back to the beginnings of modern art in the early twentieth century with the works of Braque and Picasso, arguing that the use of this technique inherently involves "transformative use" as it pertains to the fair use portion of the copyright agreement (2008, p. 37).

Dillon's work certainly features other elements besides *Minecraft* references. His desktop screen was visible from the staircase to and from the kitchen. On more than one occasion, I glimpsed clips of *Ip Man* and other martial arts movies displayed in his browser. I imagine he was searching for inspiration to fuel his animated fight choreography. Dillon also later confided in me that the title for *Gods Don't Bleed* was inspired by the scene in *The Road to El Derado* when Tzekal-Kan spots a bleeding cut on Miguel's forehead, leading him to realize Miguel and Tulio were not gods.

I suppose it is this kind of creative appropriation that has led to the popularity of *Minecraft* YouTube videos, some of which have garnered over 70 million views. These animators are feeding off an already established *Minecraft* fan base while the incorporation of other elements may attract non-*Minecraft* viewers. Yet it is precisely for this reason that they sit on the cusp of the copyright war. These videos can be considered remixes in their appropriation of existing digital works into a reformulated creation, placing them at an interesting cross section of legal and social acceptance. But they also resemble fan art and fan fiction in that most *Minecraft* animators started out as players of the game. Fan and remix works are susceptible to being legally challenged as legitimate creations because they co-opt varying amounts of unauthorized copyright-protected material. But possibly due to the sheer volume of these works, they are generally allowed and sometimes even encouraged to circulate as long as the authors don't make a move to commercialize their work (Hetcher, 1874, p. 2).

YouTube then presents an interesting predicament: account users can choose to monetize their videos, thereby crossing the threshold of commercialization. YouTube is fairly stringent in their precautions against copyright infringement, quick to remove any videos that may violate this international agreement. Yet *Minecraft* animations continue to thrive because Mojang supports individual use of their intellectual property within certain parameters (Persson). Thus, *Minecraft* animation videos on YouTube are generally accepted by both legal and social standards. But to what extent are these animations lauded as ingenuity and to what extent are they labeled as theft?

Anyone who enjoys creativity wants to make something new: a piece of art that is visually unlike anything else or a story that is compelling in its uniqueness. And of course, this is what *Minecraft* YouTube animators strive toward. The idea of originality is based in difference. In order to be original, one needs to create something different from what has been done before. Here, I mean the idea is to create something unlike and *apart* from existing works. However, the idea of creating something different from a previous work can also be thought about in terms of the "something different" *arising* from existing works.

Serres sets up all human relations as parasitic, which is especially appealing in the context of creative appropriation. In the act of appropriation, there is a constant taking involved, a one-sided taking. Yet Serres says, "the parasite invents something new. He obtains energy and pays for it in information" (1982, p. 36). The parasite is at once taking, leeching off of someone else's energies while emitting information. Something is not necessarily given in return as in an exchange but rather, given off, emanating from a particular place or center.

Even in a process of repetition and reproduction, elements change. For instance, the character of Herobrine in *Gods Don't Bleed* is actually based on a *Minecraft* myth perpetuated by the online community. Some players claim to have seen a version of the default *Minecraft* avatar named Steve with glowing white eyes and darker attire. Mojang released a statement pronouncing these claims untrue and that there has never been such a character within *Minecraft* although the company has enjoyed the development of such a legend. Certain players likened Herobrine to a God within *Minecraft*; others thought he was the King of the Endermen, villainous monsters who thrive in a world called The End. In Dillon's video, he combines these two conceptualizations of Herobrine and depicts an Endermen uprising against their deity king. He titled it *God's Don't Bleed*. After Herobrine defeats the rebels in the halls of his own palace, a drop of blood can be seen dripping down from his closed fist, humanizing this mythological character. Even though Dillon is borrowing elements from various sources, he has created a different version of Herobrine that the *Minecraft* scene was previously unfamiliar with. This fresh portrayal of Herobrine can be seen as giving off to the *Minecraft* community as opposed to giving back to Mojang.

It is also imperative to consider how images with no inherent meanings get imbued with characteristics. Even though Mojang officially dispelled the rumors surrounding Herobrine, this figure still became a hallmark of *Minecraft* lore. He may not be real in the confines of the game but what makes him less real to the people who've seen him? Within certain repeat occurrences in the *Minecraft* world, some players experienced an interference, a difference. Herobrine has been created by players of the game just as Steve, the default avatar upon which Herobrine's physique is based, was created by Mojang. He exists on the pages of online forums and fan fictions, an existence difficult to undo. Again, this conception of Herobrine can be seen as taking from Steve without giving anything back to the character of Steve, yet it introduces something new into the community of *Minecraft*. Thus we have a chain of parasitic taking and subsequent giving off. What is given off from parasitic taking can also be likened to Jenkin's use of "textual poaching," where a fan fiction writer absorbs material in a way that is meaningful to him or her, internalizing and then disseminating a version of the text unique to his or her interpretations (1992).

In general, Mojang's relaxed stance on *Minecraft* YouTube animations allows for a community driven advertising scheme. The dissemination of *Minecraft* game techniques and creative content is all based in the community of players. However, copyright and intellectual property issues arise when *Minecraft* animators try to move away from YouTube as a sharing platform. Animators Bootstrapbuckaroo, CaptainSparklez, and Slamacow are currently collaborating on a *Minecraft* episodic shorts series called *Dig Build Live*. They were considering the possibility of expanding to other media outlets i.e., doing a Netflix series or a show on Nickelodeon. The animators decided to consult with Mojang on the matter but their negotiations were tabled because of a conflict of interest (Bootstrapbuckaroo, interview). Markus "Notch" Persson recently announced on his Twitter that Warner Bros. had acquired the license to make a *Minecraft* movie. It is then in the interest of both Mojang and Warner Bros. to discourage other *Minecraft* productions from being released around the same time. Nearly a month before this announcement, an independent content creator named Brandon Laatsch attempted to rally financial support on Kickstarter.com for the making of a *Minecraft* fan-film for release on YouTube titled *Birth of Man* (Kotaku 2/06/14). But the trailer has since been removed from YouTube and the Kickstarter campaign was shut down. It is likely Mojang contacted Laatsch and informed him of the violation of intellectual property laws and recommended he not proceed with the film. This enters into ambiguous territory because the act of forbidding a YouTube movie contradicts the company's official stance on *Minecraft* YouTube videos. Yet there are obvious motivations for this mode of action, the conflict of interest with the Warner Bros. movie being a primary one.

The Web of Parasites

Dillon has spent countless nights squatting in his black leather chair, absorbed in the pixels onscreen. Almost always, he also has Skype messenger turned on in the background, minimized in the corner of his screen. The voices of his two best friends, Danny and Brandon, float torpidly from the speakers of his computer. He was constantly connected all the time—still is. No matter what he is doing—playing *Minecraft* or animating a video—he keeps an online calling program running simultaneously so he can chat with his friends, their conversations stretching across distances unseen. It was always so puzzling to me; they lived in the same city, wouldn't they rather get together in person?

Dillon and I are only two years apart but our technological engagements are vastly disparate. I believe physical interaction with a person, where our words echo in the air and a breathy secret could tickle our ears, is irreplaceable. When tensions are high and each sentence is fired with searing intent, these malicious vexes burst forth and then slow, lingering in the space between us. The air—once fraught with tension, derision, awkwardness—desires to be cleared. Compliments and idle chatter flow freely in the line from one pair of eyes to another but that space is much more resistant to negativity; it is a conduit for pleasant conversation and through an exposure of vulnerability, protects against confrontation.

From Dillon's perspective, online interactions have a certain value that is also impossible to recreate in person. A coffee shop or a friend's house does not offer the same sociability that striving for survival together in a virtual world does. So in addition to regular conversation, they can be united in a common goal on a *Minecraft* server. When I ask Dillon about how he accounts for the distance inherent in online interactions, he tells me it doesn't really feel any different. "Yeah, you can't talk to only one person if you're on Skype with a bunch of people but you can message them. You're still just talking to your friends," he says.

I can imagine being completely immersed in the cubed universe that consumes him, worrying about where to build a bed, if he has enough materials to make a contraption that kills chickens, if he can get back inside before nightfall. All the while, his friends echo these sentiments through the computer speakers, concerned about the threat of a zombie attack and whether or not they can generate enough food for themselves. I imagine him dreading the dangers of a dark screen, navigating quickly through the woods after a day of wood chopping toward the house they've started to build, but he's not fast enough and dark blue pixels of the evening sky turn black. His friends are urging him to hurry. A zombie approaches from his right and he draws his crossbow. The arrow hits and the creature collapses. He turns around to leave but there's another. This time, he's not fast enough. I imagine the *Minecraft* world falling away and pixels disintegrating to reveal a reality where he is sitting, in front of a computer screen, in the guest room of our house, alone. He can hear the faint sound of pots clanking in the kitchen below. But the speakers are silent. The game is over.

"That seems like it would be a weird feeling, you know? Like binge watching a television series and then suddenly realizing you've watched all the available episodes. Does it feel like that?" I ask. Dillon shrugs. "Not really. The game is never really over. Sometimes we start a new one. Sometimes, I go downstairs and eat dinner with you guys."

A group of people can be entirely attached to each other, their relationships interwoven. But even in the most exclusive groups, those relationships never exist in total isolation. This is apparent in my connection to Dillon and subsequent connection to the *Minecraft* scene by proxy. An investigation into how these relationships extend off-screen also reveals how Serres' parasitic relations extend to groups related and un-related to the content creators. Many anthropologists have traditionally analyzed relations through the concept of giving and subsequent reciprocity. This stems from Marcel Mauss' pivotal book, *The Gift*, where he argues that gift giving inexplicably evokes a feeling of obligation to return the gift, inciting a bond based on reciprocal exchange (1925). Michel Serres' work posits a philosophical orientation of relations completely opposite of this, where the act of perpetual taking rather than continual giving is the basis for all interpersonal connections and attachments. The integration of parasiting and poaching aside from content creation can best be exemplified by the act of viewership. In watching a movie or reading a book, we are simultaneously introduced to the author and engaging in a personalized interpretive absorption of the material presented—a connection formed as we take in the words and images.

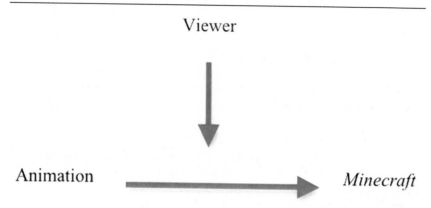

Figure 1. The parasitic relationship between a viewer, an animation, and the game.

Dillon sauntered into my room one day and announced, "Slamacow commented on my video and said he liked it!" "Who's that?" I asked. He insisted on showing me and before I knew it, I was watching a video about the interactions between a *Minecraft* stock character, an Enderman and a Creeper in a saloon.

After watching that video, Dillon moved his cursor to the 'related videos' section and scrolled until he saw another one he wanted to show me. The one I remember most vividly is the music video for an original *Minecraft* song titled "From the Ground Up." It follows the lives of two *Minecraft* characters as they navigate through the cubed world. Under the uploaded video on YouTube, Slamacow included a short description of his animation:

> The woman sees doom coming so she prepares. The man thinks she's getting kind of crazy from her old age. The doom stuff happens and he realizes she was right. They end up in the tower and see a photo of themselves with their son Steve (from cubeland) holding his pig. You realize they are in hardcore mode, so once they pass away the old world is deleted and a new world is made. They are young again because they have to start over [Slamacow].

After discovering so much about *Minecraft*, I could see the laws of physics and rules of life in the game manifest itself in Slamacow's story. In Hardcore mode, players are unable to respawn; they only have one life. To me, the video portrays this function of the game in a manner that resonates with the idea of reincarnation. They are reborn as different avatars but it seems like they maintain the same "souls."[5] In this viewing, Serres' trivalent relationship unfolds perfectly. The animation parasites elements of *Minecraft*, the original source. But there is always a last relation and the viewer then poaches upon the animation video. However, it is not simply a matter of extracting meaning from the animation video because much of the meaning is embedded in its relationship with the original source. Thus, the viewer (me) is parasiting upon the relationship between *Minecraft* animation and Mojang's *Minecraft* game. I am able to take my knowledge of the game and integrate it with what is happening to Slamacow's characters. My understanding of the animation involves absorption of both *Minecraft* game functions and the couple's story as it unfolds, allowing me to then add my personal interpretations to it.

Even in circumstances where the viewer may not understand the *Minecraft* references and background, the trivalent relationship still holds because another last relation will emerge. In the situation where the primary parasitic relationship is that of the viewer upon the YouTube animation, a third actor will always take from that relationship. YouTube animator Slamacow mentioned that parents of kids who play *Minecraft* and watch his *Minecraft* animations will often comment on his videos. They tell him that they really appreciate the clean humor he incorporates and are thankful for the content he's generating. They would much rather have their children watching Slamacow's animations than some of the vulgar content often broadcast on TV (Slamacow, Interview). In this situation, the parent is parasiting off the child's viewing relationship with the video. This trivalent model also explains how virtual relationships are never isolated or contained within the cyberspace community. There are always extensions in the form of third relations feeding off of those bonds.

Serres' parasite pays for what he or she is taking through information. This is not a direct exchange as Mauss might have conceptualized it, but rather an emission of buzz, a giving off. The viewer gives off information

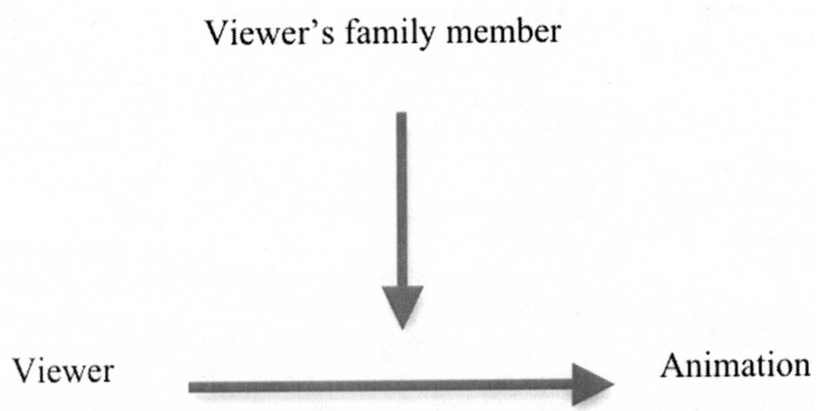

Viewer's family member

Viewer   Animation

Figure 2. The parasitic relationship between a family member, a viewer, and an animation.

through how they talk about the videos they've seen with friends, family, or acquaintances. This then generates dialogue around certain *Minecraft* videos. Because of this, there are then a group of people who come to know about *Minecraft* without engaging with the game directly–the sister who hears about CaptainSparklez' *Fallen Kingdom* from her brother, the mother who gets an earful about Slamacow from her son at breakfast, the teacher who gets a *Minecraft* update everyday in class from one of his students. Dillon, as a viewer, told me about several of the prominent *Minecraft* YouTube animators when he was thinking about becoming one himself. And in mentioning any of these videos to others, I would be parasiting upon Dillon's relationship to those videos, interpreting the videos and his captivation with them in my own way.

Similarly, Bootstrapbuckaroo, CaptainSparklez, and Slamacow–the creators of the *Minecraft* episodic series "Dig Build Live"–held a panel at MineCon 2013 to talk about their work with *Minecraft* animation and to answer questions from their fans. In response to a question about how they started making *Minecraft* animations, CaptainSparklez said he'd seen a video by Bootstrapbuckaroo, and Slamacow said he was inspired by a video CaptainSparklez and Bootstrapbuckaroo worked on together. As they were thinking about picking up animation, they might have mentioned these impressive videos to their friends; the people in the audience might now tell others about what these animators discussed during the panel. This constant spreading of information about *Minecraft* videos is what the audience of these videos give off, expanding the reach of these creations.

The parasitic relationship exists on many different levels: products with other products, content creators with other innovators, consumers (or audience) with the products, and consumers with other consumers. The *Minecraft* YouTube scene embodies the parasite in all of these relationships, even as they extend further and further away from a connection to the game itself. But the parasitic relationship never ends. Slamacow was inspired by CaptainSparklez and Bootstrapbuckaroo; now they're all working together. Dillon always admired Slamacow's videos; now they're thinking about collaborating in the future. Dillon's interactions with me during his animation process inspired this project; I ended up consulting him in reconstructing these moments for this essay. The parasite parasites the parasite. These relations are never isolated, never static. With each new permutation, the first parasite may become the last parasite.

Notes

1. Due to the scattered residency of these individuals, most of the interviews were conducted through online video calling. These animators are not at risk of legal prosecution

but in the interest of maintaining privacy, I will be referring to them by their YouTube usernames.

2. Respawning is where a player can reappear in the place they've last slept or their original spawn point after they die in the game. Thus, death outside of hardcore mode isn't permanent.

3. Creative commons licenses help "retain copyright while allowing others to copy, distribute, and make some uses of their work—at least non-commercially" (creativecommons.org). All of the environments and other creations on Blendswap are carefully modeled, textured, lit, and rendered.

4. I believe Serres speaks more to social parasitism and static than to the biological definition of parasite. Biological parasitism is when an organism feeds off another at the cost of the other. In other words, it must harm its host in some way in order to be called a parasite. If it is a harmless feeding off of, it is technically then defined as commensalism. However, social parasitism is less stringently defined.

5. This video's parallel in the real world would be a scenario where the same two people are playing with the different avatars. So the avatar's "soul" would really be the player.

References

Benjamin, W., Jennings, M. W., Doherty, B., Levin, T. Y., & Jephcott, E. F. (2008). *The work of art in the age of its technological reproducibility, and other writings on media.* Cambridge, MA: Belknap Press of Harvard University Press.

Broadfoot, K., & Butler, R. (1991). The illusion of illusion. In *The illusion of life: Essays on animation* (pp. 263–296). Sydney: Power Publications in Association with the Australian Film Commission.

Caillois, R., & Shepley, J. (1984). Mimicry and legendary psychasthenia. *October,* 31, 16.

Certeau, M. D. (1984). *The practice of everyday life.* Berkeley: University of California Press.

Dent, A. S. (2012). Piracy, circulatory legitimacy, and neoliberal subjectivity in Brazil. *Cultural Anthropology, 27*(1), 28–49.

Friel, C. (2007). The high costs of global intellectual property theft: An analysis of current trends, the trips agreement, and future approaches to combat the problem. *Wake Forest Intellectual Property Law Journal, 7*(2), 212–249.

Hetcher, S. (2009). Using social norms to regulate fan fiction and remix culture. *University of Pennsylvania Law Review, 157*(6), 1869–1935.

Jenkins, H. (1992). *Textual poachers: Television fans & participatory culture.* New York: Routledge.

Johns, A. (2009). *Piracy: The intellectual property wars from Gutenberg to Gates.* Chicago: University of Chicago Press.

Lessig, L. (2004). *Free culture: How big media uses technology and the law to lock down culture and control creativity.* New York: Penguin Press.

Lessig, L. (2008). *Remix: Making art and commerce thrive in the hybrid economy.* New York: Penguin Press.

Mauss, Marcel. *The gift: Forms and functions of exchange in archaic societies.* London: Cohen & West, 1969.

Mojang. (2011). *Minecraft* [PC game]. Stockholm, Sweden.

Person, Chris. (2014, February 6). Yep, that looks like a feature-length *Minecraft* movie [UPDATE]. *Kotaku.* Retrieved from http://kotaku.com/yep-that-looks-like-a-feature-length-minecraft-movie-1517813506.

QueenCelina33. (2013). *Minecraft*: Gods don't bleed [Fan Fiction]. Retrieved from https://www.fanfiction.net/s/9655574/1/Minecraft-Gods-Don-t-Bleed

Schneider, J., & Schneider, P. (2008). The anthropology of crime and criminalization. *Annual Review of Anthropology*, 37(1), 351–373.

Serres, M., & Schehr, L. R. (1982). *The parasite*. Baltimore: Johns Hopkins University Press.

Straw, W. (2001). Scenes and sensibilities. *Public* (pp. 22–23).

U.S. Copyright Office. (n.d.). *U.S. Copyright Office*. Retrieved February 27, 2014, from http://www.copyright.gov

"Someone off the YouTubez"

The Yogscast as Fan Producers

Esther MacCallum-Stewart

> The people who made money from the gold rush were not the gold rush miners. It was guys named Levi Strauss and Crocker, and folks who ran banks, and people who sold jeans, and sold picks and axes.
>
> I think ultimately in the long term that the money that will get made in *Minecraft* will not be about *Minecraft*, but will be about the services and products that get introduced into it. And so that's what's most interesting ... the ecosystem.
> —Rich Hilleman, as cited in Sheffield, 2012

> You can make anything you want to. You can make any game you want.
> —Lewis Brindley at *Minecon*, 2011

This chapter examines how *Minecraft* (Mojang, 2011) has altered fan behaviour within gaming to the point that it has helped to fundamentally change the reception and repurposing of gaming texts. Whilst previous studies have tended to look at *Minecraft* from within, seeing its creative purposes through the context of individual server builds or learning projects, this chapter examines the ways in which it has been increasingly appropriated by fans beyond the game. This extends beyond simply modding the game or creating artefacts within it. The blank narrative tableau of *Minecraft* has allowed fans to reinscribe it for their own ends. In particular, the webcasts created about and within the game have prompted a dramatic rise in creative gaming videos on social media sites such as YouTube. The ease of using *Minecraft* as a location for hitherto complex machinima, or visually lacking podcasts, has resulted in a huge increase in webcasting videos, which has now spread to other genres like tabletop/board gaming and film reviews. Whilst these webcast videos might originally have seemed to be a niche part of gamer culture, both the popularity of *Minecraft* and the emergent celebritization of the casters involved has caused a new type of gaming experience to emerge—that of watching games and the subsequent narratives placed on top of them—rather than that of playing itself. This chapter therefore specifically looks at one of the groups at the forefront of this development, the UK based webcasters known as The Yogscast.

"*Punch trees = 40 Million Dollars*"

Alex Leavitt describes *Minecraft* as a game with no learning curve (2011). Instead, users are thrown off a precipice and expected to discover everything for themselves, and it becomes immediately apparent that they must do this quickly in order to survive. Yet, *Minecraft* is essentially a blank narrative text. It has no underlying story; no castles to siege or tasks to fulfill. Instead, each player sets their own goals, decides what type of genre their world expresses, and collects items to build, create and explore each seed generated.[1] Despite a setting containing what rating systems might like to call "themes of mild cartoon violence," the game can be changed to look like whatever the player deems, thanks to exhaustive mods which take players to the moon, under the oceans or deep into space. Yet despite this, the first thing a player usually sees is a sunny, pastoral world and possibly a few trees.

New players to the game are often baffled by this blankness, especially if they decide to play as solo participants and encounter the eerily quiet landscapes of *Minecraft* on their own. What does one do in such a place, given that no friendly NPCs are there to show the way, and that killing monsters seems to result in so little appreciable gain? Despite introducing a levelling system and end boss in patch 1.9.4, these elements have little or no effect on the average play session. Levels do not make players appreciably faster or tougher, and the Ender Dragon end boss can only be encountered under highly specific and not particularly rewarding terms.

This narrative silence in *Minecraft* underpins the huge community of development, modification, and storytelling that surrounds it. Prior to this collection, papers have tended to focus on the educational aspect of *Minecraft*, citing its importance as a tool for schools or self generated learning. In this respect, discussions of *Minecraft* have echoed earlier studies of popular games which are at pains to emphasize the potential for them to supplement educational development, rather than seeing them as entities in their own right as objects of play and playfulness. Early papers investigate maps and mods for the game that enable learning or have been used by schools to teach specific aspects within the educational curriculum. In *Well Played* for example, Sean Duncan argues persuasively that the survival and construction (creative?) aspects of *Minecraft* are what makes it useful as an emergent tool, but he grounds this primarily in case studies of the "classic" mode of the game (which is single player and ultimately not very popular with players), and through the example of an educational mod/map called *Circuit Madness* (Duncan, 2011). Earlier critics also tend to avoid the importance of collaborative exploration or danger to the individual within each seed. Joel Levin of *The Minecraft Teacher* (http://minecraftteacher.tumblr.com/) supplies schools with the highly successful Minecraftedu mod, which helps teachers to "augment the content" of *Minecraft* when used in the classroom, and supplies a series of learning packages that share mods and maps. Mojang has been quick to embrace this hegemonic validation by allowing users to download *Minecraft* in schools for half price, and there is also a version on the Raspberry Pi, another system which strongly connects technology to learning. Whilst all these tools are undoubtedly incredibly useful, because they present *Minecraft* within a cultural sphere that is traditionally seen as having more value (i.e., education has more cultural worth than play), it means that projects that take place within these areas, rather than fan based production, tend to be the focus of studies and appreciation of the game, as well as being touted as the epitome of useful emergent play within the game.

Although the educational potential of *Minecraft* provides a useful position from which to examine it, many of the papers that examine the learning potential of games tend to accidentally obfuscate the substantial input of auteurs or less formalised modes of production. This is partly because of the fragile historical relationship between learning and games, whereby authors want to assert the importance of this connection and thus offset some of the more drastic moral panics that surround gaming as a whole. In order to do this, they choose texts which can seemingly be easily integrated into a proscribed learning environment and which preferably contain low levels of violent activity. Less formal modes of production are therefore usually mentioned in passing[2] but are seen as less useful to both cultural and learning production, especially since determining their measurability beyond the status of popular cultural artefact is problematic.

For players, the narrative blankness of *Minecraft* is not only intriguing, but it sends out a silent challenge. Although they may inadvertently follow a learning pathway, or find themselves engaged in aspects of unintentional stealth learning (Sharp, 2012), the functionality of the game allows players not only to tell their story, but to produce ludic and paiedic constructs in order to give it coherence. Storytellers can make narratives, and coders can use the source code to implement functional changes in the game, and both can draw equally usefully from the other to fill in any gaps. The vast amount of modification and experimentation that allows the game to proceed far beyond its rather basic initial appearance is generated almost entirely around the need to give this world not only a voice, but to force it to adhere to more traditional modes of gameplay and storytelling.

Digging a Hole—Beyond Maker Communities *in* Minecraft

Sips Co. For All your Quality Dirt Needs.
—Trailer for The Yogscast "Sips Co" series, 2012

The ways in which the community of *Minecraft* exhibit their creations is, as many have already noted, extraordinary (Dean, 2013). This began with very simple articulations of crafting, which escalated as the game granted more potential. At first, *Minecraft* was unstable for multiple players, and although huge builds are now created by teams of players working together, early creations could only be witnessed by their authors. In *Making is Connecting*, David Gauntlett (2011) discusses how crafting communities need to share the tangible artefacts they have created. They do this via websites that enable them to display the objects that they have created in a virtual manner but which highlight their originality and effect upon the senses (with visual and aural content obviously predominating). The importance of "show and tell" means that members create community and a sense of pride by showing the artefacts that they have created, even if they are exhibiting versions of the same thing (for example a knitted jumper or Arduino pattern). The prevalence of crafting websites online is testimony to this need for sharing, and players of *Minecraft* were early adopters of a similar technique through their use of YouTube to demonstrate their creations.

For *Minecraft* modders and designers, demonstrations of complex objects made within the game were important exhibits of how individuals could manipulate the game in creative ways. Exhibits of the Starship Enterprise were followed by those of fully operational calculators or fruit machines. Builders began to make time delay videos as a sign of authenticity (demonstrating the effort and time required to create these marvels), and also to help others replicate their work. These were quickly followed by more complex recordings with the beginnings of narrative discussions, whereby players explained their design processes and problems, and at this point the recordings began to change.

One of the first viral *Minecraft* LP (Let's Play) recordings is *Minecraft FIREE WTFFFFFFF!!!!!* (MinecraftFTW, 2010). In it the hapless recorder visits his friend's server whilst he is away and sets a fire in the fireplace of their newly built house. Because the walls behind the fireplace are made of wood, the entire house catches alight by increments and rapidly burns to the ground, whilst the player desperately tries to put it out. The recording demonstrates a classic moment of tendentious humour, which marries with the ethos of the game in an unexpectedly comic way; things in *Minecraft* frequently go wrong, most often at the expense of others. The recording establishes a crucial emergent aspect of the game; stories are not only possible, but there is huge currency in the surviv-ability (or not) of each world and the friability of the player within it.

As soon as the servers became stable enough (around December 2010) individuals and groups of players began to make videos of their play, addressing the lack of *Minecraft's* tutorial by creating their own. However, two webcasters took this further, realizing the potential of the game to entertain through the more accidental failures seen in videos like *Minecraft FIREE WTFFFFFF!!!!!*. In the same month, webcasters Lewis Brindley and Simon Lane (collectively known as The Yogscast) began uploading a series of videos onto their YouTube channel explaining how to play the game. After making a base and moving into the YogCave, however, their videos began to change in tone. As Simon Lane explains, the rather flat nature of simple playthroughs had not only lost its appeal, but the two wanted each episode to stand out from the crowd:

> things were getting a bit boring. With a *Minecraft* walkthrough it starts off quite interesting because you're in a race to get shelter and to set yourself up, but then once that's done, then you're not really in an awful lot of danger ... things were in danger of getting a bit stale [Lane, interview, 2011].

Thus the duo introduced a nemesis called Israphel to the narrative. In "Minecraft—Part 6: The Mysterious Tree" (Brindley & Lane, 2010), the two entered their private server to find that someone appeared to have been playing on it, perhaps a friend or someone who had chanced upon the server when access to it was left open. However it became quickly clear that the threat came

Figure 1. The house burns in *Minecraft FIREE WTFFFFFF!!!!!* (MinecraftFTW, 2010) (Minecraft ®/TM & © 2009–2013 Mojang / Notch).

from within and was in fact a sinister figure called Israphel. At first Israphel was unseen, although he gradually menaced the two by leaving threatening messages, booby trapping the YogCave, building weird structures that put Honeydew and Xephos in peril, and finally attacking them in their base. Israphel's identity and motives were never clear, and the narrative gradually suggested that he was not another player, but instead a malevolent being that had "leaked out from the portal" to the Nether that the two had spent some time building in early episodes.

The series quickly developed into a popular adventure story called *Shadow of Israphel*, with episodes released on a daily basis. The videos still explained how to play the game, but they also presented a series of engaging comic characters, frequently subverted their own plots (meticulously crafted with the help of friends working behind the scenes), and celebrated the relaxed, wry demeanour of the two hosts. This combination drew in viewers keen to watch both aspects—the rather inept how-to nature of the show supported the notion that not everybody was capable of building artistic structures on their first go, that the game was relatively hard to play, and the storyline provided an engaging way to view the game as a springboard for adventurous play. As *Shadow of Israphel* become more production intensive, requiring huge sets and large amounts of NPC players to be present at any one time, the series found other ways to release daily content and to please fans willing to watch Simon and Lewis explore other games or different iterations of *Minecraft* itself.

Yogscast shows therefore also began to explore other mods, document changes to the game, and play adventure maps; seeds built up by other players and containing their own narratives. Secondary episodes also saw the duo playing other games together such as *Fable III* (Lionhead Studios, 2010) and *Portal 2* (Valve, 2011b), returning to the style of their earlier videos and podcasts, but this time with a fanbase that was virally expanding through gaming and *Minecraft* communities. The *Minecraft* series combined slapstick with more practical how-to elements, showcased other fans' good work, and dominated the ratings for videos about *Minecraft* itself, whereas the more general videos expanded the content outwards to more general gamers. All of these videos were overseen by the charismatic, witty banter of the two presenters, allowing viewers to experience each game vicariously and to listen to the equivalent of a comedy podcast at the same time.

A typical episode of The Yogscast is about twenty to twenty-five minutes long. Xephos and Honeydew play through either a game of their own devising (such as *Moonquest*, in which they embark on a lengthy endeavour to send Simon/Honeydew to the moon), or one created by fans (such as *Calmere Nightmare*, an adventure map based on the stories of H.P. Lovecraft). Each episode is usually part of a series—as of December 2013 *Moonquest* was over 50 episodes long with a six hour special planned for later in the month.[3] The two protagonists, often with the help of friends both behind the scenes and acting out their own characters within each webcast, explore each map and comment as they do so. This commentary interchangeably switches between discussions of the game itself, roleplay of each character,[4] and normal conversation about games and the lives of the two players. This is interspersed with moments of improvised comedy that respond to events (usually unfavourable or unexpected ones) within the game. A fairly typical example of this is as follows from "Minecraft—'Shadow of Israphel' Part 11: The Crumbling Ruin" (Brindley & Lane, 2011):

> [Xephos and Honeydew are trying to rescue Honeydew's current love interest, the geriatric Granny Bacon, from the cultists of Israphel who have imprisoned her in an underground base. The cultists have been infecting people with a plague that turns people into zombies. Granny Bacon is an NPC played by one of the cast who does not speak, but instead types responses, which Honeydew then vocalizes.]

> Xephos / Lewis Brindley: Open the door, let her out.
> Honeydew / Simon Lane: I ... should we?
> Lewis: Yeah! It's Granny!
> H: What if ... what if she's been afflicted by the taint? [He opens the door. Granny Bacon edges out.] She looks really weird. She looks... She's making weird noises. Lewis, I'm freaking out.
> Xephos / Lewis Brindley: I'm freaking out as well!
> [Granny Bacon starts to menace Honeydew, edging towards him.]
> H: Look at her, look at her. What's going on?
> X: I don't know!
> H: See, I bloody told you! I TOLD YOU, "What if there's something wrong with her?" Look at her!
> ...

> [Granny Bacon chases the two around the dungeon. They build a wall but she smashes it down. Honeydew hides in a cell, and she locks him in. Xephos frees him, as the chase escalates...]

> ...
> H: [Outraged] She's hittin' me! She's hitting me with bacon, Lewis!
> X: See if you can knock her out of her trance. Just hit her!
> H: Okay, okay. Oh God. Forgive me for doing this.

> [When he strikes Granny Bacon, the player behind the scenes controlling her puts on a different piece of armour which makes Granny appear to have a zombie's head].

> AaaaHHHH! Oh my God! That ... that is not good.
> X: That is very bad news indeed. Shall we just leave her? D'you reckon she might turn back?
> H: Nooo! She's gone mad, she's GONE MAD, SHE'S GOING TO KILL ME! [crying] Oh my God kill her KILL HER! Oh God I'm sorry! [Granny Bacon chases him around the dungeon] OH GOD I'M SORRY I'M SORRY!

The Yogscast rapidly became successful, regularly drawing in over a million viewers per video every day. Within a few months, they were the most subscribed YouTube channel in the UK, and usually featured in the top ten for the U.S. In the UK, viewing figures regularly surpassed those of comparable television programmes, including the driving show *Top Gear* and the children's programmes which were usually broadcast in the same time slot. As a result of this, revenue generated from the videos made Brindley and Lane two of the first YouTube millionaires, able to support themselves independently via money made through the subsidiary advertising that YouTube channels must display.

Viewers tuned in for a variety of reasons. People came for the tutorial, but stayed for the story and the presenters. The narrative of getting things wrong, being blown up by creepers, and facing off against Israphel was overlaid with a secondary one of stories about daily life, gaming geekery, and apparent ineptitude. The series was both endearing and instructional, and the regularity of content meant that fans always had something new to watch. Brindley and Lane rapidly became gaming celebrities. The series escalated as word of mouth from fans started to increase their popularity, and in turn, The Yogscast began to expand. In order to cope with the demand for videos, they invited new members from amongst their friends, many of whom they had met online.

Three years later in December 2013, The Yogscast had 6.5 million dedicated subscribers and over 2 billion hits on their main channels. The main Yogscast channel had produced nearly 4000 YouTube videos, most of them about *Minecraft*. The group was now comprised of 30 staff members producing at least five shows daily across eleven different YouTube channels. They covered many aspects of gaming culture, from playthroughs of new releases to interviews at conventions and gaming news. Alongside the rest of their staff, Brindley and Lane worked full time from their YogTowers offices in Bristol. They were not alone. The popularity of gamer videos had spread around the world to other groups. Other presenters like Jesse Cox, TotalBiscuit, and PewDiePie all dominated YouTube ratings. Similar geek cultures like tabletop boardgaming and roleplaying had also found YouTube playthroughs a useful way to discuss and review games. Personality driven shows like *Tabletop, ShutupandSitDown,* and *Dice Tower* frequently emulated the tried and tested formula of two slightly geeky friends whose obvious friendship helped drive the show and make viewers feel as if they were amongst friends. These videos were not only successful, they were now a fundamental part of gaming culture.

Screw the Nether: The Impact of the Yogscast

To understand this meteoric rise to fame, it is important to understand the ways that fan relationships are critically important within subcultures without spokespeople, and to appreciate *Minecraft* as a text that apparently endorses a reciprocal relationship with its players.[5] *Minecraft* has always prided itself on its dynamic relationship with fans, allowing them to modify and enhance the game since its inception. This extended to fan-producers such as The Yogscast who were now making what were essentially episodic, daily entertainment shows for YouTube that advertised the potential of *Minecraft* itself. As Hilleman suggests in the introduction to this paper, *Minecraft* also allowed these groups to move beyond the confines of the game and forge their own identity, which both informs understandings of the game and moves beyond it. This also overrides previous critical understandings of machinima and YouTube videos, which have often seen such expressions as entirely subsumed into promoting the core text (Schott & Yeatman, 2011).

For viewers however, The Yogscast were a new, and surprising type of spokesperson. Their modes of address were friendly and informal, drawing players into the world of each presenter and creating an intimate dynamic with them. Fans knew, for example, that Simon was terrified of spiders and loved Jaffa Cakes, but in return there was a direct reciprocity to the relationship whereby fans contributed adventure maps, fan art, and suggestions. As former fans themselves—what Matt Hills called "elite fans" or "producer-fans" (Hills 2002, 2006) and which I have dubbed "fan-producers" (MacCallum-Stewart, 2014)—The Yogscast and their peers actively utilized these objects, appropriating useful maps and recording their own adventures within them, hiring promising artists and editors, and regularly monitoring less direct activities such as the discussion on their forum or SubReddit. If fans did not like a particular show, or objected to its content, the Yogscast would alter the subsequent content accordingly. Meet-ups and other social events at gaming conventions (also rapidly growing in popularity due to the rising interest in gaming as a social activity beyond the game itself) reinforced the approachable nature of the group even if only a small percentage of fans ever experienced them. And fans watched, imitated, and trusted the shows.

The impact of The Yogscast and their peers might seem to be confined to the realms of internet phenomenon or niche gamer culture until one considers both the viewing habits of users and the ways in which the shows have permeated popular culture. Since 2010, consuming gaming culture through online videos has become a huge part of gamer culture. In 2013, Google metrics showed that 95 percent of gamers watch a video on YouTube before purchasing a title (Getomer et al., 2013). Playthroughs are one of the central ways in which this is done, since gamers get an idea of the game as well as being able to compare their own skills to those of players they consider their peers. A fundamental part of The Yogscast, and other groups like them, is that they are imperfect as gamers, giving a more accurate picture of play as well as what is considered an honest perspective. Developers actively pursue these reviews, since they allow them to reach a broad spectrum of gamers, to showcase their work and to advertise their product with relatively little input on their behalf. For viewers, videos like those by The Yogscast inject an aura of authenticity into the critique, as well as allowing them to partially gauge the games for themselves.

In 2013, YouTube promoted themselves with a huge internet and terrestrial campaign that saw The Yogscast plastered across the hoardings of London buses and the London Underground, two of the most lucrative advertising locations in the UK. Lewis, Simon, and Hannah (Brindley's partner and fellow caster) were well-known enough for their lifestyle to be parodied in a series of television advertisements for broadband access. These campaigns demonstrate the ubiquitousness of the group as well-known celebrities, since they used The Yogscast as a familiar brand or social identity in various contexts.

But most of all, watching The Yogscast and their peers for news, reviews, playthroughs and entertainment became a normative practice for a huge demographic, with their core groups ranging from 13–17 to 45–54 years of age (YouTube analytics, "BlueXephos," 2012). As Schott and Yeatman argue when examining *Half Life 2* (Valve, 2011a) machinima, the Yogscast "contributes to the articulation of a shared community of game-player interests and investment" and "combine emergent digital authorship with cultural appropriation in a manner that seamlessly and effectively integrates and absorbs other texts" (2011, p. 312).

Conclusion

The Yogscast are a hugely influential group of entertainers who represent a new type of gamer. Their ability (and luck) in tapping into the cultural currency of *Minecraft* and using it as a springboard text for their own work demonstrates several things. Firstly, it points to the importance of *Minecraft* as a text that engenders creativity and emergent play beyond the game. Secondly, the blank narrative of the game enabled The Yogscast to implant their own brand of humour onto a text that needed both story and ludic explanation. Thirdly, as Hilleman prophesied, the game allowed many people to benefit from the game's popularity, acting as a springboard to The Yogscast's own brand of humour and entertainment. It is perhaps telling that the row that broke out between Mojang and the Yogscast in 2011 was a direct result of this friction— possibly prompted in part by a quote from Brindley in which he stated that the success of the game was in part due to their videos (Brown, 2011). This clearly touched a nerve, as Notch later described them as "isolated island of egos" (Persson, 2011). Yet, it is undeniable that their recordings of the game have had a huge influence on the ways that the game is perceived and must have boosted sales as a result.

What The Yogscast recordings mean for gaming as a form of entertainment also has important repercussions. The Yogscast have been at the forefront of several power shifts in the games industry; raising the fan-producer to a position of power, and also positioning them as highly visible spokespeople for gaming beyond the text of the game itself. Subsequent responses, which have seen the Yogscast nominated for BAFTAs and the recipient of several Golden Joysticks, suggest that the industry recognizes webcasts as a rising force in gaming criticism and entertainment. This is especially important when one considers Brindley's claim that Mojang are indebted to the Yogscast and the vital importance of YouTube celebrities as arbiters of taste in gaming culture.[6]

Notes

1. Each random iteration of the *Minecraft* world created can be identified by a unique number, called a seed. Players are able to share these numbers if the content proves particularly interesting or unique.
2. The Yogscast in particular are often mentioned in academic papers, but Duncan (2011) misspells their name, for example.
3. The Yogscast livestreamed every night in December for charity and have raised over $1 million for various causes.
4. Honeydew is an oversexed, rather shy dwarf with a penchant for TNT, while Xephos is the brave although regrettably irascible leader.
5. Elsewhere I have discussed the rather illusory nature of this relationship (MacCallum-Stewart, 2013).
6. I am indebted to Lewis Brindley, Simon Lane, Hannah Rutherford, and Mark Turpin of the Yogscast for their help in writing this paper.

References

Brindley, L., & Lane, S. (2010, December 7). *Minecraft*—Part 6: The mysterious tree [Video file]. *The Yogscast*. Retrieved from https://www.youtube.com/watch?v=AvrNUFoBl9U

Brindley, L., & Lane, S. (2011, February 10). *Minecraft*—"Shadow of Israphel" part 11: The crumbling ruin [Video file]. *The Yogscast*. Retrieved from http://www.youtube.com/watch?v=80GSvackaxk

Brown, N. (2011). Yogscast: Credit us for *Minecraft's* success. *Edge Online*. Retrieved from http://www.edge-online.com/news/yogscast-credit-us-minecrafts-success/

Dean, P. (2013). The best *Minecraft* projects ever: 30 incredible builds. *PCGamesN*. Retrieved from http://www.pcgamesn.com/minecraft/best-minecraft-builds-ever-30-incredible-projects

Duncan, S. (2011). *Minecraft*, beyond construction and survival. *Well Played*, *1*(1), 1–23. Retrieved from http://www.etc.cmu.edu/etcpress/content/volume-1-number-1

Gauntlett, D. (2011). *Making is connecting; The social meaning of creativity, from DIY and knitting to YouTube and Web 2.0*. Oxford: Polity Press.

Getomer, J., Okimoto, M., & Johnsmeyer, B. (2013). Gamers on YouTube. Evolving video consumption. *Google Think*. Retrieved from http://www.google.com/think/articles/youtube-marketing-to-gamers.html July 2013.

Hills, M. (2002). *Fan cultures*. London: Routledge.

Hills, M. (2006). Not just another powerless elite? When media fans become subcultural celebrities. In Holmes, S. & Redmond, S. (Eds.), *Framing Celebrity: New directions in celebrity culture* (pp. 101–118). London: Routledge.

Leavitt, A. (2011, August 9). *The hidden value of punching trees. Minecraft and the future of game culture.* Paper given at PAX 2011, Seattle, WA.

Levin, J. (2011). *The* Minecraft *teacher.* Retrieved from http://minecraftteacher.tumblr.com/

Lionhead Studios. (2010). *Fable III* [Xbox 360]. Microsoft Game Studios.

MacCallum-Stewart, E. (June 2013). Diggy holes and jaffa cakes: The rise of the elite fan producer in videogaming culture. *Journal of Gaming and Virtual Worlds, 5*(2), 67–85.

MacCallum-Stewart, E. (forthcoming 2014). *Players vs. games: Online narratives, virtual communities.* New York: Routledge.

MinecraftFTW. (2010, September 18). *Minecraft FIREE WTFFFFFFF!!!!!* [Video file]. Retrieved from http://www.youtube.com/watch?v=LnjSWPxJxNs

Mojang. (2011). *Minecraft* [PC game]. Stockholm, Sweden.

Persson, M. [notch]. (2011, November 21). Everyone else in the *Minecraft* community is all about respecting and caring. They're not. They're an isolated island of egos. [Twitter]. Retrieved from https://twitter.com/notch

Robertson, M. (2010, October 21). Five minutes of ... *Minecraft. Gamasutra.* Retrieved from http://www.gamasutra.com/view/feature/6179/five_minutes

Schott, G., & Yeatman, B. (2011). Participatory fan culture and *Half Life 2* machinima: A dialogue among ethnography, culture and space. In. Lowood, H, & Nitsche, M. (Eds.), *The Machinima Reader* (pp. 301–314). Massachusetts: MIT Press.

Sharp, L. (2012). Stealth learning: Unexpected learning opportunities through games. *Journal of Instructional Research, 1,* 42–48. Retrieved from https://cirt.gcu.edu/jir/documents/2012-v1/sharppdf

Sheffield, B. (2012, March 26). Getting EA ready for the future. *Gamasutra.* Retrieved from http://www.gamasutra.com/view/feature/167196/getting_ea_ready_for_the_future.php

Valve Corporation. (2011a). *Half-Life 2* [PC Game].

Valve Corporation. (2011b). *Portal 2* [PC Game].

Videogames
in the White Cube

MICHAEL ST. CLAIR

The essentially religious nature of the white cube is most forcefully
expressed by what it does to the humanness of anyone who enters
it and cooperates with its premises.
—O'Doherty, 1986, p. 10

Some decades after it became common for people to spend hours manipulating mass-produced arrangements of colored light, it has finally become
mainstream to actively display and market videogames as aesthetic objects.
Wielders of cultural capital ranging from Apple to the London Philharmonic
trumpet the beauty of videogames. In 2012, the MoMA—principally at the
direction of Paola Antonelli, senior curator of the MoMA's Department of
Architecture and Design—made one of the boldest and strangest maneuvers
in this direction. It "acquired" 14 videogames and put them on display in its
Applied Design exhibition. It used a spare, minimalist gallery design:
unadorned screens set into black walls; the bare minimum of control surfaces
for those games short enough that they can be played meaningfully in a gallery
setting at all, or explanatory videos for those that can't; and white informational cards discussing their respective game's provenance and peculiar virtues.
Since then, the MoMA has acquired 7 more games, including *Minecraft*
(Mojang, 2011)—though they are not yet on display.

Response from gamer and game design communities was overwhelmingly
positive: now, at last, videogames' long taxonomic twilight was over. No
less an authority than the MoMA had spoken. Videogames could now be
ensconced in the highest temples of art. I should be clear that Antonelli
(2012) has emphasized that she does not want to acquire videogames as merely
art:

> Are video games art? They sure are, but they are also design, and a design approach
> is what we chose for this new foray into this universe. The games are selected as
> outstanding examples of interaction design.... Our criteria, therefore, emphasize
> not only the visual quality and aesthetic experience of each game, but also the many

other aspects—from the elegance of the code to the design of the player's behavior—that pertain to interaction design.

The particular mode of display Antonelli chose, however, is passionately "arty." And, no matter how welcome this enthusiastically arty display is to gamers, it nevertheless performs a peculiar violence on videogames. Critic Gabriel Winslow-Yost (2013) wrote:

> as an exhibit it doesn't quite work. To make any sense at all, games need to be not just played but played seriously, with a sweaty, childish abandon totally unlike the cool passivity of an art viewer. Tucked into a corner of MOMA's sleek architecture and design gallery, the games seem bedraggled, and ... played only tentatively.

This highly traditional mode of gallery exhibition fundamentally performs a suppression of play. The ideology of the gallery space works against interactivity.

This is the ideology of the so-called "white cube," the anonymous and alienating mode of gallery exhibition developed in the late nineteenth century. The white cube is both highly traditional and distinctly modern. Brian O'Doherty (1986) characterized it as a "technology of flatness" (p. 22) that worked to pull paintings from their illusionistic premodern origins to their modern status as infinitely precious and infinitesimally deep objects. The MoMA chose to display videogames basically as paintings, as flat objects, as essentialized "art" in the most conservative modern conceptions. The delicious flatscreen displays of the new millennium here serve only to recapitulate the *fin de siecle* ideology of the white cube, its "essentially religious" and separating qualities. This is to say that they instantiate "videogames" as dimensionless objects that the viewer cannot enter, in contrast to the logic of videogames themselves. As Michael Nitsche writes in *Video Game Spaces*, "In contrast [to cinema], it is a defining characteristic of video game spaces that they allow this step into the represented space" (2008, p. 85). Even the notion of "acquisition" as applied to a videogame implies a similar absurdity: how can an evanescent and infinitely replicable piece of interactive software become a fixed, stable component of a collection?

Minecraft has, perhaps fortunately, not yet been displayed in this way. It seems to me that the epistemic violence of the white cube would be more appalling when applied to *Minecraft* than to virtually any other game. *SimCity* (Maxis, 1990), *EVE Online* (CCP Games, 2013), and *Dwarf Fortress* (Bay12 Games, 2006), for instance, cannot be treated, as *Pac-Man* (Namco, 1980) and *Passage* (Rohrer, 2007), basically as interesting arrangements of lines to be placed on walls. They require extensive disquisition. To "display" them in a gallery setting is merely to display a commentary about them. But they are merely incompatible with the gallery's logic of display, while *Minecraft* is directly opposed to it. *Minecraft* is about walking around and placing cubes. It is not about walking into a cube and being placed by it.

Videogames "sure are" art. They're design, too. But the question remains: what kind of art are they? Well, they're certainly not paintings. *Minecraft* perhaps least of all.

Minecraft *as Installation, Gallery, and Medium*

Minecraft is, rather, a logical progression of many anti-pictorial trends in modern art. It works as a radical gesture in sculpture, performance, and most specifically, *installation* art. It expands the borders of the gallery far beyond traditional museum sites (and even beyond location as such). It does not require special skill or virtuosity. Generally speaking, *Minecraft* continues a trend of increasingly open access to both the means and the ends of artistic production.

Of course, all videogames—at least those with 3D worlds—perform some of these functions, not to mention many nondigital games and toys. To use Claire Bishop's language, installation art both activates and decenters its spectating subjects (2005, p.11). Every videogame map is a kind of installation piece in this sense. Videogames demand participation; the specific visual stimuli they present vary depending on the character of that participation, and there is no specifically correct camera angle or position to view a videogame map from.

Minecraft experience does not simply involve navigating and viewing its procedurally-generated worlds, or the gorgeous *Minecraft* constructions of others. There are certainly enough published *Minecraft* worlds that you could simply treat *Minecraft* and its community as an art gallery. *Minecraft* wouldn't fit very well in a white cube, but it makes a perfectly good white cube of its own. Most *Minecraft* aficionados use it in this way at least occasionally. Sculptures, murals, architecture, and earthworks are all popular *Minecraft* marvels. Museums are beginning to recognize this: the Tate Modern is, at the time of this writing, considering *TateCraft*, a proposal by Adam Clarke to entirely recreate the Tate and its holdings in *Minecraft*.

But viewing such things is not the core of *Minecraft* play. Making them is. As early Mojang marketing copy put it: "*Minecraft* is a game about placing blocks to build anything you can imagine." Even watching *Minecraft* streams, possibly as popular an activity as actually playing *Minecraft*, generally involves viewing processes of active building. *Minecraft* is a set of tools and materials, a visual style, a method of creation.

This is to say that *Minecraft* is perhaps the first truly mass-market, democratic, ubiquitously available installation art medium. Of course, various sandbox building videogames existed long before *Minecraft*, as did many construction kits before them. And *Minecraft* is even partly translatable into such tangible components, as demonstrated by Cody McCabe and Jeffrey Kam's installation *Real World Minecraft*, formerly *Meatcraft*. But *Minecraft* surpassed all such videogames in their popularity, and *Minecraft* constructions are replicable and distributable in a way that LEGO and similar constructions are not. Furthermore, the vast field of imitations of *Minecraft* suggests that *Minecraft*-like software may even be a viable new *category* of medium.

Modernist Blocks

So, how does one trace *Minecraft's* genealogy in visual art? It seems sensible to consider that most fundamental and characteristic unit of *Minecraft* worlds: the block. *Minecraft* worlds are entirely made of blocks. Most are cubes, but some are not. All are cuboids with a 1x1 "meter" base, but some have heights other than 1 "meter": see "Solid Block" on the *Minecraft Wiki* for a table. Although high-resolution textures and shaders can disguise *Minecraft's* unapologetic blockiness, it is generally considered a salient component of its aesthetic and its widespread appeal.

The ostentatious use of blocks has a distinguished pedigree in modern art. The *cube*, of course, lent its name to *Cubism,* the most famous modernist rupture with traditional styles of visual representation. But is *Minecraft* an implementation of Cubist aesthetic ideas? No. Definitely not. Cubism was too much about the fragmentation and multiplication of perspectives in a single image. *Minecraft* does not incorporate this, not least because, like the vast majority of videogames with 3D worlds, it visually organizes itself around the viewpoint of a single virtual camera. Turning back to Nitsche:

> this virtual world is not the slave of the image. Players are free to explore and interact with it directly.... The necessary eye of the virtual camera makes these spaces cinematic and the interaction makes them accessible much like architectural structures. The player experiences game spaces in a combination of both continuous navigable space and cinematic space [2008, p. 85].

And as Rosalind Krauss (1998) noted, cameras overwrite Cubism: "Cubism was, after all, the painstaking and thoroughgoing dismantling of unified, perspectival space that the camera, with its particular optics, could not but reproduce again and again" (p. 114). The unary, cinematic viewpoint of the vast majority of 3D-world videogame cameras is deadly poison to Cubism's explosion of perspectives. *Minecraft* engages in perhaps the most anti–Cubist uses of cubes possible. Even as it refuses to open itself to the simultaneous apperception of all points of view that Cubism promised, it automatically generates classically organized, rationalized space that is broadly accessible to a wide variety of users.

This being said, *Minecraft* does share certain themes with Cubist sculpture and collage, and with related forms like Marcel Duchamp's readymades. Duchamp's readymades were prefabricated industrial objects typified by his *Fountain* pieces (urinals he signed and mounted in galleries). Duchamp's design for the 1938 International Surrealist Exhibition at the Gallerie des Beaux-arts in Paris is especially worth mentioning. Its centerpiece was a huge mass of coal sacks which obscured light and created a subterranean atmosphere. The piece is often cited as *1200 Sacks of Coal* and identified as an early piece of "installation" art, in the sense that it both utterly transformed a gallery and also created an affectively rich architectural space. Performing these functions through the three-dimensional tessellation of mass-produced, roughly identical, messy objects is fairly *Minecraft*.

Benjamin Buchloh observed that Duchamp's readymades exemplify a distinctly modern fusion between mass production or duplication and creativity:

> the fragmentation of representation and of the production process and the juxtaposition of heterogeneous materials ... emerge as the dominant phenomena of modernist sculpture ... in Cubism and Futurism the combination of mechanically produced anonymous objects and fragments with individually produced aesthetic signs became a quintessential production procedure, resulting ultimately, it would seem, in the final takeover of the aesthetic construct by the mechanically produced object in Duchamp's ready-mades [1983, p. 280].

This kind of fusion is also characteristic of *Minecraft*. These tendencies are not, of course, uniquely shared between *Minecraft* and Duchamp's readymades; this "final takeover" was the full beginning of an artistic tendency, not a conclusion. These tendencies have remained persistent themes in installation and sculpture continuing to today.

These "anonymous objects" have often in fact been blocks. Duchamp's body of work contains many blocks in the form of boxes, although often the box is a vehicle or container for artistic work, as in his final work *Étant donnés,* in which peepholes in a freestanding door block afford visual access to an interior scene. When the Duchamp box does not work in this way, it generally still avoids the simplicity of the block *qua* block and instead uses rectangularity as an organizing principle—as in *Green Box,* an artist's multiple packaged and shipped in a box but which is not actually made of boxes.

Green Box furthermore begins a modern tradition of using regular blocks as representatives of the spectacle of ostentatious regularity in general. Duchamp, in an interview, noted:

> I wanted to reproduce them [the *Green Boxes*] as accurately as possible. So I had all of these thoughts lithographed in the same ink, which had been used for the

originals. To find paper that was exactly the same, I had to ransack the most unlikely nooks and crannies of Paris. Then we cut out three hundred copies of each lithograph with the help of zinc patterns that I had cut out on the outlines of the original papers [cited in Cros 2006, p. 122].

Some of the best-known descendants of this tradition are that family of artworks that present blocks that are visually striking by virtue of their excessive blockiness. Early examples of this type included Larry Bell's glass and metal cubes; Robert Morris's column and cube pieces, including his *Untitled (mirrored cubes)* and his 1960 *Column;* and Andy Warhol's *Brillo Boxes.* Despite their apparent similarities with *Minecraft*, these might be even less *Minecraft* than *1200 Sacks.* Let me explain why.

Bell began making cubes in the 1960s and continues today. His cubes have continuously remained on the cutting edge of material science, using increasingly complex polymers and metal deposition techniques to make them more ostentatiously cubic. These are attempts at a more perfect cube, or cube-shaped intervention in perception. Like many of the efforts of the '60s and '70s West Coast sculptors and installation artists associated with the "Light and Space" movement, Bell's cubes evoke a single ideal form. It is "ideal" in the sense that it is precise, weightless, singular, and stunningly unreal. This mode of idealization prefigures a certain type of digital aesthetic in the physical world. It does not, however, prefigure *Minecraft*'s aesthetic, which relies on roughness, low-performance graphics, and multiplicity.

Morris's cubes tend to violently obtrude into and reorder perception. The mirrored cubes of *Untitled* push back against the viewer's visual field, reflectively distorting their surroundings according to the viewer's position. *Column* was a "dance piece" for a single, six-foot-tall featureless gray block: it appeared on stage, paused for several minutes, and then suddenly fell over. Rosalind Krauss comments that this motion meant that the column "had to be reinterpreted as a body inhabited by something like its own volitional center, or 'mind'" (2013, p. 84). Morris's blocks are agents; they are profoundly non-instrumental and resist simple objectification. They are in this way utterly unlike the blocks of *Minecraft.*

In Warhol's *Brillo Boxes*, the *citationality* of the blocks is central to the aesthetic function of the work. These blocks are representational, not simply functional materials. Despite having a varied, bold, and simplistic visual appeal, along with the appearance of mass production and potentially infinite replicability, they do not work in the same way as *Minecraft* blocks.

It is also worth mentioning that despite the visual anonymity of all of the blocks I have just mentioned, they are owned, named, and presented under strictly controlled conditions. They are not only Brillo boxes, they are Warhol's *Brillo Boxes*; not just a gray block, but Morris's *Column.* No one is allowed to walk into Tate Liverpool and rearrange Morris's mirrored cubes into a more personally pleasing form. These works do not involve the same kind of participatory building as *Minecraft;* it remains crucially important that only the artist, or their legions of unmentioned but authorized assistants, have created and placed the blocks. These are profoundly undemocratic works.

Minecraft *and* Fluids

Not all block art from the 1960s had this character. Allan Kaprow's 1967 *Fluids,* like Morris's *Column,* presents another point of contact between visual art and live performance via blocks, but of a very different character. *Fluids* involved a highly coordinated but participatory use of blocks. *Fluids* was profoundly more *Minecraft* than *Column.* I will explain why.

Here is the "score" for *Fluids* that Kaprow printed on flyers:

DURING THREE DAYS, ABOUT TWENTY
RECTANGULAR ENCLOSURES OF ICE
BLOCKS (MEASURING ABOUT 30
FEET LONG, 10 WIDE AND 8
HIGH) ARE BUILT THROUGHOUT
THE CITY. THEIR WALLS ARE
UNBROKEN. THEY ARE LEFT TO MELT [in Hermann, p. 189].

Here is another way to describe *Fluids:* people, working according to a firm but flexible framework of rules, traversed a vast and challenging environment. Their goal was to make structures out of blocks. This mission had no practical purpose. These structures didn't *do* anything. They were just for fun. And they didn't last for long, because shortly after their handlers ceased to attend to them, they disappeared forever.

My point is obvious. This abstract, generalized description of *Fluids* could also describe *Minecraft.* They are not direct cognates, of course. The blocks were made of ice, not data and light; the structures were interventions in Los Angeles County, not in digital space; the rules were based on written instructions and physical law, not the emergent effects of computer code. Nevertheless, this connection is worth following further.

One immediate observation is that, at least for a participatory art event like *Fluids,* it's not much of a stretch to read the "game as art" equation I began this essay with backwards and describe "art as game." How so? *Fluids* had an ostentatiously durational, embodied, and laborious character. Kaprow's participants built the ice enclosures in public; the enclosures melted over time (even as the participants were building them), and no attempts were made to prevent them from melting.

This is all partly to say that although *Fluids* generated short-lived installation art, it was also a species or method of performance. Specifically, it was a member of that short-lived genre of performance known as the Happening. Happenings have traditionally been analyzed by critics as modes of aesthetic performance related to theater and dance, which is perfectly sensible, especially for those Happenings that were meticulously scripted and took place in gallery or theater-like environments, and especially if one is examining Happenings as precursors to or early examples of what we now refer to as "performance art."

But there is no particular reason not to analyze them as game or play forms instead. The experimental theater director and performance scholar Richard Schechner distinguished Happenings from theater proper by noting that Happenings and related activities are "formally ... very close to play" (p. 16). Like play, Schechner notes, Happenings only sometimes have a symbolic reality, can be grouped or solitary, have a loose special relationship to time, tend to rely on an inner, private logic and set of rules rather than received scripts or rulesets, and do not have to be performed in a special place, which this is not to say that they are not site-specific, but rather that there is not a special category of buildings in which most Happenings and play are traditionally performed. Here Schechner means play as distinct from games and sports. It is important to note, however, that Schechner was not thinking of contemporary game design practices, and certainly not of videogames. He was thinking of traditional games and sports, like chess and soccer, that rely on rules that have a long body of tradition and are received by entities perceived as radically prior to and generally also hierarchically superior to their players.

Kaprow, however, made gestures towards the possibilities of the expanded field of game design we enjoy today, thinking of the flexibility that ludic rules structures could afford to Happenings. In his 1966 *Assemblage, Environments, and Happenings*, he pointed to the possibility of using rules structures to score Happenings:

> In the near future, plans may be developed which take their cue from games and sports, where the regulations provide for a variety of moves that make the outcome always uncertain. A score might be written, so general in its instructions that it could be applied to basic types of terrain such as oceans, woods ... and to basic kinds of performers such as teenagers, old people ... and so on, including insects and the weather. This could be printed and mail-ordered for use by anyone who wanted it [pp. 194–195].

And if, by 1967, *Fluids* was not quite here, it was certainly working in this direction. The complex but open act of enclosure-building with ice gave rise to a host of unexpected play potentialities. It's still more proper, I think, to call it "play" rather than game.

Most engagement with *Minecraft* is also considerably more like play than like game in the narrower senses of these words. In fact, under many strict definitions of *game*, *Minecraft*, at least in Creative Mode, and perhaps even in Survival Mode prior to the addition of The End in B1.9pre4, is not a game at all. Salen and Zimmerman's influential definition in *Rules of Play*, for instance, clearly excludes Creative Mode: "a game is a system in which players engage in an artificial conflict, defined by rules, that results in a quantifiable outcome" (2003, p. 81). Creative Mode fails to produce a disequilibrial outcome. It even fails to bound itself firmly enough in time and space that it can be said to produce, in and of itself, a particular outcome of any kind. Jeff Kelley, referencing Walter de Maria, identifies *Fluids* as the first of Kaprow's "meaningless work" pieces (2004, p. 120). It is not just a piece about labor, it is a piece that is primarily composed of nonproductive labor that refuses to produce a meaningful outcome or useful objects. "Meaningless work" could equally be a description of the play form that is building in *Minecraft*.

More generally, as Celia Pearce has emphasized, there are deep continuities between contemporary videogames and all the games and playful art of the post–World War II avant garde. These include not just scores of Kaprow's kind but also what Pearce has identified as mods, notably by artists associated with Fluxus, such as Yoko Ono's 1971 *White Chess Set,* an "elegantly placed anti-war statement" from the "modding category of unplayable games"; or George Maciunas's 1966–1973 prepared *Ping Pong Rackets* which "added awkward, bizarre, almost slapstick obstacles into the game" (28). The continuities Pearce identifies are based not only on the activation and decentering of the viewer common to installation and modern sculpture generally, but also on the dislocation of the artist's agency. This dislocation preempts the undemocratic qualities I noted in works by Warhol, Morris, and Bell. As Pearce writes, "In creating game art, the artist is making a choice to invite the viewer in as a co-creator of the work. Although it can be said that all art does this, game art does it in a very explicit way. It questions the relationship of art and artist to the viewer/spectator" (2010, p.16).

Minecraft—and for that matter *Fluids*—are of course not merely instructional pieces like, say, Fluxus artist Alison Knowles' 1962 *Proposition*: "Make a salad" (Cited in Hendricks 2008, p. 88). Nor are they simply mods, though they can of course be modded: *Minecraft* of course has countless mods, and *Fluids* has been "modded" in recreations by arts organizations twice in the past decade: in 2005 at Arts Unlimited Basel and in 2008 at the Tate Modern (bizarrely, in a fenced-off enclosure).

Making and Perceiving in Minecraft

Minecraft and *Fluids* are building kits. *Minecraft* and *Fluids* are, specifically, *architectural* building kits. They focus on the labor of creating spaces, affording players the capacity to make meaningful shifts in perspective through navigating space. Unlike most architectural labor, this is *meaningless* work; it creates space with form but without extrinsic function.

It's worth mentioning here that both *Fluids* and *Minecraft* use rough blocks. By this I mean that their blocks are explicitly marked as distinct from the most perfect block technology could create. *Fluids* creates flaws in its blocks through irregular exigencies of delivery, stacking, salting and melting; *Minecraft* creates flaws in its blocks through its self-consciously retro, 16x16 default textures. In this way they are aesthetically distinct from the aesthetic of perfection / detail / regularity that characterizes the classically modernist uses of the block described earlier. They are also distinct, for that matter, visual uses of blocks in videogames, like the lovingly detailed, faceted, specular Weighted Companion Cube from the *Portal* (Valve, 2007) series. And, significantly, they are also distinct visual uses of clean blocks in digital interface design generally, including social media that works as online gallery space.

But *Minecraft* and *Fluids* also do not partake of that thread of modern art that begins with Cubist collage and bricolage. *Minecraft* and *Fluids*, even when nonsensical and useless, are above all *coherent*, self-similar, made of their own regularly-shaped materials and not a conglomeration of irregular found externals.

Rough-but-regular cubes are easy to build with for the specific reason that they tessellate space easily while covering visual imperfections. Situations and maps in *Minecraft* can certainly have cognitively challenging aspects, but the act of building is itself not the challenge: *Minecraft* is not a digital version of a 3D jigsaw puzzle. This maps roughly to the classic distinction in human factors analysis between task complexity and interface complexity (Kirwan, 1994), where "task complexity" refers to the cognitive difficulty of the problems in a given scenario, and "interface complexity" refers to the operational difficulty of addressing those problems via the provided control surfaces and graphical displays.

"Interface," of course, here generally refers to menus, heads-up displays, analog meters, and other such output devices. But in the context of gaming, it could be applied a layer deeper. "Interface" could name all the apparatus of a video game that exists perceptually prior to significant action, the boring controls that give access to the richer complexity of the world. Walking, moving the camera, and switching equipped items are common examples in 3D games. Some videogames intentionally have extremely fiddly and intransigent controls, and as such have little content at this level of action-interface. Examples include most car racing games, or, for a very extreme instance, *Octodad* (DePaul University Students, 2010) which pushes even the simplest acts of walking past this level of action-interface. Under this definition of "interface," *Minecraft* makes stacking cubes a basic, user-friendly component of its interface.

Large amounts of interface complexity of course do not prevent people from building extremely complex environments, otherwise, architects could not use AutoCAD. But this interface complexity is precisely why *Minecraft* is not AutoCAD and why AutoCAD is not *Minecraft*. *Minecraft* relies on making a world in which simple assumptions make sense.

This rough, easy-to-use, versatile, retro aesthetic and implementation connects *Minecraft* to the so-called "maker" culture. Maker-associated outlets and periodicals, from Etsy to *MAKE* and *Boing Boing* commonly feature interesting *Minecraft* levels, kitschy craft items, and assorted paraphernalia. *Minecraft* levels so featured are almost always aesthetically rather than ludically interesting: impressive visual constructs, not fun things to play in.

This is because construction in *Minecraft* is basically aesthetic rather than utilitarian. This is not to say that *Minecraft* cannot model utilitarian architecture. To argue this would be patently absurd. Early *Minecraft* construction efforts tended to focus on notionally functional construction, building at the bare limit of architecture. This probably remains true for the vast majority of *Minecraft* players now—but, of course, most *Minecraft* players are now playing in survival mode. You need to build a shelter if you are worried about night monsters.

But, even in Creative Mode, does *Minecraft* evoke a primal impulse towards utilitarian architecture? I suggest that it's exactly the opposite. Going back to some of the very first public uses of *Minecraft*, user behaviors in the 2009 TIGSource thread in which Notch released the original alpha of *Minecraft* revealed quick impulses towards constructing forms reminiscent of functional architecture that users rapidly framed and recognized as *aesthetic*.

User Muku (possibly the first person to publicly report building a structure in *Minecraft*), wrote "This is way too much fun... Built a bridge." User Increpare (Stephen Lavelle, a famous indie developer in his own right) responded:

> I can't remember if this was possible in infiniminer (probably due to the extended range in your version), but yeah, the 'bridges' thing is great. I actually started experiencing mild vertigo as I was building a really tall/narrow tower (I had to edge out over each ledge to attach a new block).

The first function of *Minecraft* construction is to afford a change in motion and perception, and it does so by itself affording a wide range of motion and perception—a first-person game with just enough of the extended range of a top-down god game to grant players perception-warping powers of construction. This is installation art at its essence: transforming one's own (and potentially others') perceptions of a space by building within it, the creation of a radically subjective but not purely interior world.

Within days, people were creating representational sculptures, albeit of dubious aesthetic value, that explored the limits of the *Minecraft* model of space; Türbo Bröther wrote: "The cock I made was just massive, much larger and more bulbous than the first one I made. Where the bottom of the level cuts off to the maximum height you can build to." Citational earthworks, traditionally characteristic of the interface between installation, architecture, and sculpture, like Robert Smithson's *Spiral Jetty,* appeared soon after, when MisterX posted a massive earthwork depicting the iconic *Dwarf Fortress* dwarf-with-pick. Shortly after, MisterX, commenting on another user's village, wrote: [That] shows what I really love about games like Minecraft: The ability to create little really atmospheric worlds out of nothing. While the houses themselves aren't as spectacular as some other, more complex buildings, the whole village looks just so sweet ... I think if you weren't able to walk around in those worlds, or couldn't even build them from that perspective, the whole game would lose a lot of its charm. MisterX here perfectly summarizes the way that *Minecraft* democratizes and distributes the work of installation art. Anyone can create sites "out of nothing." These sites have specificity. They are "atmospheric worlds."

Minecraft *as Non-Art*

The marketing promise is true. *Minecraft* does let you build anything you can imagine—and also walk around in it. And if you share it, anyone else can walk around in it too. *Minecraft* is a highly advanced and maximally accessible form of creative exchange. Allan Kaprow becomes relevant here again, particularly via his notions of "non-art" and the "un-artist" as expressed in his 1971 essay "The Education of the Un-Artist, Part I." Here, Kaprow identified an "art-not-art" dialectic in which artists like George Brecht, Max Neuhaus and Wolf Vostell worked outside of art establishments, "in their heads or in the daily or natural domain," while still informing art institutions of their activities. Of course, most of these artists eventually saw "their work absorbed into the cultural institutions against which they initially measured their liberation" (p. 98–99). *Fluids* began to melt itself out of this dialectic, absorbed only into the ground—though the Tate still managed to fence it in by 2005.

But *Minecraft* is a more advanced kind of block-based non-art, of precisely the kind predicted by Kaprow: "It can be pretty well predicted that the various forms of mixed media or assemblage arts will increase, both in the highbrow sense and in mass-audience applications such as light shows ... toys, and political campaigns. And these may be the means by which all the arts are phased out" (p. 104). Crucially, Kaprow identified non-art as not only a fad or art-world phenomenon but as a cultural and technical process centered on sandboxy software systems:

Agencies for the spread of information via the mass media and for the instigation of social activities will become the new channels of insight and communication, not substituting for the classic "art experience" ... but offering former artists compelling ways of participating in structured processes that can reveal new values, including the value of fun... Systems technology involving the interfacing of personal and group experiences ... will dominate the trend. Software, in other words. But it will be a systems approach that favors an openness towards outcome, in contrast to the literal and goal-oriented uses now employed by most systems specialists... Playfulness and the playful use of technology suggest a positive interest in acts of continuous discovery [p. 106].

Minecraft radically fulfills this promise. Notch's block art offers everyone the capacity to build locations, to create site-specificity fundamentally outside of institutionally-controlled galleries, site-specificity without sites. It allows "art," or in other words creative play, to become an integrated component of life: with the popularity of *Minecraft* on mobile devices, this is not just site-specificity for everyone, but site-specificity everywhere.

Minecraft is one conclusion of modern sculpture, installation, and non-art. *Minecraft* is not struggling to escape the gallery; the gallery is struggling to incorporate or even enter *Minecraft*. Indeed, *Minecraft* and its sandbox relatives are a new potential set of galleries. But they're not white cubes either; they're more open than other, more visually neutral but much more tightly ideologically controlled digital spaces. Blockiness resists the faux transparency and value-neutrality of YouTube, Facebook, and of social media platforms generally. A maximally flexible but instantly recognizable aesthetic is, in and of itself, a form of digital site-specificity. I don't want to be monotonically utopian here. Like every other popular medium, *Minecraft* is also a sensory weapon working to impose a new hegemony on perception. It will do something to the "humanness of anyone who enters it and cooperates with its premises" (O'Doherty, 1986, p. 10). But its hegemony will at least be gentler than many others, for the nontrivial reason that it is structured by an ethic of fun.

References

Antonelli, P. (2012, November 29). Video games: 14 in the collection, for starters [Blog]. *Inside/Out*. Retrieved from http://www.moma.org/explore/inside_out/2012/11/29/video-games-14-in-the-collection-for-starters/

Bay12 Games. (2006). *Dwarf Fortress* (Unspecified version number in MoMA collection) [Videogame].

Bishop, C. (2005). *Installation art*. New York: Routledge.

Buchloh, B. (1983). Michael Asher and the conclusion of modernist sculpture. *Art Institute of Chicago Museum Studies, 10*, 276–295. Retrieved from www.jstor.org/stable/4104341

CCP Games. (2003). *EVE Online* (Unspecified version number in MoMA collection) [Videogame].

Cros, C. (2006). *Marcel Duchamp.* London: Reaktion Books.

DePaul University Students. (2010). *Octodad* [PC game].

Duchamp, M. (1917). *Fountain* [Readymade (urinal)].

Duchamp, M. (1934). *Green box* [Artist's multiple].

Duchamp, M. (1938). *1200 sacks of coal* [Gallery installation].

Duchamp, M. (1969). *Étant donnés* [Mixed-media box].

Hendricks, J. (Ed.). (2008). *Fluxus scores and instructions: The transformative years.*

Hermann, E., Perchuk, A., & Rosenthal, S. (2008). *Allan Kaprow: Art as life.* Los Angeles: Getty Publications.

Jturtles. (2013). *Minecraft tribute to Andy Warhol* [Image / *Minecraft* level]. Retrieved from http://imgur.com/hnj4K

Kaprow, A. (1966). *Assemblage, environments, and happenings.* New York: Harry N. Abrams.

Kaprow, A. (1967). *Fluids* [Happening].

Kaprow, A. (1971). The education of the un-artist: Part I. In J. Kelley & A. Kaprow (Eds.), *Essays on the blurring of art and life* (1993). Los Angeles: University of California Press.

Kelley, J. (2004). *Childsplay: The art of Allan Kaprow.* Berkeley: University of California Press.

Kirwan, B. (1994). *A guide to practical human reliability assessment.* Bristol, PA: Taylor and Francis.

Knowles, A. (1966). *Proposition* [Instructional art piece].

Krauss, R. (1998). *The Picasso papers.* New York: Farar, Straus & Giroux.

Krauss, R. (2013). The mind/body problem: Robert Morris in series. In J. Bryan-Wilson (Ed.), *Robert Morris.* Cambridge, MA: MIT Press.

Maciunas, G. (1966–1973). *Ping pong rackets* [Series artwork: Modified ping pong rackets]

Maxis. (1990). *SimCity.* (Unspecified version number in MoMA collection) [Videogame].

McCabe, C., & Kam, J. (2011). *Real-world Minecraft* (Also cited as *Meatcraft*) [Installation].

Mojang. (2011). *Minecraft* [PC game]. Stockholm, Sweden: Mojang.

Mojang. (2009). *Minecraft (Alpha)* [Videogame]. Stockholm, Sweden. Mojang.

Morris, R. (1960). *Column* [Sculpture / dance].

Morris, R. (1965). *Untitled* [Installation of mirrored cubes].

Namco. (1980). *Pac-Man* (Unspecified version from MoMA collection) [Videogame].

Nitsche, M. (2008). *Video game spaces.* Cambridge, MA: MIT Press.

O'Doherty, B. (1986). *Inside the white cube: The ideology of the gallery space.* Los Angeles: Lapis Press.

Ono, Y. (1966). *White chess set* [Modded chess set].

Pearce, C. (2010). Games as art: The aesthetics of play. In C. Touchon (Ed.), *Fluxhibition #4.* Retrieved from http://lmc.gatech.edu/~cpearce3/TenureReview/7-Pearce_FluxhibitionCatalog.pdf

Persson, M. [notch]. (2009). *Minecraft (alpha)* [Forum thread]. Retrieved from http://forums.tigsource.com/index.php?topic=6273.0

Rohrer, J. (2007). *Passage* (Unspecified version from MoMA collection) [Videogame].

Salen, K., & Zimmerman, E. (2003). *Rules of play: Game design fundamentals.* Cambridge. MA: MIT Press.

Schechner, R. (2003). *Performance theory.* New York: Routledge.

Smithson, R. (1970). *Spiral jetty* [Earthwork].

"Solid Block." (Jan 4, 2014). *Minecraft wiki.* Retrieved from http://minecraft.gamepedia.com/Solid_block

Valve Corporation. (2007). *Portal* [PC game].

Warhol, A. (1964). *Brillo boxes* [Installation].

Winslow-Yost, G. (2013, April 11). *SimCity*'s evil twin. *The New Yorker Culture Desk.* Retrieved from http://www.newyorker.com/online/blogs/culture/2013/04/simcitys-evil-twin.html

Fine Arts, Culture and Creativity in *Minecraft*

JAMES MORGAN *and* R. YAGIZ MUNGAN

In *Language of New Media*, Lev Manovich describes five principles of new media. He uses these principles to explain how new media is different from imitation of older media forms in cumulative style. The fifth principle, transcoding, dictates that "the logic of a computer can be expected to have a significant influence on the traditional cultural logic of media" (Manovich, n.d., pp. 63–64). The influence between the digital and the physical works both ways. Actions in *Minecraft* should not be observed and committed as recreations of the physical world but instead recognized as emanating from the code that is *Minecraft* (Mojang, 2011). The act of translating from physical to virtual is not a derivative; instead, it is the process that defines the meaning. Thus transcoding is the precursor to the new meanings, ideas, and aesthetics.

This chapter investigates select projects created in Orwell, a private *Minecraft* server inhabited by artists and students. These projects included student sculptural work, an international collaborative art biennial, and a live performance series presented in the U.S. and Europe. In studying these examples we identify a set of unique attributes that make *Minecraft* different from other virtual platforms. Through openness and gameplay, *Minecraft* as a system initiates a fractal, recursive state, where transcoding and translation makes new meanings and aesthetics possible.

Creativity and Society

> A creative man is motivated by the desire to achieve, not by the desire to beat others.
>
> —Ayn Rand

Built upon stacking and crafting, *Minecraft* provides limitless, open-ended, non-linear play as a sandbox game.[1] Gameplay in survival mode[2] is initiated based on the expectation that the avatar will have to respond to hardships in the environment in order to survive. Thus, creating a dwelling space represents a significant issue but also directly leads to creation of secondary needs (Huitt, 2007). These needs are satisfied through exploring and finding new materials, crafting new items, building new places and exploration of the virtual world. Exploration not only is necessary for continued survival but it also enables the acquisition of resources, which makes new designs possible. Although *Minecraft* includes an endgame scenario (ender dragon), play neither ceases nor culminates there. Instead, the dragon presents a focus for narrative and a goal for survival play, a narrative end.

Stacking blocks and crafting actions are innate skills, aided by the automatic alignment of blocks. There is little sense of physics although players, water and lava fall, most blocks do not. Constructions are untethered and stationary. Block stacking in *Minecraft* is thus a natural, native and necessary process. It is the most visible creative aspect and is a core mechanic along with crafting. Objects, which are placed, have a relative scale to the player and the voxel placement only takes on significant resolution at large scale. The inflexibility of resolution is more of an acceptable challenge than an obstacle and fits within the concept of character controls and units in a 3D design tool. This structured constraint is liberating to the artists of *Minecraft*. The familiar "natural" beginning space creates an initial context for the player's builds and the survival environment establishes both tension and necessity

The basic act of building is satisfying and fulfilling as it is possible to realize large ideas and experience them in 3D when they are finished. Moreover, it is also easy to share via screenshots, video walkthrough, and live feeds. *Minecraft* benefits from the integrated online communities such as reddit,[3] where the community not only discusses the *Minecraft* of-game but also shares and inspires builders in addition to recruiting for servers. It is key to realize that the environment is compelling; the voxel would permit many interpretations, various narratives, and possibilities within the space such as spatial and environmental storytelling. Many of these can be created by the player in a straightforward manner and others might need more engineered or collaborated approaches. Data can be inserted and extracted through editors and other tools, which is to say that *Minecraft* becomes a toolset built upon a virtual environment with an embedded game. *Minecraft* creates relatively small file sizes, which makes it easier to share. This shareability opens the work to critique, which is part of iterative design and the art production process.

In *Minecraft*, the society is made up of avatars connecting from different parts of the physical world, individuals who are disconnected from their physical form and location. They share a common goal, trying to survive while exploring and shaping the procedurally generated world. This sandbox model changes the dynamics by making everybody a creator and an owner of that creation, at the same time giving all the avatars the same basic abilities. These dynamics encourage collaboration and a community that is productive and supportive. Players become connected through a series of shared experiences, mining, exploring, searching for rare minerals, building, defending one's castle.

Minecraft characters do not improve their skillsets, but the player improves theirs relying more on their imagination and building larger more challenging objects. Even though crafted items can alter the productivity of an avatar, at its core each avatar has essentially the same powers and abilities. This helps in crafting and creating, the main mechanic of *Minecraft*, in two ways: Players do not need to invest time to improve their characters and instead can start creating and block stacking. The constant skill set allows different players of varying experience to collaborate. Different materials and recipes play an important role in providing expression and variety. Because there are no explanations of recipes included with *Minecraft*, the player is expected to explore and research these. In this respect, *Minecraft* pushes players out to the networked community. In most cases, this knowledge is transferred from avatar to avatar on the servers.

Naturally, sharing recipes is not the only reason for communication; cities and the function of large social spaces are also a category of collaborative building. These tend to take on an emergent property as their use is discovered during play. Additionally, these larger-scaled constructions have the ability to extend beyond the confines of *Minecraft*. They can be imported from other pieces of software but are often executed on large-scale creative servers. These builds are complex coordinated machinations that require engineering and forethought. A good example of this is the themed servers that recreate sites from J. R.R. Tolkien's Lord of the Rings trilogy. The cities that we evolved in Orwell are no less detailed, but lack the initial plan and had a tendency to grow organically with use.

The collaborative and open social structure of *Minecraft* also brings the question of ownership. As a platform and a virtual world, *Minecraft* moves the role of governance and censorship from traditional power structures. This power is placed into the hands of the residents and the server administrator who has choice over where and how the server runs. The server of a *Minecraft* world can be operated by any individual, group or organization. Any public *Minecraft* server can be visited by other *Minecraft* players. Governmental sovereignty is achieved when all of the rules for self-governance are contained within the hosting environment requiring no additional support. This in effect makes the world its own record of its history, law, and culture.

In short, the low-pressure sandbox dynamics coupled with the initial high-pressure situations requires the users to create and encourages users to collaborate. The ease of creation helps the process, which results in objects that satisfy the creator through experiencing them in 3D or sharing them with people in different ways of forms. Minecraft presents a fulfilling cycle of creation that starts with block stacking, crafting and exploration and ends with virtual self-determination and self-governance.

Mining and Data

> It is the function of art to renew our perception. What we are familiar with we cease to see. The writer shakes up the familiar scene, and, as if by magic, we see a new meaning in it.
> —Anais Nin

Data creation and visualization is an integral part of *Minecraft* as a system. Each *Minecraft* world is generated from a seed value through algorithms. Later this data is represented as the 3D dimensional *Minecraft* worlds through infamous *Minecraft* blocks (voxels). However, the generation of data does not stop here. A second wave of data creation happens with the human factor: The environment inspires the players to go in, explore, and shape the world thus changing the bits that form the experienced environment. Modifications allow a server to track (undo and redo) the placement or destruction of every block, including the location, orientation, and communication of every avatar on a server, and heat maps of activity. While this certainly brings up issues of surveillance and privacy, data from the actions of the players can yield information about human behavior as well as become the source for new objects through visualization and sonification. There is a fantastic level of ad hoc culture that can be captured in this environment. Imagine visually mapping a community build or every action that a class takes on a server.

On our server, player data is primarily used for rule enforcement. When something is vandalized or when someone builds in a restricted area, the admins are easily able to find out who placed/destroyed the blocks in question. It is interesting that this data does not equate to direct identification of a culprit. In our most recent case, the perpetrator had given his account credentials to a less than reputable friend. This does not prevent punishment / banning of the offenders, but does create complications.

The data does not only stay in *Minecraft:* notably, the data for objects created in *Minecraft* can be exported to the real world using 3D printing and other methods. The data exported to the physical, is based on the volumetric pixel or voxel,[4] and can be located in the single player saves (hidden away in the players library) or in the region[5] files of the server. Depending on the data source and the size of the object to be extracted whole regions from the target world can be moved or identified. Whereas it is possible to use a bukkit[6] mod on a bukkit server to edit and copy portions of the world, we

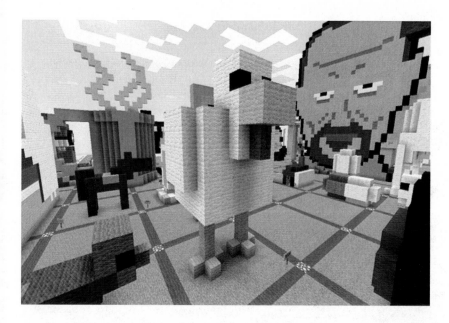

Figure 1. El Pollo Loco, wool, 2013, by Leonel Medrano (Minecraft ®/TM & © 2009–2013 Mojang / Notch).

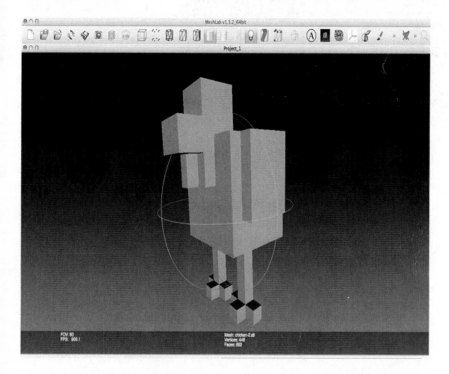

Figure 2. El Pollo Loco (imported into meshlab, 2013, by Leonel Medrano).

have found it easier to just give players access to the target region containing the data.

We use the software Mineways[7] to extract and do the initial translation from voxels to a more standard 3D file format. Extracting data from the voxel

environment is a big deal, and currently Mineways is the most common way to do this. We use another program, Meshlab,[8] to do voxel cleanup and to translate the file into a more common format. Using Mineways and Meshlab it is easy to setup files for printing on 3D printers or for use with Pepakura,[9] a program for printing foldable creations on paper. Neither process is easy. Translation to 3D print requires an awareness of materials and nuances of the design. For example, building excessive undercuts can result in structural material being created as scaffolding, which can be difficult to remove. The primary issue with paper crafting is related to the number of voxels and how they are used. If the artist takes into account that the object is paper, she can make construction an order of magnitude easier by avoiding too many difficult structures (recessed areas) and extending lines to make folding and cutting easier.

Figure 3. **El Pollo Real (3D Print, 2013, by Leonel Medrano).**

With regards to construction of an installation, the scale of *Minecraft* is epic in the real world. The one-meter voxels would create huge sculptures and in a large enough space may work, but for most implementations, this is impractical. Material considerations also have to be taken into account. Does the structure need internal support? How will people engage the space? What are the traffic patterns? In this case, *Minecraft* becomes a plan, a walk thru, and a starting point.

Valley to Valley

Valley to Valley, which combines the creative, social and data aspects of *Minecraft*, took place in Orwell. Valley to Valley (V2V) was an art project commissioned to connect two cities and two biennials[10] held at the same time through an artist residency. The Silicon Valley, which encompasses San Jose (a place) and the Zero1 Biennial (an event), was built in the mid–20th century. The Titanium Valley, near the Russian city of Yekaterinburg (again a place), hosts the Ural Industrial Biennial of Contemporary Art (and the associated event). At the time of the project, the Titanium Valley had not broken ground. The goal was to find an intersection and build connected projects for both biennials.

The project was built on the foundations of previous work. Through virtual world projects Ars Virtua[11] and Third Faction,[12] we had a history of working collaboratively online. At the outset of this project we recruited groups including artists, historians, scientists and project managers in the U.S. and Russia. The Yekaterinburg team was recruited from the Ural Federal University and was organized by the Ural branch of the NCCA.[13] The Silicon Valley team was made up of members of previous performances and students of SJSU. James Morgan[14] was the only member to visit both teams introducing concepts, software and hardware, and recruiting participants. Of the 25 people who participated, we covered 13 time zones and had varying degrees of comfort in spoken English. We met frequently to make sure that both teams were working in a complementary fashion and to share designs.

Minecraft became the key to the project's success. Operating on our own server, we took time to get to know the environment as players. We built cities, explored the landscape, survived, and began to work as a community. *Minecraft* gave us a common experience and a point of interaction. We talked about events, struggled together to keep our cities safe, and shared architecture and build secrets with each other. We learned a common vocabulary as players in the same world.

Our first milestone was to share our process with a Russian audience as part of the Innoprom showcase. The Russian team built out a tradeshow booth with media and technical support from the American team. To work out design aspects, an interactive model of the showcase was built in *Minecraft*. The final presentation of the space was a mash up of the white cube gallery and the grass of *Minecraft*, where videos, graphics, and 3D renders from the environment were displayed.

During the next phase, we prototyped iconic objects and transformed them into *Minecraft*'s blocky style with the goal of eventually creating installations as commissioned by the two arts organizations. The teams met together in *Minecraft* every other week to align our projects and to critique what had

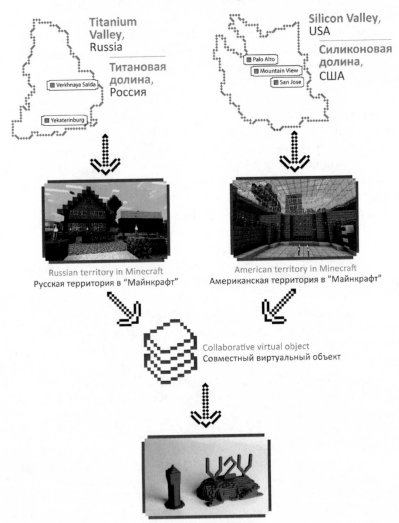

Figure 4. **Innoprom Poster detailing overview of V2V (Infographics by Vera Fainshtein and Ars Virtua).**

been built. The Silicon Valley team looked back at the history of the Silicon Valley. We marveled at how similar a board covered with transistors was to the orchards that used to cover the valley, even lines and uniform rows. Thomas Asmuth drew up the plan for the work, which was primarily built out by Jenene Castle, and it was modeled to scale in *Minecraft* based on the size of the exhibition space. We knew we wanted the transistors to tower over the visitors. We also knew we could provide on-site access at the biennial to the *Minecraft* build and that viewers would be able to engage both spaces.

The Titanium Valley team camped, out for three days in the region and visited the local city with the titanium plant to understand the regional concerns about corruption and the impact on the environment and their way of life. Our first build was Alex's[15] radio tower, the only man-made object in the valley as we camped there. Conversation ranged from people to nature to technology. Finally, Nikita[16] built a giant half tree. The tree embodied everything that we had thought about the tension between nature and technology; it had the distinct fingerprint of *Minecraft* on it in both its blocky nature and one-side flat surface. In our conversation, we became aware of the missing element ... people. We setup a swing in the exhibition space to let the visitors bask under our tree.

When we were done creating virtual objects, we used various means of data extraction to create 3D printed models and paper crafted art. Buildout became a challenge, as both spaces required some adjustment to the materials.

Figure 5. Some of the TV & SV collaborators (Minecraft ®/TM & © 2009–2013 Mojang / Notch).

The tree, for example, needed a sturdy frame to hold the swing, and the transistors needed thinner legs. With very short deadlines, the SV team adopted a production line model. TV chose a lead who oversaw the construction. The SV project would stand alone and the TV project would be in a room of other works from the biennial. In the end V2V presented two installations inspired by the valleys; trees became natural themes but were interpreted differently on either side of the collaboration. The structures reached out to the audience, talked about the nature of the valley and the hopes and expectations of the future. Both spaces proved popular; the TV site became a great place to relax with Wi-Fi and the SV place was a quiet space for contemplation.

Performance and Performing Arts

> A picture is a secret about a secret, the more it tells you the less you know.
>
> —Diane Arbus

Performance art and the performing arts both employ movement and body in ways to convey ideas and/or entertain. Similar effects are achieved in the virtual world using avatars,[17] where the virtualization is not a limited translation; instead, it alters the nature of performance and the range of motion. Scott deLahunta argues that performing arts in virtual realities encourage and explore interaction, participation, audience-led dynamics, space and gaming (deLahunta, 2002). These are observable even in the earlier virtual reality based artworks with low resolution and awkward interfaces. In addition, these new dynamics of personal and direct audience interaction and participation coupled with the experimental nature of virtual performances blur the line between performing art and performance art.

Virtual worlds and games are often used as platforms for performance-based art of various types. The usage of popular virtual environments[18] such as *Second Life* (2003), massively multiplayer games like *World of Warcraft* (WoW) (2004), and sandbox games like *Garry's Mod* (2004) enhance the reach of the work and encourage audience attendance and participation by removing the limitations of the physical world and accessibility. The platform chosen tends to control the type of interactions that are possible and the ability of the avatar to manipulate the environment. For example, in a game like *WoW*, the interaction is well defined and is specialized for the game's mechanics. The actions and interactions are specific to the genre and narrative they serve; the world is a closed system and players are limited to what has already been developed into the system, persistence is for the world and not for the players' interactions. In other words, depending on your character creation, the avatar is loaded with a posture and certain skills and animations that are highly specialized to the genre of the game, and this can limit the expressiveness of the avatars. On the other hand, *Second Life* allows customization of everything; however, much of the customization frequently happens with the use of tools like Maya outside the virtual environment.

This also resonates with our experience in *Minecraft*. The core mechanics of *Minecraft* are crafting, exploring, and building. Compared to other games, *Minecraft* presents a more natural environment that is not focused on combat or competition. This directly affects the animations of the characters and what the avatars can and cannot do. In *Minecraft*, the avatars have a more natural posture; they move in a certain style that is free of the combat stance observed in most games. The simple movements of the avatars are accompanied by highly stylized graphics. This abstraction gives *Minecraft* its visual quality that does not aim to mimic realism and avoids the pitfalls of realism such as the uncanny valley.[19] In addition, the ability to shape the space very easily adds to the expressiveness of the space and allows the artist to create a complete work of art where each individual element matches the main idea.

Performance in *Minecraft* benefits from the game mechanics (including limits). The game provides an easily accessible common space that can be shaped to a person's will such that the space can be considered as the part of the body as the player can not only change the way it looks but also can design the way it behaves. This allows very specific environments for each experience. In addition, being able to change the space and craft properties for the performance inside the game on the fly is a tool that hastens the iteration process. This also encourages the artist to think within in the game world rather than trying to emulate physical reality and create new expressions that do not exist in the traditional sense.

Performance in *Minecraft* is also social in multiple ways. Since every avatar has the same skills, the line between the performers and the audience is based on the choice and availability. Active participation or being present in *Minecraft* is not the only way to enjoy the performances. The performance, which in essence is data, can be shared using the traditional forms of multimedia or new media such as YouTube.

Ars Virtua Artist in Residence (AVAIR)

AVAIR was originally founded by New Radio and Performing Arts, Inc., in 2005 to support and promote arts in the virtual worlds. It is considered by its founder and supporters to be a form of extended performance in a virtual space to understand what it is to be resident within a space that does not exist. AVAIR has utilized various virtual environments as platforms for exploration.

Earlier residencies took part in platforms such as *Second Life* and *World of Warcraft*. Since 2011, AVAIR is hosted on a private *Minecraft* server called Orwell. For the residency of 2013, AVAIR featured Yagiz Mungan,[20] whose work experimented with sound in virtual worlds. The artist investigated the objects and actions in *Minecraft* and their ability to produce sound within the environment.

The soundscape of *Minecraft* is subtler than most games. After all, there is no action pumping music. This makes the environment similar to the physical one where simpler sounds such as keystrokes of a keyboard define the soundscape. Mungan identified two types of sound objects:

Musique Concrète:[21] Like most other games, every action and interactable object in *Minecraft* has an associated sound. These common sounds define the world of *Minecraft* from an auditory perspective. For example, when a player is mining deep under the ground; the change in the sound of mining defines the soundscape. It can be accompanied by lava flowing near, the sound of a monster on the other side of a wall, or of a sheep that lost its way into an underground cave.

Note Blocks:[22] Note Blocks are musical blocks in Minecraft and are used by players to recreate songs or create objects, which make musical sounds in a more traditional sense. However, they are only one part of the soundscape in *Minecraft*.

The artist's experimentations with sound in *Minecraft* led to the creation of musical instruments that utilize Note Blocks and Musique Concrète. With the Note Blocks, the artist created more traditional instruments such as pianos, drum kits, bass guitars and chord-instruments; while with the daily sounds (such as water, crates, grass), the artist created instruments such as remote-controlled surround doors. The instruments were intended to cover a variety of sounds to serve as a vocabulary and structure an auditory narrative.

The residency also produced a public performance structure, the music hall called Enderman Arena of Music.[23] In *Minecraft*, sound is not reflected and only propagates from the initial source. For this reason the regular concert hall design evolved into arena style architecture with the musicians/performers in the middle and the audience forming a circle around. The arena and the instruments were made in order to provide the residents of Orwell a musical playground, where they could create new sound objects and perform.

Enderman Arena of Music is both an architectural project that responds to the nature of the environment and a platform for performance. Due to the collaborative and virtual nature of the performance, each performer was joining *Minecraft* from a different physical location through different connections. This made it hard to coordinate and keep a perfect synchronization. As performers, we devised a framework, an algorithm composed of *Minecraft*

Figure 6. Enderman Arena of Music from outside (Minecraft °/TM & © 2009–2013 Mojang / Notch).

steps and actions, which became the composition for our music or organization of sound following Cage's description (Cage, 1937). Manovich's concept of transcoding was again important in encouraging us to use an algorithmic approach to performance and to devise other ways to communicate through a performance. The performance itself reflected the general experience of *Minecraft*: a plan that is being attacked by the temptation of new discoveries.

Through the social channels of Orwell, Mungan was also recruited to join in the Diamond Boots Ensemble, a group led by D.C. Spensley.[24] Minecraft provided a common work space where the group could create, collaborate, and build new connections. Mineopticon,[25] a performance-based artwork in *Minecraft*, was produced and directed by Spensley and performed by the Diamond Boots Ensemble live for YouIn3D, Germany, and AvaCon Metaverse Cultural Series 2013. It was also exhibited in various places through recordings of the performance.

The story of Mineopticon follows through the narrative of a court case. The choreography is composed of symbolism, seriousness and absurdism that unite the aesthetics and mechanics of *Minecraft* with the subject matter. The stage plays with the idea of panopticon and casts the audience in the center on a viewing platform. It contains the path for the choreography, machinations, fire pits, slamming doors, and other theatrical properties, which are part of the performance. Mineopticon is one of the few public performances where

Figure 7. Rehearsing Mineopticon (Minecraft */TM & © 2009–2013 Mojang / Notch).

there is a possibility of a performer setting himself/herself accidentally on fire or dying of hunger during the 30-minute performance.

Conclusion

> The work you do while you procrastinate is probably the work you should be doing for the rest of your life.
>
> —Jessica Hische

Virtual worlds have moved along to the point of productivity in the hype cycle ("Hype cycle," n.d.), which is a direct reflection on innovation within the space. The conversation is not so much about advances in technology but about the practicality and useful function. Through its unique world, *Minecraft* enables new possibilities for applications based on the aesthetics and mechanics. *Minecraft* codes a culture of creativity, collaboration, and performance into the environment which when adopted by an artistic community flourishes in a myriad of forms including musical performance and other types of performance art.

In this context, data resonates as a source of intellectual and artistic inspiration. Data traces are part of the technical DNA of all online spaces and *Minecraft* is no exception; however, through game mechanics and 3D printing *Minecraft* creates a full circle between the physical and the virtual that does not exist in other environments. The resulting object carries ideas of *Minecraft*, the initial inception in the physical world, and multiple layers of transcoding and translation. The cycle back to physical creates a new discourse on the change of meaning in translation. The state of positive feedback makes *Minecraft* go beyond its initial capabilities and creates fertile ground for emergent behavior within the realm of the fine arts. This extends past the game element but does not remove it or downplay its relevance. *Minecraft* is thus a game and a tool. A palette. A stage. A drum. A place to swing.

Notes

1. Sandbox game is a type of game that allows the player to roam freely.
2. Throughout the chapter, we will be focusing on the survival mode.
3. Readers can visit http://www.reddit.com/r/Minecraft/ to look into this community. The statistics of the group can be observed at http://stattit.com/r/minecraft/
4. A voxel is a volumetric pixel, representing a position in space and a volume.
5. A map unit is 512x512 voxels.
6. Bukkit is a reverse engineered *Minecraft* server, the primary purpose of this work was to facilitate add-ons and plugins.
7. Mineways is a voxel extraction software http://www.realtimerendering.com/erich/minecraft/public/mineways/
8. Meshlab is a 3D file translation software http://meshlab.sourceforge.net/
9. See http://www.tamasoft.co.jp/pepakura-en/
10. In this case a biennial is an art festival and presentation that happens every other year.
11. More information about Ars Virtua can be found at http://arsvirtua.com/
12. More information about Third Faction can be found at http://thirdfaction.org/
13. More information about NCCA can be found at http://www.ncca.ru/en/main?filial=5
14. More information about James Morgan can be found at http://www.sjsu.edu/art/community/faculty/digitalmedia/jamesmorgan/
15. More information about Alex can be found at https://www.facebook.com/alexkiryutin
16. More information about Nikita can be found at http://www.rokotyan.com/
17. The human body must move for the avatar to move. We are talking about a puppet show, where the movement of the puppeteer is awkward and alien to the audience as well as hidden.
18. For the arguments of this chapter, we are omitting single-player platforms as they lack the collaborative aspects that we discuss earlier.
19. Uncanny valley is a term about the relation between the likability of robot, 3D model or a similar humanoid design, and the realism it provides. As these models get more realistic, they face the risk of causing an immense dislike after a point where they look like a human being to be accepted as one, but at the same they have fundamental problems (such as jittery movements) that cause a negative reaction. For more information read Mori's www.movingimages.info/digitalmedia/wp-content/uploads/2010/06/MorUnc.pdf
20. More information about Yagiz Mungan can be found at http://yagizmungan.com/
21. Musique Concrète is defined as the concrete sounds of daily objects as opposed to abstract sounds.

22. More information about Note Blocks can be found at http://minecraft.wikia.com/ wiki/Note_Block

23. More information about Enderman Arena of Music can be found at http:// yagizmungan.com/EAoM.html

24. More information about DC Spensley can be found at http://www.dcspensley.com/ art/

25. More information about Mineopticon can be found at http://www.dcspensley.com/ art/?portfolio=mineopticon and http://www.avacon.org/blog/events/metaverse-cultural-series/#toggle-id-3

References

Blizzard Entertainment. (2004). *World of Warcraft* [PC game]. Irvine, CA: Blizzard.

Cage, J. (1937) *The future of music—credo*. Retrieved from http://www.medienkunstnetz. de/source-text/41/

deLahunta, S. (2002). Virtual reality and performance. *Performing Arts Journal, 24*, 105–114. doi:10.1162/152028101753401839.

Facepunch Studios. (2004). *Garry's Mod* [PC game]. Bellevue, WA: Valve Corporation.

Huitt, W. (2007). Maslow's hierarchy of needs. *Educational Psychology Interactive*. Valdosta, GA: Valdosta State University. Retrieved from http://www.edpsycinteractive.org/ topics/regsys/maslow.html

Hype cycle research methodology. (n.d.). Retrieved January 18, from http://www.gartner. com/technology/research/methodologies/hype-cycle.jsp

Linden Lab. (2003). *Second Life* [PC game]. San Francisco, CA: Linden Lab Entertainment.

Manovich, L. (n.d.). *The language of new media*. Retrieved from http://www.manovich. net/LNM/Manovich.pdf

Mojang. (2011). *Minecraft* [PC game]. Stockholm, Sweden.

Building a Case for the Authenticity vs. Validity Model of Videogame Design

ADAM L. BRACKIN

Authenticity refers to a simulated experience that is realistic or believable regardless of aesthetic concerns. Validity is defined as a scenario that is standardized or normalized even at the expense of the realistic. In one sense, highly validated linear game forms like platformers and plot-driven games can be considered to have more epic meaning and may employ much more recognizable story models, but are not necessarily best for promoting active player agency. Whereas games with open worlds, especially those that give creative tools to the player, will feel much more authentic but may not rise to the level of meaning expected from a quest-driven narrative.

One example of this spectrum can be found in character dialogue that we are all very used to. Highly validated prosaic dialogue in Shakespeare can often be considered to have epic meaning but not be especially realistic for daily interaction, whereas discussions around the water cooler will feel much more authentic but not rise to the level of meaning expected from a quest-giver. More than just finding the right words during dialogue, the design concept of the authentic and the valid stretches across the entire range of aesthetic decision making during the video game design process to include many other forms of agency promotion. As applied to games, authenticity vs. validity explains the difference between playing a game like *The Sims* (Electronic Arts, 2000) and *Half-Life* (Valve, 1998).

The authenticity vs. validity model is also a way of clarifying intent towards the level of audience participation in the authorship process. Figure 1 is a visualization of the model that I proposed in 2012. In this model, as authenticity of the experience increases, so does the potential for authorship. Conversely, as the validity of the experience increases the player is cast as an audience member.

While the core un-modded vanilla game of *Minecraft* (Mojang, 2011) in its many iterations has done very well in promoting authentic experiences for

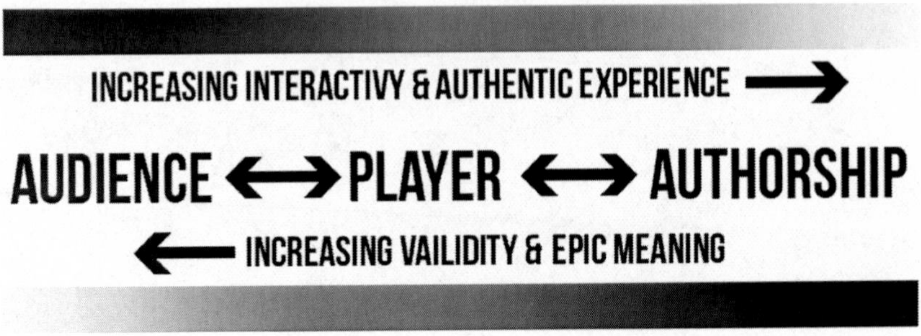

INCREASING INTERACTIVY & AUTHENTIC EXPERIENCE ➔

AUDIENCE ⟷ PLAYER ⟷ AUTHORSHIP

⟵ INCREASING VAILIDITY & EPIC MEANING

Figure 4. The authenticity vs. validity model of game design.

players, what is perhaps most fascinating is how the *Minecraft* community has leveraged the crowd-sourcing power of mods, adventure maps, and YouTube giants like the Yogscast in order to create the valid player experience. The key concept within the model that is so well illustrated by the *Minecraft* phenomenon is that while traditional authorship implies that a creator develops content experiences for an audience who either accepts or rejects the story, authentic gameplay gives functional agency to the player resulting in emergent gameplay decisions, and if pushed far enough with non-linear and ergodic models of gameplay, effectively gives authorship to the audience. This shift in authority in *Minecraft* has driven Mojang's content development process itself. Ultimately the case of *Minecraft* demonstrates how concepts of authenticity and validity as applied to games are really generational, cultural, micro-cultural, and audience-driven, which suggests that we need a much more complex way for understanding the game.

Minecraft's *Unique Form of Authentic Gameplay*

Assuming that all player experience is a form of storytelling, gameplay can be defined as the place where the mechanics of the game meets the story being told by the game developers. To put it another way, it's also anything the player does to change the story the developers were trying to tell. The result is the player's story at whatever level of immersion and/or emergence allowed by the game's fundamental design and structure. In many ways, this is the very definition of *Minecraft's* gameplay.

As it turns out, we can begin to discuss a "good" game and a "bad" game of *Minecraft* without opening up a dangerous discourse on subjective aesthetics on the part of the designer, because with *Minecraft*, it is that very aesthetic subjectivity that is at the core of the game experience. Meaning, *my* game is enjoyable because of what *I* do and what *I* find, the mods I have installed, and the texture pack I'm using, as opposed to how well a level designer, creative director, writer, or so forth scripted my experience. It is much more common to hear "I found this really great world seed" than to hear "I'm having trouble getting past this one part in the game" as with other games.

Arguably, this level of authentic gameplay is the holy grail of design, and thus one way to design towards it becomes to think not in terms of systems and stories as opposing forces, but rather as the necessary framework for either a very realistic simulation based authentic experience, or a very holistic scenario based on valid experience within an interactive story construct that is the sum of the game's parts. In other words, *Minecraft* represents one of our first and best entries to date of a game that allows players to experience the full spectrum between gameplay with high validity, which feels right for the game one is playing, and authenticity, which models reality as a simulation or serious game might.

Jenova Chen is a game designer notable for his highly unusual games such as *flOw* (Thatgamecompany, 2006), *Flower* (Thatgamecompany, 2009) and more recently *Journey* (Thatgamecompany, 2012). His research on flow theory has been instrumental in designing games that find the zone between frustration and ability for the player by giving them control over the most basic gameplay experience. This ability to adjust the "difficulty level" intuitively and naturally while playing has strong connections to the tabletop RPG experience, which has by definition an open-ended capability. It does not take long then to realize that the choice built into the idea of flow theory is exactly what we mean when we talk about *Minecraft*. Being completely open-ended, non-story driven, and user-directed is the entire point of flow theory's "flow channel" of gameplay (Chen, n.d.).

Similarly, writer Jeff Howard (2008) calls this kind of in-between space "Quest," declaring: "A quest is a journey across a symbolic, fantastic landscape in which a protagonist or player collects and talks to characters in order to overcome challenges and achieve a meaningful goal." Worth noting is Howard's mention of the necessary components for quest to occur. Namely some sort of hero in a place where others provide a challenge for said hero—in other words a plot hook story mechanic. He goes on to clarify that quest is a "middle term" in which gaming overlaps with literature, technology with mythology, meaning with action, and yes ... game overlaps with narrative. The model is not about defining borders like the yin and yang define each other, but about recognizing shared space like in a Venn diagram. As it is with *Minecraft* when goals are set and challenges must be overcome, Howard's model may be a good way of visualizing the self-imposed "quests" that a *Minecraft* player engages in during their free-form gameplay.

In their 2009 PICNIC presentation "Once Upon These Times: New Stories for New Media Audiences," Ettinghousen and Locke (2009) proposed a new set of guidelines for telling stories in new media summarized here:

- Hide stories in unexpected places.
- Give yourself ridiculous constraints.
- Experiment outside your comfort zone.
- Invent a character without a storyline.
- Give the fans stuff to play with.
- Give them stories to snack and binge on.

In the presentation, Ettinghousen and Locke are quick to point out that stories can be told in disjointed chunks through bus stops and SMS as with "We Tell Stories"[1] or "Surrender Control,"[2] via unexpected and real world means as with "I am Cherry Girl"[3] or "You Suck at Photoshop,"[4] and often as with most of these examples, imbedded into other media entirely as noted with "Yu-gi-oh!"[5] More significant for us though is the fact that these principles are all deeply rooted in authentic experience, and as it turns out, evident within *Minecraft's* fundamental design, since we can find examples of every one of these things within the context of its authentic gameplay.

Minecraft has always been about exploring the next area while strategizing survival. We have seen this through procedurally generated landscapes and features from the earliest builds of the game. The mere presence of randomly generated biomes and unexplored caves, of a fashion more mysterious and unknown than the earliest of Interactive Fiction entries like *Colossal Cave Adventure,* was revolutionary design. Now in current builds, with the more recently added NPC towns, abandoned mines, temples, and the illusive stronghold with its end portal and the terrors beyond it, emergent story lies potentially behind every block.

Ridiculous constraints are also a part of *Minecraft's* core gameplay. While many potentially frustrating elements are abstracted out—such as the ability to carry metric tons of supplies in stacks of sixty-four in the inventory—other constraints that enhance gameplay remain. The food bar which was added to require players to eat is an example. The durability of tools and weapons is another. These elements add dramatic tension without being overly frustrating, and so contribute to the overall gameplay positively via the element of restraint. Put simply, this is the fundamental difference between *Minecraft* and other builder examples such as *Gary's Mod* (Facepunch Studios, 2004) in which the tools are infinite and the canvas blank. It is fair to say that the fear of a creeper attack when finishing a tricky element in SMP is always there, and as such, the dramatic tension created by the mere possibility enhances the gameplay.

The *Minecraft* experiment is fascinating because of how different it is from other games. Despite being imitated a number of times now, there is still that fundamental experience that all players must remember when they either figured out they could punch trees and dirt to remove and take the blocks, or were told, saw a video, or read a wiki explaining the process. The very concept of allowing players to destroy the world in order to subsequently rebuild and recraft it to their own desires is so far outside of the fundamental expectations of the gaming comfort zone, that even the most experienced gamer can recall this early moment in their first *Minecraft* playthrough. Add to that the subsequent challenge created by every crafting recipe, technique, and game rule which does not exist within the context of the game, but only as out-of-game content, and there is a fundamental quality to *Minecraft* that is "uncomfortable" as Ettinghousen and Locke described.

A good character can exist inside a writer's head across storylines, or even without a storyline at all. This is precisely what Steve the empty, mute, reskinnable default avatar is. A shell to be filled by the player's every move, the *Minecraft* character is essentially a non-entity, a pure reflection of the player himself and a character with a story that only exists through the player's experiences in the game. *Minecraft's* star is not a known "package" character like Link, Kratos, or Solid Snake; nor a stock stereotype "mute" like Claude Speed, or Gordon Freeman, but a blank slate for the player to engage in much more authentic roleplay.

Giving the players something to play with is the very point of *Minecraft,* and more intrinsically so than in other games. Indeed there is nothing in the game which cannot be manipulated by a player, and that in and of itself has been genre-breaking and unusual. Even the most detailed game in which all items are fully rendered and interactable such as *Skyrim* (Bethesda, 2011) cannot make the claims that *Minecraft* can with billions of diggable dirt blocks on any given random map. Yet it goes even deeper than this. As mentioned above, the recipes themselves are mysterious and enigmatic without the help of a wiki, let's play, or friend; and no game guide map can exist since every map seed is unique. Infinite possibility means infinite play is possible.

Finally, Ettinghousen and Locke suggest giving the players something to do quickly and something to spend a great deal of time on. *Minecraft* does this without fail, for no matter how big or small the build project a player undertakes, there will always be something to do for some minutes, some hours, and apparently some many years since the game's popularity and reach seems to only be increasing. Other games have come and gone, having been binged and snacked upon until the story was told or the gameplay grew stale, but through a combination of game updates, a strong core community of modders and multiplayer servers as well as other factors, *Minecraft* has so far outlasted them all, transcending systems as well as its own humble prior iterations.

The Case for Validity in Minecraft

So it is clear then that publishers are experimenting with new ways to tell all sorts of stories more authentically and with a focus on the "real," but not all content choices are right for a story any more than A1 sauce is right for all foods—it just doesn't work on breakfast cereal. Likewise, some stories are a good fit for a given format, such as film and games, and some stories aren't based on the elements of the story and the characteristics and purpose of the media type. The challenge for media creators is to find the "right" combination of content and format for a specific intellectual property. More to the point, how can *Minecraft* be used to both tell authentic stories and as a tool for valid experience?

When we engage with static media, many of the meaningful decisions are already made through writing, visualization, acting, editing, and in many other ways. What we are allowed to contribute often varies by the media type. This is why some audience members saw the Harry Potter film for the first time and thought "Wait! That's not what Hogwarts Castle is supposed to look like" (Rose, 2011). For those who read about Rowling's Hogwarts School of Witchcraft and Wizardry and imagined something less grand than the iconic wizard's castle that came to be in the Warner Bros.' release, the movie was better. And while the later film entries in the series did shirk valid continuity with the earlier entries by taking liberties with the layout of the castle for narrative reasons, most audience members did not notice or care because it was right for that moment, and thus validated the story being told. Regardless, the imagination is a powerful tool. So powerful in fact that however we visualize something first, it often becomes the best and true version, even when presented with another option later on. So despite the now iconic vision of Hogwarts, there still exists a select group dedicated to teasing out the "real" layout of the castle based not on production decisions from the film, but from the only truly valid core material: the books (HPL, 2006).

However, the translation of static media into a digital game is often even more disastrous as the creators find themselves needing to invent content and will often shoehorn in "something for the player to do" that was not needed when the audience was merely a passive viewer/reader attaining a different kind of agency from the main character's thoughts and actions. This departure from the validity of the original author's narrative is damaging and in fact often disastrous to the attempted translation. If this is true, then perhaps Tom Hall was right when he nudges us in his 10 Commandments of Game Design that the most important rule of thumb for the budding designer is simply: If the media being translated is not highly interactive write a book or make a movie out of it. Don't try to make a video game (Hall, 2005).

Yet *Minecraft* is not that sort of game; it has a different language for validity even when engaging other texts. It doesn't try to tell stories, and unapologetically changes every time we generate a world. In many ways it feels more like a design tool than a traditional valid linear narrative experience, but in fact it is this ability of players to recreate to spec a particular piece of architecture or other design, then publish the map or a video of play that gives it its own brand of validity. How many times has the iconic Hogwart's castle been recreated in *Minecraft* worlds? I must admit that I myself am one of these fans who did this very thing. This freedom to create is—in a way—simply shifting the validity of the authorship experience to the player by shifting where choice occurs. Instead of canonizing and homogenizing the content, the player is left to their own subjective devices to interpret and translate the content—visual or otherwise—which is one of the fundamental building blocks of an authored interactive experience.

But what of media that is not subject to translation? Consider the early days of YouTube giants: The Yogscast. Originally "Ye Olde Goon Squad," a *Warcraft* guild who filmed themselves raiding and acquired a following on YouTube, the Yogscast crew soon discovered *Minecraft* and their following exploded. The keystone to their success was the webseries "Shadow of Israphel," in which the two main channel personalities Simon and Lewis—call them personas or even characters if you prefer—spent many hours building a "Yogcave" only to be attacked by some unknown player named Israphel who had appeared on their open server! In the process of investigating this, they discovered first a town, then an entire subsequent world populated by "NPC" individuals who were in fact real people playing parts, and the entire series quickly evolved into an online RPG within the *Minecraft* world including a quest line, characters, and live action style roleplay (LARP). It was later revealed that this was largely a constructed fiction for Simon's behalf, and that while his reactions were genuine, Lewis had been in on the prank from the beginning. Though the story has not ever been concluded, the fame acquired by the stunt was enough to launch the group—now a company—into stardom, and many new series and episodes have been notable for their unusual, funny, and innovative elements. Most of these subsequent series have occurred using *Minecraft* or a modded variant such as Tekkit or FTB, all further attempts to create validity for their popular content.

The lesson here is that willing suspension of disbelief combines with the fourth wall when the audience engages in fiction, or any story really, and we have a better chance at succeeding as storytellers when the audience understands what we are attempting to communicate via authentic language and approachable storytelling. For those highly literate logophiliacs, reading is still preferred in almost every case because of the inherent authenticity imbedded in the act of reading and this is because of the intimate level of agency provided by the experience of engaging the imagination without pre-formed and biased visuals. But new game forms like *Minecraft* are changing this, giving the same level of creativity and agency to the player to actually transform them into authors of their own right via publishing channels like YouTube. So while a picture may be worth 1000 words, our imagination is worth an uncountable, perhaps infinite, number of words and images, including all the ones there are no words for. This is the level of validity that should be aspired to in games, perhaps not in translation title pieces but in original works at the very least.

Connecting the Authenticity vs. Validity Model to Agency

While traditional authorship implies that an author writes for an audience who either accepts or rejects the story, many digital games can give functional agency to the player and more authority to participate in story decisions, and if pushed far enough with non-linear and ergodic models of gameplay, effectively gives authorship itself to the audience as gameplay transcends to roleplay. In the context of *Minecraft*, the previously discussed authenticity vs. validity model may be more usefully broken into quadrants (see Figure 2). As mentioned before, if Jeff Howard's assertions that story and game meet in a border zone called quest are true (Howard, 2008), then it is a simple matter to draw a hypothetical quest point out into a y-axis of validity and authenticity.

When mods, adventure maps, in-game RPGs, and spin-off building games are considered, it becomes clear that *Minecraft* is the perfect illustration of the model in all four areas. Recognizing of course that the placement of these

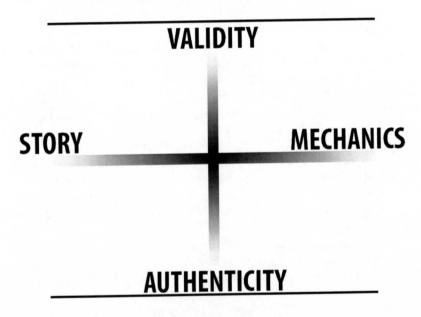

Figure 5. The quadrant model of the authenticity vs. validity model of game design.

examples are my own choices, derived from my own experience and therefore my own critical aesthetic perspective, I believe the following are very good popular examples of each of the four categories as relates to *Minecraft*.

QUADRANT: MECHANICS AND AUTHENTICITY

Vanilla *Minecraft* itself is a curious game that in many ways is no game at all. During its dubious open paid alpha and beta phases many things changed with the game, in an ever steady progression towards validity. Indeed at the time of this writing, it still continues to evolve and change with new content added every few months even though alternate versions now exist on pads and consoles seemingly locked in to now dated beta version builds. The PC version now has an ending dimension called unapologetically "the end" with a massive boss dragon to beat in order to be presented with credits, but the game claimed its status and funding not through these things but by presenting a massive sandbox and very logical set of tools to the player without any identifiable goals or purpose beyond creating. Every imaginable thing has been created in Minecraftia now, including emergent full RPG stories, extremely complex working computers from virtual circuitry, and all kinds of architecture imaginable including my own year-long project: a faithful scale recreation of the Hogwarts as seen in the films.

QUADRANT: STORY AND VALIDITY

Minecraft adventure maps have existed for as long as maps could be exported and posted online. While every imaginable work-around from redstone mechanics to NPC dialogue written on signs has been employed, it is now considered a completely valid form of gameplay supported in full by the game's Adventure Mode setting, and the introduction of command blocks to control the major dynamic settings in the game. This extremely popular form of play lends itself to the traditional author-designer / player relationship construct, and is true evidence to the fanbase's ability to turn out large quantities of quality content extremely quickly. While certain top designers and authors have arisen as being the best at creating adventure maps, this is really no different from any other content creation driven entertainment form, and is the ideal example of how *Minecraft* can be used for highly valid story.

QUADRANT: STORY AND AUTHENTICITY

The Yogscast's early recognition that *Minecraft* could be used to tell valid story was likely what inspired them to put on their in-game RPG "Shadow of Israphel." While it cannot be considered an adventure map, for it was being played in real time by the team within a fictional world they created, the open-ended nature of the game-turned-story is a perfect example of what can happen when story and mechanics are made to work in tandem. Much like a tabletop roleplaying game, the literal tools available in an open system are only as limited as one's own imagination and the fundamental mechanics of the RPG itself. In the case of Simon and Lewis of the Yogscast, while they were limited to the mechanics of *Minecraft* as they interacted with characters and explored the unexpectedly well-developed world around them, they were still able to interact with characters being played by real people, and therefore engage with the roleplay in a way that conventional computer RPG video games do not allow since computer-controlled NPCs are still ingloriously bound to the limited responses written for them in advance.

QUADRANT: MECHANICS AND VALIDITY

This is the most difficult quadrant to define, but perhaps it can be understood in the context of the above. Following their adventures in "Minecraftia" and the land of "Shadow of Israphel," The Yogscast felt frustrated by the limitations of *Minecraft* to tell these types of stories, and set out to create a much less abstract version of the game. The result was the highly successful Kickstarter project for Yogventures—essentially *Minecraft* with Voxel art—followed by the lackluster reception of the actual game. Unlike *Minecraft*, a loyal and dedicated fanbase to the tool did not arise, and though available for purchase in its Alpha state, the tool is not likely to find funding for continued development any time soon. The idea of a valid mechanic for implementing storytelling is an interesting one though, but what seems to have been forgotten by the team is that they are already engaging in valid mechanics every day by playing with *Minecraft* mods. It has in fact been so long since the Yogscast played with vanilla *Minecraft* that they freely admit to not knowing many of the newer potion or item recipes, while having become highly affluent in major builds such as Tekkit, Feed the Beast, and even their own proprietary Yogscraft build.

Conclusion

By using this quadratic framework as a guide for aesthetic reasoning and critique, it becomes possible to identify trends within whole genres by asking questions of a mapped out array of games. Did Bioware's choice for a dialog-free toggle in *Mass Effect 3* (BioWare, 2012) in order to provide an "action oriented game option" effect sales in any meaningful way? Their choice to deny choice in the ending certainly resulted in player outrage. Moreover, by identifying gaps in the distribution, such a model allows for new types of games to be envisioned in gameplay spaces that have not been explored, even within a given game like *Minecraft*.

In short, we need more games like *Minecraft*. It's not that we need another *Minecraft*, or a better *Minecraft* ... on the contrary that's the last thing we need since *Minecraft* will continue to evolve and change on its own with no signs of stopping soon. Rather, the best thing we can do is to design a game which is born of a complete understanding of the nature of authenticity and validity as tools for design, and provide new ways for the audience, players, and content authors to experience these kinds of games in ways we can't even envision right now—except of course through the one-of-a-kind *Minecraft*.

Notes

1. *We Tell Stories* is a digital fiction experiment published by Six to Start for Penguin Books in which six authors told six stories and a hidden seventh were written specifically for the internet in six weeks in 2008 via the website www.wetellstories.co.uk

2. *Surrender control* was a 2001 interactive work comprising an escalating sequence of text message instructions delivered direct to the mobile phones of individual users who opt in by sending a message to a particular number, then were drawn into an evolving game of textual suggestions, provocations and dares.

3. *I am Cherry Girl* is a global project by MTV, presenting an open, loose approach to using social media to tell a story with no focus on a big narrative, instead presenting a strong character in the real world. Cherry Girl is on Twitter, Facebook, has a blog and interacts with everyone who wants to interact with her.

4. *You Suck at Photoshop* is the dramatic yet humorous story of a normal guy named Donnie Hoyle who vents about his marital problems, cleverly discoverable within a Photoshop tutorial spread over a series of YouTube movies.

5. *Yu-gi-oh!* is a vastly popular children's Anime franchise which was originally part of a Japanese manga in the 1990s, based around gaming and gameplay. The franchise spawned innumerable spinoffs, ranging from a set of gaming collector cards to a TV series and games on all available gaming platforms of the time.

References

Bethesda Game Studios. (2011). *SkyRim* [PC game]. Bethesda Softworks.

BioWare. (2012). *Mass Effect 3* [PC game]. Electronic Arts.

Chen, J. (n.d.). Welcome to Jenova Chen's homepage. *Welcome to Jenova Chen's homepage.* Retrieved May 11, 2012, from http://www.jenovachen.com/

Electronic Arts. (2000). The *Sims* [PC game]. Electronic Arts.

Ettinghausen, J., & Locke, M. (2009). *Once upon these times: New stories for new audiences* [video]. FORA.tv. Retrieved from http://fora.tv/2009/09/23/Once_Upon_These_Times_New_Stories_for_New_Audiences

Facepunch Studios. (2004). *Garry's Mod* [PC game]. Bellevue, WA: Valve Corporation.

Gilmore, J. H., & Pine, B. J. (2007). *Authenticity: What consumers really want.* Boston: Harvard Business School Press.

Hall, T. (2005). *Tom hall's ten commandments of game design.* U.S.: Wordware.

Howard, J. (2008). *Quests: Design, theory, and history in games and narratives.* Wellesley, MA: A. K. Peters.

HPL: Atlas of Hogwarts. (n.d.). *HPL: Atlas of Hogwarts.* Retrieved May 11, 2012, from http://www.hp-lexicon.org/atlas/hogwarts/atlas-h.html

Mojang. (2011). *Minecraft* [PC game]. Stockholm, Sweden.

Rose, F. (2011). *The art of immersion: How the digital generation is remaking Hollywood, Madison Avenue, and the way we tell stories.* New York: W.W. Norton & Co.

Salen, K., & Zimmerman, E. (2003). *Rules of play: Game design fundamentals.* Cambridge, MA: MIT Press.

Schell, J. (2010). DICE 2010: "Design outside the box" presentation. G4tvwww. Retrieved May 11, 2012, from http://www.g4tv.com/videos/44277/dice-2010-design-outside-the-box-presentation/

Thatgamecompany. (2006). *flOw* [PlayStation 3]. Sony Computer Entertainment.

Thatgamecompany. (2009). *Flower* [PlayStation 3]. Sony Computer Entertainment.

Thatgamecompany. (20012). *Journey* [PlayStation 3]. Sony Computer Entertainment.

Valve Corporation. (1998). *Half-Life 2* [PC Game]. Sierra Entertainment.

Where Game, Play and Art Collide

Rémi Cayatte

[*Minecraft* is] every nerd's dream, like an endless video game.
—Lia, 14 years old (as cited in in Fine, 2011)

The main difference between a chess game and a chess video game logically is the video component; onscreen representation of the current state of a play session replaces the traditional chess board and pieces. In the case of a chess video game, the onscreen information is just a substitute for the traditional representation. However, interestingly, chess can be played without any representations at all, using annotations only to describe the pieces' current positions and the players' different moves. This comes in especially handy for players engaged in correspondence chess, and also makes chess a rather easy video game to program. Another important difference between a traditional game of chess and one of its numerous video game counterparts is the fact that the computer—or any other electronic device—takes into account a user's input. This cybernetic element allows chess to be played alone, enables players to set the game's difficulty, and permits saving progress without having to carefully preserve a tangible board.

According to our rather simple illustration, any game that takes into account its user's input to render it onscreen can be understood as a video game. On the one hand, the very simple definition used here can be a rather satisfying one because it enroots video games to their intrinsic common denominators. On the other hand, such a definition is problematic since it does not exclude gaming activities that are not generally considered as video games, such as the *Atmosfear* board game series for instance (Clements & Tanner, 1991–2006). These "video board games" basically enhance traditional board games with the addition of a video tape that both gives instructions to the players and serves as a timer. One could argue that such video board games are merely board games played while watching a tape and that they lack the interactivity with the onscreen data that is the essence of most video games. *Atmosfear* games do not actually take into account users' actions in what can be seen on the television screen while playing, and these games only fake the creation of an interactive link between the screen and the players. This is indeed true, but it is also what software we usually call video games actually do, they merely fake it in a better way.

Among other challenges to this broad definition is an experimental game boy advance game, *Soundvoyager* (Skip Ltd., 2003), which is meant to be played without looking at the screen. *Soundvoyager* is composed of several mini-games that consist in navigating in a virtual space that has to be heard, as opposed to traditional video games in which the virtual space is mostly seen. In disconnecting the link between player and screen, this experimental video game becomes more an audio game than anything. *Soundvoyager* and the *Atmosfear* video board games are both exceptions that can potentially neutralize even the most inclusive definition of video games.

But on the matter of its relationship to video, *Minecraft* (Mojang, 2011) is not problematic. Let us address this right away: *Minecraft* is a "video something," simply because it is meant to be used with a screen or any device that provides visual feedback, such as a projector. This video nature of *Minecraft* is not one that calls for a debate or even for a lot of thinking. Video conferences, for instance, do not confuse anyone as to their video nature. The real issue in considering the nature of the interactive opportunity presented by *Minecraft* is whether or not *Minecraft* is a game. This chapter explores the nature of interactivity in both *Minecraft's* creative mode and survival mode in light of various popular definitions of both game and play to ultimately reveal a unique core duality that thrusts *Minecraft* into a new realm where the classic binary of game vs. play confronts art.

Creative Play in Minecraft

> First and foremost, then, all play is a voluntary activity. Play to order is no longer play.
> —Huizinga, 1949, p. 7

Depending on the options selected before the creation of a new world, avatars in *Minecraft's* creative mode will appear in a virtual space that can feature biomes, endless flat and grassy land, or randomly generated structures such as mineshafts and temples. In this mode users have access to any kind of block they want, and there is unlimited access to items, including animals in the form of eggs. Last but not least, avatars can fly, which makes navigating the virtual space easier, in addition to making building any kind of structure much simpler. Furthermore, avatars cannot die in creative mode unless they fall into the void (ie. below the generated world). These specificities allow users to fully express their creativity. Many online videos document recreations of the *Star Trek* Enterprise (Halnicholas, 2011), for instance, or even entire fictitious landscapes such as the *Lord of the Rings* (Cox, 2012). The latter consisting of multiple different locations interconnected without clear boundaries between them, which gives to the users who enter these landscapes a real sense of virtual navigating in an immense lifelike place, a feeling that can be quite difficult to convey using traditional tangible construction sets.

This type of creative activity differs greatly from traditional definitions that aim to define video games. In the following extract taken from Manovich's *The Language of the New Media* (2001, pp. 221–222), the author aims at differentiating the inner mechanisms of video games and databases:

> In games, the player is given a well-defined match-winning task, being first in a race, reaching the last level, or attaining the highest score. It is that task that makes the player experience the game as a narrative. Everything that happens to her in the game, all the characters and objects she encounters, either take her closer to achieving the goal, or further away from it. [...] While computer games do not follow a database logic, they appear to be ruled by another logic—that of the algorithm. They demand that a player execute an algorithm in order to win.

How Manovich defines the essence of video games and of how they are meant to be played is characteristic of many other definitions of video games that insist on the performance aspect of such cultural products: video games are meant to be finished, to be won.

Yet, most of the features of video games according to Manovich's definition are absent from sessions of *Minecraft*. There is nothing to win in the creative mode of *Minecraft*, no real ending, nothing that the users do brings him closer to a certain outcome, simply because there is no outcome. Consecutively, *Minecraft's* creative mode does not offer any story. The gameplay mechanisms do not encourage any kind of actions, or behavior, and the users' avatars simply are in the middle of a virtual nowhere, with an unlimited landscape to explore, to terraform, and to build upon.

Instead, the creative mode of *Minecraft* mainly consists in what could be called free play. This type of interactivity has been categorized as early as 1958 by French sociologist Roger Caillois who coined the term "paida"to describe playful activities that are not necessarily focused on a specific set of rules that aim at deciding how players can or cannot achieve game-ending goals. Paida refers to games and playful activities that are centered on the pursuit of mere joy for itself: "[Paida is] an almost indivisible principle, common to diversion, turbulence, [in which] free improvisation and carefree gaiety is dominant." Caillois then opposes this principle to that of "ludus" which "is a growing tendency to bind [paida] with arbitrary, imperative, and purposely tedious conventions" (Caillois, 2001, p. 13). These two opposed poles coexist within many playful activities. While some interaction is principally aimed at the pursuit of carefree pleasure, most interactions also feature elements that can be associated with Caillois' ludus, which, to put it simply, is more about rules, conventions, and restrictions, restraining free play in order to transform it into games as we most commonly understand them.

While Manovich's depiction of games as task-achieving endeavors well reflects this idea of ludus, as far as *Minecraft*'s creative mode is concerned the player is engaged in free play and restrained by very few rules when compared to most games. *Minecraft*'s creative mode does however resemble other playful activities that are usually referred to as toys, probably because they lack the systemic restraining that turns free play activities into games. Playing—or maybe toying with—*Minecraft*'s creative mode could thus be seen as a virtualized version of construction sets such as LEGO, Kaplas, or even mere cubes that can be found in any toy store. All the while, Mojang's rendition of such construction sets enables multiple improvements, such as an acute feeling of infinite possibilities both regarding the number of blocks available—that is as much as your computer can handle—or the potential for modding the core mechanics of the software.

While toying with LEGO, Kaplas, *Minecraft,* or mere cubes, is an activity that involves a lot of "free improvisation" and that appears as an interesting illustration of what Caillois called *paida*, it does not inherently prevent the implementation of a system of rules. Toying can easily become game playing, even with mere cubes, when goals and rules are included with such an activity. Trying to determine, for instance, who can build the tallest construction, or the construction that most resembles a picture, are common occurrences of toys being transformed into games by their very users, and *Minecraft*'s creative playful experience does not neutralize such possibilities. To be more precise, the amount of goals and rules featured in *Minecraft*'s creative mode entirely depends on the users' will. If some tangible games feature level design elements delegated to the players (such as the size of the board, and thus the duration of a game in a board game such as *Cranium* for instance), *Minecraft*'s creative mode delegates to its users the entirety of what is commonly called game design. The delegation of such an essential feature, of what the game is about when it ceases to be a toy, is amplified by the countless possibilities offered by various mods that allow users to deeply alter *Minecraft*'s core visual and gameplay elements. When users seize this opportunity to make their own game in altering its inner mechanisms, *Minecraft*'s creative mode becomes a game and potentially fits Manovich's definition of what games are about. But until then, such creative mode in its "natural" state cannot be truly referred to as a video game, but only as a video *toy*.

That being said, if a toy like this creative mode is an experience that can easily be transformed by its very users into a game, the opposite is possible as well and most games can be turned into toys when users disregard rules and conventions. *World of Goo* (2D Boy, 2008) for instance, is a video game that, like *Minecraft*, is very similar to traditional construction sets especially because it places the building of various constructions as the core—and unique—gameplay feature. 2D Boy's game consists for its users in creating structures using only a set of similar pieces, namely Goos, virtual creatures that have the propriety of solidly attaching to one another. The concept of building with only one kind of material is very similar to *Minecraft*. In *World of Goo*, different creatures of different colors have different physics and specificities, just like *Minecraft's* various blocks that are only differentiable thanks to their colors. While both games have this common central gameplay mechanism, users are placed in very different positions when interacting with the two. While *World of Goo* players can freely choose to turn the game into a toy in disregarding the game's goals—build structures using Goos to join two places—they cannot progress in the game if they do so. Here, toying with games marks a clear halt regarding players' progression within the game, while in *Minecraft's* creative mode, toying with blocks actually is what is expected on the users' behalf and an integral part of their progression. Since this progression is not commanded by any specific goals to achieve or tasks to complete, play here indeed is a voluntary activity that no formal instructions frame.

Gaming in Survival Mode

Minecraft's survival mode differs in many ways from creative mode. In survival mode, avatars have hunger and health bars, the latter diminishing when an avatar is hit by hostile NPCs (Non-Player Characters), if they fall from high ground, or if they become too hungry. Death of an avatar follows when the health bar is depleted. In order to avoid such a tragic outcome, users have to direct avatars to build a shelter to protect themselves from hostile creatures and hunt animals and forage for consumable vegetables to refill their hunger gauge, which results in slowly replenishing their health bar.

Survival mode does not allow for an unlimited supply of blocks, and users are limited to the possibility of storing a finite number of blocks and items that they find. This requires them to explore their surrounding and to harvest resources or to find a way to produce such resources, cultivating plants or breeding animals for instance. Harvesting large amounts of resources such as minerals or wood is a gameplay mechanic that works in synergy with that of crafting, and users willing to defend themselves against the hostiles NPCs that lurk outside at night have to discover how to craft various pieces of equipment, from mere doors to different sets of armors and weapons and powerful enchanting tables. This second mode of *Minecraft* is—not surprisingly—

mostly about surviving, and to that extent, it could be compared to some recent survival horror games such as *DayZ* (Bohemian Interactive, 2013) that feature similar gameplay mechanisms, principally crafting and exploring a hostile environment in order to gather useful items, albeit set in a much more realistic virtual environment than *Minecraft*.

Survival mode, which was first alpha tested as early as September 2009, has constantly evolved. Regular updates to *Minecraft* have expanded the features of survival mode in order to propose to the players an increasingly deep and interesting experience of surviving its virtual wilderness. These evolutions came in the form of updates that either benefited both survival and creative modes, such as the implementation of automatically generated natural biomes and the addition of new blocks, items, and creatures, or that mostly changed the survival mode alone. Among the updates that principally concerned the survival mode of *Minecraft* was one that introduced achievements to the game. Achievements were first implemented in the 1.5 beta update of *Minecraft* in April 2011. Although completing any achievement is completely optional and awards nothing except the possibility to complete other more complicated achievements, this simple addition to *Minecraft*'s survival mode nonetheless brings this game mode closer to Manovich's depiction of games in which a gamer moves "closer to achieving the goal, or further away from it." The difference here with more traditional video games is that at the time of this implementation there still was nothing to win or to finish in survival mode. This changed with the implementation of "The End" with the 1.9pre4 beta update of the game. *Minecraft*'s End is both a dimension of the game, which is a virtual environment that can be explored, and two distinct achievements. Entering this alternative virtual space awards player with the completion of "The End?" achievement, and killing the Ender Dragon that dwells there completes an achievement called "The End." The first time a player manages to kill what cannot be called anything but the game's "boss" and to escape the End, credits in the form of a long poem appears and the player's avatar then reappears in the very first location it first spawned.

The implementation of such a goal in survival mode well illustrates the slow evolution of *Minecraft*'s survival mode into what can be truly called a game—as opposed to a toy. New computer-controlled hostile characters and randomly generated structures, as well as health and hunger bars and experience points, achievements, and the End dimension, transformed *Minecraft* into a rather traditional video game played in a completely different way than the creative mode. Players who aim at completing all survival mode's achievements find themselves engaged in quite a difficult endeavor, in a long quest which climaxes in nothing less than battling a dragon, a grand final outcome that does not put an end to the game per say, but that can nonetheless provide players with a sense of completion that creative mode cannot.

If creative mode's users can turn the free play experience into a game simply in inventing their own set of rules and objectives, survival mode's players can choose to experience this mode as a more difficult version of creative mode and still let their imagination and creativity run free. Nevertheless, if traditional games' users can decide to toy with any game, to choose to put *paida* over *ludus* for a while, this always marks a stop to their progression towards the end of the game, or is an interaction that occurs entirely outside the borders of gaming. In the case of *Minecraft's* survival mode however, there is no ending, but an "End" that ironically sends players back to where they came from, as if mocking *Minecraft's* own lack of closure and definite goals as well as reminding players that the game mostly consists in making one's own game.

The Art of Configuration

> To generalize: in art we might have to configure in order to be able to interpret, whereas in games we have to interpret in order to be able to configure, and proceed from the beginning to the winning or some other situation.
>
> —Eskelinen, 2001

Minecraft can be a surprising and even challenging experience for those accustomed to more authoritarian video games that feature fixed and unavoidable goals and rules, a more or less hidden *ludus* that players have to abide by in order to proceed from the beginning of a game to its ending. What is to interpret here are the rules of games that can be very prosaic, such as determining if or when one's avatar is able to fly, or double jump, or what happens when Mario hits lava. Interpreting this allows players to make the best out of any situation, according to their understanding of such rules and to their skills with handling a joystick or a keyboard. The better the interpretation of the rules, the more adequate the configuration and the easier it is to reach the "winning or some other situation."

Eskelinen's vision that clearly considers (video) games as elaborated puzzles requiring configurative actions appears highly relevant as far as the survival mode of *Minecraft* is concerned. Yet, what users can experience playing *Minecraft's* creative mode is deeply in contradiction with Eskelinen's definition, simply because there is next to nothing there to interpret that would help players to freely configure whatever virtual world they fancy. What makes *Minecraft* so challenging is that it is both art and game, to paraphrase Eskelinen. More than a mere toy, creative mode is a way for users to express themselves building virtual structures, be they mere shacks, or entire towns or landscapes. And more than a traditional scavenger hunt game, survival mode still allows players to set their own rules in a less peaceful environment, in a potentially more readily goal-focused experience when compared to creative mode.

However challenging that may be for those used to more linear and authoritarian productions, this dichotomy between free creation and not-so-free gaming is not new. While Manovich situates the difference between video games and databases on what is required on behalf of the users, Gonzalo Frasca, in his essay *Simulation versus Narrative: Introduction to Ludology* (2003, pp. 232–233), focuses more on the game developers' authority and not on what tasks a software demands that users perform, but on what parts of such a software they are allowed to alter:

> A meta-rule is a rule that states how rules can be changed.... Some [games] only allow you to do cosmetic changes while others permit more drastic modifications. Still, it is important to keep in mind that meta-rules do not imply neither the death of the author nor the player's freedom.... Nevertheless, with or without meta-rules, the simauthor always has the final word and remains in charge because total player freedom is impossible since it would imply that no rules are unchangeable and therefore the game could literally become anything.

A game like *Warcraft III* (Blizzard Entertainment, 2002), for instance, came with additional software that, in a user-friendly fashion, allowed users to create their own maps (or levels) using the game's visual assets. The software also included a trigger editor to help users set their own rules regarding interactions with visual assets. This gave birth to what came to be known as *Multiplayer Online Battle Arenas*, also known as MOBA, a genre that began with the creation of a user-generated map called *Defense of the Ancients* (*DotA*). This map completely changed the original game's rules and ultimately created a new product the origins of which were only recognizable by the visual assets common to both games. Later on, what the *DotA* creators started was continued by other game developers who kept *DotA's* gameplay but implemented their own visual assets, the most well-known examples being *League of Legends* (Riot Games, 2009) and *Dota 2* (Valve, 2013). Thus, if Frasca was certainly right in pointing out the impossibility for users to immediately disconnect their modifications from an author using what freedom of creation this author allowed, this disconnection can be achieved on the long run, time and constant changes slowly erasing the author's presence from a game, or renewing it differently.

Furthermore, while such editing software is only meant to allow users to create maps and levels that will be playable later on, *Minecraft's* creative mode is inherently a seemingly authorless toy, and an immediate playable experience of carefree pleasure, exploration, and building. More importantly, its two sides, creative and survival, are not entirely discriminate entities but are overlapping modes that can be triggered on and off at will by users.

This blurring of the lines between survival and creative modes might be the reason why *Minecraft* has become so popular for online videos and live retransmissions of game sessions—there are simply many different opportunities for commentary. Demonstrations of one's prowess at *Minecraft* can be found on video sharing websites. Some of those take the form of tutorials for beginners, either aimed at helping players create functioning and/or beautiful structures, or providing gamers with survival tips. Other *Minecraft* videos have nothing to do with helping viewers learn about the inner mechanisms of creative and survival modes, but simply are recordings of what appears onscreen when someone else interacts with the software. Such videos, can be organized in episodes similar to traditional TV shows, or merely are raw recordings of someone playing. Although game live retransmissions and recordings are present on the internet for many different games, there is a uniqueness in some of those focused on *Minecraft* that is directly linked to this game being both interpretative and configurative, both art and game. The example of the French *Minecraft Hardcore* series of videos available on the *millenium.org* website is a good example of this.

Millenium.org mostly proposes e-sport video, that is programs centered on the competitive aspect of video games. The website thus sponsors three video channels that retransmit live tournaments or competitive multiplayer games such as *League of Legends* and *Starcraft II* (Blizzard Entertainment, 2010) in a way very similar to the more traditional broadcasting of sport events. In addition to these streams, a sizeable part of the website's videos and written articles focus on tutorials and advice aimed at viewers who want to become better e-sportsmen and e-sportswomen.

The *Minecraft Hardcore* program (2011–2013), however, is neither devoted to competitive gaming nor to tutorials but to the adventures of a *Minecraft* player known as iplay4you. *Minecraft Hardcore* is described on the *millenium.org* website as a series "aiming at proposing to players a new way to play *Minecraft* consisting in completing a set of goals in *Minecraft*'s most challenging mode: Hardcore mode." In these videos, iplay4you navigates in an environment that has been previously created especially for this series with mods adding new elements to the game such as deadly creatures or items. These structures, landscapes, and mods are created by both a team associated with the online *Minecraft Hardcore* series of videos and other *Minecraft* users who volunteered to help to create iplay4you's challenge. The first episode of each season of this web video series consists of a presentation of both the map corresponding to the current season and of a list of the objectives associated with this map. Such goals vary from one season to another but usually consist in gathering specific resources in the environment created by the *Minecraft Hardcore* building team, which are found by completing challenges and riddles as well as exploring the map and defeating various hostile NPCs. Although such goals may appear quite simple at first, because the video-maker plays in hardcore mode game saves are prohibited, death is permanent and automatically concludes the season. Furthermore, the video-maker is only allowed to gather blocks and items that can be found in chests disseminated in the environment, and he cannot deconstruct his surroundings in order to fill his inventory.

Minecraft's core duality of creative and survival mode hence enables a new kind of entertainment that is a mix between traditional sports broadcasting, TV shows, and multiplayer online video gaming. Furthermore, the same duality allows viewers to both watch iplay4you struggle with the building team's creation and to potentially experiment the same challenges, the maps built for the series being made available to anyone after the current season is over. Viewers who followed the series online can then use these maps in creative mode to fully explore and modify them or to attempt the same challenges iplay4you faced in hardcore mode. The *Minecraft Hardcore* series, meant both to be watched and interacted with, can be seen as the junction between what Eskelinen defined as art and games, two seemingly opposite poles that Mojang successfully merged into one game/toy experience that places user-delegated level and game design as its very essence.

Since its early beta released, *Minecraft* has mostly drawn the attention of numerous commentators because of its aesthetic specificities. This visual uniqueness has also inspired many game developers to create what has been commonly referred to as voxel games. However important this particular contribution to modern video games has been, Mojang's creation has been often summed up to this visual aspect alone, which went against the current evolution of video games towards increasingly more realistic onscreen representation of life. But *Minecraft's* principal artistic quality is to be found somewhere else. In allowing its users a tremendous degree of freedom regarding game design, without being editing software, *Minecraft* brought creating and playing together, and this is its true artistic quality. *Minecraft* is not an artistically elaborated game, but simply art, as well as game and toy, and its artistic quality resides in this software's potential to question the lines that are usually drawn between interactive and narrative. In such a field as the academic analysis of video games, much time has been spent debating on the nature and extent of video games' narrative components as opposed to their configurative aspects, and an interactive experience such as *Minecraft* proves that at least some part of modern video game industry already overcame these considerations to address less obvious distinctions.

A New Type of Video Game

In summary, the creative mode of *Minecraft* truly allows for limitless play. One could indefinitely stack and destroy its virtual blocks, and finding the borders of *Minecraft*'s world can be as difficult as catching a rainbow. With such an open structure, players are also free to impose upon it any number of consensually agreed upon rules making the gameplay also endless. While the existence of survival mode built on top of creative mode can be identified as a tendency toward more traditional definitions of game, it enabled much more by creating a duality that cannot be dismissed.

If LEGO construction sets successfully transitioned from mere toys to games—especially board games that involve a little bit of construction—and most recently to art with *The Lego Movie* (2014), those three different aspects of what might be called the LEGO universe remain discrete entities. What *Minecraft* achieved, in putting delegated game design and users' independence from fixed rules at the center of its gameplay, is to merge those entities into a unique software that is always simultaneously art game and toy.

Minecraft's inner duality between creative and survival mode positions it as a challenge to our very understanding of what video games are. In being a game of both interpretation and configuration, *Minecraft* is closer to traditional paper-based role-playing games—during which players both strive to overcome difficulties using definite sets of rules and collectively create their own imaginary diegesis—than most role-playing video games. While the latter usually merely borrow settings and rules from paper-based role-playing games, *Minecraft*'s duality captures the very essence of what *Dungeon and Dragons* started decades ago. And, like *Dungeons and Dragons*, because of the possibilities that the game's hybrid nature offers to its users both in terms of actual gameplay and of entertainment at large, *Minecraft* is indeed every nerd's dream—an endless video game.

References

Alexander, W., & Tait, R. (1998). *Cranium* [Videogame]. Seattle: Cranium, Inc.

Blizzard Entertainment. (2002). *Warcraft III* [PC game]. Irvine, CA: Blizzard Entertainment.

Blizzard Entertainment. (2010). *Starcraft II* [PC game]. Irvine, CA: Blizzard Entertainment.

Bohemian Interactive. (2013). *DayZ* [PC game]. Prague: Bohemian Interactive.

Caillois, R. (2001). *Man, play, and games*. Champaign: University of Illinois Press.

Clements, B., & Tanner, P. (1991–2006). Atmosfear [Board game series]. El Segundo, CA: Mattel.

Cox, J. (2012, November 13). *The two towers (and 10 thousand hours): A* Minecraft *middle earth special* [Video file]. Retrieved from http://youtu.be/2M9Sc8zhoBQ.

Eskelinen, M. (2001, July). The gaming situation. *Game Studies*. Retrieved from http://www.gamestudies.org/0101/eskelinen/

Fine, B., & R. (Creators & Directors). (2011, November 13). Kids react to *Minecraft*. In The Fine Bros, React [Video file]. Retrieved from http://youtu.be/g1tBXe0JGyc

Frasca, G. (2003). Simulation versus narrative: Introduction to ludology. In M. J. P. Wolf & B. Perron (Eds.), *The video game theory reader* (pp. 259–273). New York: Routledge.

Halnicholas. (2011, March 30). *New tour of the* Minecraft *enterprise* [Video file]. Retrieved from http://youtu.be/lXUkdrcey-w

Huizinga, J. (1949). *Homo ludens: A study of the play-element in culture.* London: Routledge.

Iplay4you, et. al. (2011–2013). *Minecraft hardcore.* Retrieved from http://www.millenium. org.

Lord, P., & Miller, C. (Directors & Screenwriters). (2014, February). *The Lego Movie.*

Manovich, L. (2001). *The Language of new media.* Cambridge, MA: MIT Press.

Mojang. (2011). *Minecraft* [PC game]. Stockholm, Sweden.

Riot Games. (2009) *League of Legends* [PC game]. Santa Monica, CA: Riot Games.

Skip Ltd. (2006). *Soundvoyager* [Videogame]. Kyoto: Nintendo.

2D Boy. (2008). *World of Goo* [Videogame]. San Francisco: 2D Boy.

About the Contributors

Adam L. **Brackin** is a research assistant professor of arts and technology at the University of Texas at Dallas. His areas of research include new media and transmedia games and stories, non-linear and ergodic story models, and video game design and studies.

Jeffrey E. **Brand** has a Ph.D. from Michigan State University and is a professor of communication and creative media and chair of the Bond University Higher Degree Research Committee. His research explores the social psychology and behaviors of interactive media users and content regulation issues arising from presumed media effects.

Joseph Alexander **Brown** has a Ph.D. in computer science from the University of Guelph in Guelph, Ontario, Canada. He has over twenty-five peer reviewed publications on evolutionary computation, bioinformatics, mathematical game theory, videogame design, and Canadian poetry.

Iris Rochelle **Bull** has an M.A. from the University of Oregon and is a doctoral student at Indiana University. Her research interests revolve around videogames, virtual worlds, new media, and Westerns.

Rémi **Cayatte** is a Ph.D. student at the French Université de Lorraine. His doctoral thesis analyzes the nature and inner mechanisms of post 9/11 political discourse in video games. His current work focuses on the links that can be drawn between a game's discourse, its gameplay features, and eventual narratives, as well as players' freedom of action and interpretation within modern games.

Peter **Christiansen** is a Ph.D. student at the University of Utah and teaches courses in videogame studies. In addition to working on numerous game jams and personal projects, he has been making games professionally since 2005. He also works for the ASPIRE program, creating educational games to teach children physics.

Jeremy **Colangelo** is a Ph.D. candidate in English, at the University of Western Ontario. His research interests lay primarily in twentieth century literature and literary theory. His academic work has appeared in *The James Joyce Quarterly* and *Joyce Studies Annual*. He has published over a dozen poems and short stories, as well as four chapbooks.

Penny **de Byl** has a Ph.D. from the University of Southern Queensland and is a professor of interactive media and design at Bond University. Her research areas of interest include games-based learning, gamification pedagogy, and game development. She is co-owner of Aardbei Studios, an indie mobile game development company focusing on the creation of educational games.

Colin **Fanning** is a curatorial assistant at the American Federation of Arts in New York City. He holds an M.A. in decorative arts, design history, and material culture from the Bard Graduate Center where his research focused largely on the material culture of childhood, twentieth-century studio craft, and European graphic design.

Nate **Garrelts** has a Ph.D.from Michigan State University and is an associate professor of English at Ferris State University. His research focuses primarily on critical approaches to digital games, cultural studies, and computer hacking. He regularly contributes to the website *Bad Subjects* and other similar publications.

Jandy **Gu** is a Ph.D. student in anthropology at the University of Florida. Her research interests include social and legal legitimacy, visual aesthetics and media, and space and place theory. Most of her work revolves around urban graphic forms, but digital creations and virtual sociality are also topics of interest.

James **Hooper** is an experienced multimedia artist, 3D modeler and animator, game designer and software developer with undergraduate degrees in information technology and multimedia design. He is working toward a Ph.D. in computer games, and teaches website design, 3D animation and modeling, graphic design, and games development at Bond University.

Scott J. **Knight** is an assistant professor of film, television, and videogames at Bond University. He teaches courses in film and videogame form, style, and culture. He has authored papers on fan cultures, exploitation film, censorship issues, and videogame history and aesthetics and is engaged in research on the formal characteristics of film-to-game adaptation.

Esther **MacCallum-Stewart** is a senior lecturer in digital media arts at the University of Surrey, UK, and a research fellow for the Digital Cultures Research Centre at the University of West England. Her work investigates the ways that players and gaming communities understand and reform game narratives, and she has written widely on videogame players and communities, gender, roleplay and deviant practices in online communities.

Rebecca **Mir** began writing about the visual and material culture of video games during her studies at the Bard Graduate Center, where she earned an M.A. in decorative arts, design history, and material culture. She is dedicated to using videogames (and digital media in general) for educational good.

James **Morgan** is an instructor for digital media art at San José State University. His work involves social interaction, coded culture and democratic structures in gamespaces and simulations. He curates art and games in physical and simulated spaces and also serves as the director of Ars Virtua, a gallery and collaborative project executed in virtual worlds.

R. Yagiz **Mungan** is a new media artist and scholar interested in games, generative art, and interactive sound. He holds an MFA in electronic and time-based art from Purdue University and an M.S. in integrated electronic system design from Chalmers University of Technology. He works at Float Hybrid Entertainment.

Amanda **Phillips** is a Ph.D. candidate at the University of California, Santa Barbara. Her interests are in queer, feminist, and race-conscious discourses in and around technoculture, popular media, and videogame studies. In addition to her academic work, she has been involved with the #transformDH Collective's efforts to encourage and highlight critical cultural studies work in the digital humanities.

Dennis **Redmond** has a Ph.D. in communications from the University of Illinois Urbana-Champaign and is a lecturer in communications at the Miami Dade College at Kendall. His main research interests include contemporary videogame culture, transnational media, the politics of digital democracy and anti-neoliberal mass mobilizations, and the digital media cultures of the industrializing world.

Michael **St. Clair** teaches in theater and performance studies and the d.school at Stanford University. In addition to having an active installation and design practice, he also studies the intersections between games, art, and performance.

Michael **Thomét** is a digital game designer and researcher interested in how games and narratives can work together and research methods in games studies. He holds an M.A. in English from Arizona State University, where he developed the Player-Game Descriptive Index, a method of describing videogames and their players.

Alexandra Jean **Tremblay** is an avid *Minecraft* player working on an M.Sc. in computer science at the University of Guelph in Guelph, Ontario. Her research interests include human-computer interaction and educational data mining. She is specifically interested in improving student engagement and educational data visualization.

Index

219